P9-CLC-064

R03102 80930

DISCARD

	DATE DUE		

ALBERT EINSTEIN

Other titles in the
People Who Made History series:

ALBERT EINSTEIN

Clarice Swisher, *Book Editor*

Daniel Leone, *President*
Bonnie Szumski, *Publisher*
Scott Barbour, *Managing Editor*

Greenhaven Press, Inc., San Diego, CA

Library of Congress Cataloging-in-Publication Data

Einstein, Albert, 1879–1955
    Albert Einstein / Clarice Swisher, book editor.
        p. cm. — (People who made history)
    Includes bibliographical references and index.
    ISBN 0-7377-0893-X (lib. bdg. : alk. paper) —
    ISBN 0-7377-0892-1 (pbk. : alk. paper)
    1. Einstein, Albert, 1879–1955. 2. Physics—History—
19th century. 3. Physics—History—20th century.
4. Physicists—Biography. I. Swisher, Clarice, 1933–
II. Title. III. Series.

QC16.E5 E3917   2002
510'.092—dc21   2001028925
[B]

Cover photo: © Bettmann/CORBIS
Library of Congress, 18

Copyright © 2002 by Greenhaven Press, Inc.
10911 Technology Place
San Diego, CA 92127
Printed in the U.S.A.

CONTENTS

Chapter 1: Major Influences on Einstein's Development as a Scientist

Einstein's family instilled in young Einstein an interest in science and mathematics and a love for music. A family friend, Max Talmey, launched Einstein into serious study of physics, higher mathematics, and philosophy by bringing him books and discussing the contents with him. The rigidity of his high school made him suspicious of authority, an asset when he began doubting accepted scientific theories.

Einstein began searching for a satisfying way of viewing life at an early age. He rejected religion and replaced it with wonder about the riddles of the great yonder world that was the curiosity of men he admired. Two childhood experiences activated his own wondering, which led to thought about the world.

Recognizing Einstein's talent, Marcel Grossmann overlooked Einstein's faults and helped him study for university examinations. Two years later Grossmann and his father helped Einstein obtain a full-time job at the patent office in Bern, Switzerland.

Chapter 2: Einstein's Work in Physics

In 1905 Einstein, the little known physicist working in a patent office, published four papers in *Annalen der Physik,* a scholarly journal of physics, and overturned long-held theories. He proved the existence of atoms, showed that light is composed of particles, declared that space and time are relative, and showed that energy and mass are different forms of the same thing.

Chapter 3: The Public Einstein—His Fame and Causes

Chapter 4: Einstein in America

search was going on in Germany, and Einstein knew an atomic bomb available to Hitler would be more dangerous if America was unprepared.

Chapter 5: Assessing Einstein's Contributions

FOREWORD

In the vast and colorful pageant of human history, a handful of individuals stand out. They are the men and women who have come variously to be called "great," "leading," "brilliant," "pivotal," or "infamous" because they and their deeds forever changed their own society or the world as a whole. Some were political or military leaders—kings, queens, presidents, generals, and the like—whose policies, conquests, or innovations reshaped the maps and futures of countries and entire continents. Among those falling into this category were the formidable Roman statesman/general Julius Caesar, who extended Rome's power into Gaul (what is now France); Caesar's lover and ally, the notorious Egyptian queen Cleopatra, who challenged the strongest male rulers of her day; and England's stalwart Queen Elizabeth I, whose defeat of the mighty Spanish Armada saved England from subjugation.

Some of history's other movers and shakers were scientists or other thinkers whose ideas and discoveries altered the way people conduct their everyday lives or view themselves and their place in nature. The electric light and other remarkable inventions of Thomas Edison, for example, revolutionized almost every aspect of home-life and the workplace; and the theories of naturalist Charles Darwin lit the way for biologists and other scientists in their ongoing efforts to understand the origins of living things, including human beings.

Still other people who made history were religious leaders and social reformers. The struggles of the Arabic prophet Muhammad more than a thousand years ago led to the establishment of one of the world's great religions—Islam; and the efforts and personal sacrifices of an American reverend named Martin Luther King Jr. brought about major improvements in race relations and the justice system in the United States.

Each anthology in the People Who Made History series begins with an introductory essay that provides a general overview of the individual's life, times, and contributions. The group of essays that follow are chosen for their accessibility to a young adult audience and carefully edited in consideration of the reading and comprehension levels of that audience. Some of the essays are by noted historians, professors, and other experts. Others are excerpts from contemporary writings by or about the pivotal individual in question. To aid the reader in choosing the material of immediate interest or need, an annotated table of contents summarizes the article's main themes and insights.

Each volume also contains extensive research tools, including a collection of excerpts from primary source documents pertaining to the individual under discussion. The volumes are rounded out with an extensive bibliography and a comprehensive index.

Plutarch, the renowned first-century Greek biographer and moralist, crystallized the idea behind Greenhaven's People Who Made History when he said, "To be ignorant of the lives of the most celebrated men of past ages is to continue in a state of childhood all our days." Indeed, since it is people who make history, every modern nation, organization, institution, invention, artifact, and idea is the result of the diligent efforts of one or more individuals, living or dead; and it is therefore impossible to understand how the world we live in came to be without examining the contributions of these individuals.

ALBERT EINSTEIN: MAN OF THE TWENTIETH CENTURY

Albert Einstein—scientist, icon, symbol of genius—was *Time* magazine's choice for the "Person of the Century" at the end of 1999. Famous foremost for his theory of relativity, Einstein also called attention to the causes of freedom and peace and enlisted support for international government and Zionism. He was famous throughout the world; wherever he went people loved him for his courage, kind face, humor, and humble attitude. Who he was at the end of his life was much like who he was as a boy—a dreamer fascinated by the workings of the universe.

Albert Einstein was born on March 14, 1879, in Ulm, Germany, a village on the banks of the Danube River in the foothills of the Swabian Alps. He was the first child born to Pauline and Hermann Einstein, a couple devoted to each other but inattentive to their Jewish religion. Einstein's father, an easygoing man, owned a small electrical and engineering shop, which he tended with marginal seriousness. Einstein's mother, better organized and more ambitious than her husband, played Beethoven and read German literature and valued education.

CHILDHOOD IN MUNICH, GERMANY

In 1880, when Einstein was one year old, the family moved to Munich, Germany, where Hermann and his brother Jacob set up a small electrochemical factory. The next year the Einsteins had a second child, a daughter named Maja, before Hermann and Jacob moved their business to the suburb of Sendling. There, the two families lived in adjoining houses with a large shared garden where the children had space to play. As an adult, Maja remembered her brother as a daydreamer who liked play activities that required patience, such as building complicated structures with blocks and houses of cards fourteen stories high.

Einstein developed normally as a child in every way but in speaking. His parents worried when their three-year-old son had not learned to talk, and they took him to a doctor, who found nothing wrong. Einstein eventually talked, but the delay in his speech affected him. When he was school age, he often repeated words and sentences to himself before he spoke, practicing in order to avoid mistakes. As an adult, he never felt confident as a speaker and joked about his inability to be an orator. Though he talked little as a child, he did not lack curiosity and imagination. At age five he was fascinated with a pocket compass his father brought to his sickbed. Einstein noticed that no matter which way he turned the compass, the needle always pointed north. He remembered the incident years later:

> That this needle behaved in such a determined way did not at all fit into the kind of occurrences that could find a place in the unconscious world of concepts. . . . I can still remember—or at least believe I can remember—that this experience made a deep and lasting impression upon me. Something deeply hidden had to be behind things.[1]

Einstein referred to this experience as the first "wonder" of his childhood.

When still a preschooler, Einstein resisted coercion and harshly imposed authority. He exhibited this attitude while watching a military parade of soldiers marching in formation to the accompaniment of drums and fifes. Many parents used the soldiers as models and told their children that they could grow up to be like them. Einstein opposed the suggestion and cried, "When I grow up I don't want to be one of those poor people."[2] Intuitively, he sensed that they were forced to act in this machinelike way. This skepticism toward authority and hatred for militarism characterized Einstein's personality throughout his life.

GERMAN SCHOOLS AND PRIVATE STUDY

Violin lessons and school became part of Einstein's life when he turned six. He took violin lessons because his parents insisted, but he hated the teacher, who made him memorize musical techniques by rote. After seven years of lessons, he saw the underlying structure of musical compositions, and from then until the end of his life he enjoyed playing the violin, though he never achieved professional musicianship. Because the nearest Jewish school was too far away, Einstein attended a neighborhood Catholic school, where he was the only Jewish boy. At first he enjoyed school: He learned Catholic traditions and beliefs, heard stories from the Bible, and even helped his Catholic classmates study for quizzes. But his enthusiasm for school was short lived. He soon hated the rote learning and the authoritarian rules that required students to stand at attention when a teacher spoke to them. When he left elementary school, he compared it to military barracks where teachers emphasize obedience.

Although the rigidity of organized education irritated young Einstein, the flexibility and independence of private study fascinated him. He found a school mathematics book that taught Euclidean plane geometry, and he worked through the whole book, making notes and solving problems. Later he wrote,

> I experienced a second wonder of a totally different nature. . . . Here were assertions, as for example the intersection of the three altitudes of a triangle at one point which . . . could nevertheless be proved with such certainty that any doubt appeared to be out of the question; this "wonder" rested upon an error. Nevertheless, for anyone who experiences it for the first time, it is marvelous enough that man is capable at all to reach such a degree and purity in pure thinking as the Greeks showed us for the first time to be possible in geometry.[3]

Einstein found further encouragement for independent study from family friend Max Talmey, a medical student who came to dinner every Thursday. He brought five or six volumes of Aaron Bernstein's *Popular Books on Natural Science,* which covered the animal world, astronomy, geology, and climate. Unlike Einstein's fragmented school studies, these books stressed the wholenesss of nature. Talmey next brought books by the philosopher Immanuel Kant and explained, "At the time he [Einstein] was still a child, only thirteen years old, yet Kant's works, incomprehensible to ordinary mortals, seemed clear to him."[4] These private studies helped Einstein develop a view of an interconnected, unified world, plus a way to reason about it.

Einstein continued his formal high school education at the Luitpold Gymnasium, which he entered at age ten, a school that displeased him even more than his elementary school. Because he found the emphasis on obedience and rote learning to be even greater, he resisted the authorities and retreated into his own study of differential and integral calculus. He developed a poor reputation at school, especially with the Greek teacher, who did not understand Einstein's poor memory for words and texts; consequently, Einstein chose to endure the teacher's punishments rather than obey the rules, and the teacher told him, "You will never amount to anything."[5] Similarly, when Hermann Einstein inquired how to advise his son toward a profession, the headmaster told him that it did not matter because Albert would never make a success of anything.

RELATING RELIGION AND SCIENCE

Einstein's schooling in Catholicism had a temporary impact that led to a lifelong religious outlook that, in turn, influenced his attitude toward science. His enthusiasm for Catholic study sparked his interest in his own Jewish religion, about which he was ignorant since his father thought that attending synagogue and following Jewish food traditions were nothing more than ancient superstitions. In a course in Judaism at the gymnasium, he studied the Old Testament and learned about Jewish holidays and rules about food. He liked wise Solomon, became a serious practicing Jew, and urged his parents to join him; however, they did not, and he ended up being religious alone.

This religious experience, which gave him temporary security, he later called "the religious paradise of youth."[6] Through his science reading and his own thinking, he soon concluded that Bible stories could not be literally true because they did not fit the world of nature. With this discovery he became embittered at authorities who, he thought, manipulated children into unreality with religious lies. He switched his allegiance to nature and to those who studied it and vowed that he, too, would study nature. Reflecting late in life on this experience, he said,

> Out yonder there was this huge world, which exists independent of us human beings and which stands before us like a great, eternal riddle, at least partially accessible to our inspection and thinking. The contemplation of this world beckoned as a liberation. . . . The road to this paradise was not as comfortable and alluring as the road to religious paradise; but it has shown itself reliable, and I have never regretted having chosen it.[7]

UNCERTAINTY BETWEEN HIGH SCHOOL AND THE UNIVERSITY

In 1894, when Einstein had only one year left before graduation from the Luitpold Gymnasium, the family business failed, and the brothers sold it. Hermann moved his family to Milan, Italy, but left Einstein behind to complete his studies under the watch of a distant relative. Living alone in a room, Einstein became lonely and depressed, and the school routine became insufferable. His father helped him obtain a medical certificate designating that depression required his return to his family in Italy. The school authorities were very happy to comply; the homeroom teacher's words to Einstein, "Your mere presence spoils the respect of the class for me,"[8] encapsulate the entire school's attitude toward Einstein. So bitter was Einstein that he wanted to give up his German citizenship and sever all ties with the country. His plan was to enjoy his family and Italy for a brief time, take the university entrance exams, and continue his education in science.

His plans, however, did not go as expected. He did enjoy Italian culture and the countryside. Then his father's business failed again, and because he could no longer support his son, Hermann urged Einstein to prepare for a practical profession and earn money. Nevertheless, Einstein, who was sixteen, took the entrance exams at the Swiss Federal Polytechnic School, exams intended for eighteen-year-olds. He failed the tests in languages, zoology, and botany, but because he scored so well in mathematics and physics, the director, Albin Herzog, recommended that he get a diploma at the Swiss Cantonal School of Aargua in Aarau, Switzerland, and then retake the exams. The Swiss school, unlike the German Gymnasium, had an atmosphere of freedom, and teachers conversed with students and urged them to think independently. In a conversation with his physics teacher, Einstein posed the question: What would a light beam look like if a person could travel alongside it at the same speed? Would the light beam appear to be standing still? He did not know at the time that the question would form the idea for his special relativity theory a decade later. At this school Einstein was happy, successfully earned a diploma, and obtained the knowledge to pass his second try at the entrance exams.

A UNIVERSITY DEGREE LEADS TO UNEMPLOYMENT

Einstein entered Zurich Polytechnic in October 1896 planning to prepare for a teaching career in science. He took many different kinds of science classes as well as literature and philosophy, and because physics was his favorite subject, he spent many hours in the laboratory working on research. Gradually, his old habits returned. Because he thought lectures were poorly prepared and omitted the latest findings in science, he cut classes and studied privately. Biographer Anton Reiser says of these times, "With a veritable mania for reading, day and night, he went through the works of the great physicists—[Gustav] Kirchhoff, [Heinrich] Hertz, [Hermann] Helmholtz."[9]

These times were also times of poverty. His only means of support was a small allowance provided by his mother's relatives in Geneva, out of which he saved a fifth so that he could eventually pay the fees for a Swiss citizenship. He lived in a single room, ate at soup kitchens, and entertained himself with his violin and any free concerts he could find. He developed three close friends from the university—Marcel Grossman, Mileva Maric, and Michele Besso—who shared serious conversations about science. They considered Einstein an eccentric since he wore unconventional clothes and cared little for social manners.

When it came time to take his final exams to determine his graduation status, he was unprepared because he had missed so many classes. Grossman, who recognized Einstein's intelligence and talent, offered to let Einstein study from his complete, well-organized notes. Einstein accepted, and he passed the exams with an average score of 4.9 out of a possible 6.0 and graduated in August 1900. He did not, however, receive the usual offers for assistantships from his former professors. His physics professor, whom Einstein had insulted by addressing him improperly, told Einstein, "You're a clever fellow! But you have one fault. You won't let anyone tell you a thing."[10] With no money and no job, he rejoined his parents in Milan and wrote letters asking for work.

Meanwhile, he continued his private study and wrote papers on atoms and thermodynamics, which he sent to the scholarly journal *Annalen der Physik;* the journal published one of them in 1901 and the other in 1902. He also sent these papers to universities hoping they would help him get a job, and he sent the one on thermodynamics to the University of Zurich in an application for a doctoral degree, but nothing came of any of his requests. Einstein became very depressed during this period; as biographer Banesh Hoffmann explains, he "felt himself sinking helplessly in the quagmire of a world that had no place for him."[11] The only bright spot occurred when his application for Swiss citizenship was accepted on February 21, 1902, after being a person with no citizenship for five years.

A JOB AT THE PATENT OFFICE

Gradually, Einstein's fortune changed. He first found temporary jobs as a substitute teacher and tutor, which provided him with some money. The real break came when Grossmann and his father recommended Einstein for a job at a patent office in Bern, Switzerland, which he began on June 23, 1902. The job as a patent clerk was perfect: Einstein learned it easily, analyzed the patents quickly, and had the time between patent requests to work on scientific ideas and to develop equations. Between 1902 and 1904 he wrote three new papers on thermodynamics, all of which *Annalen der Physik* published. In addition, he completed his dissertation papers for his doctoral degree for the University of Zurich, making a total of six papers published since graduation. As biographer Ronald W. Clark writes, "It was a good record for a failed teacher who had ended up in a patent office; it was surprisingly little for a man who was about to shake the scientific world."[12]

The early 1900s also brought changes in his personal life. On October 10, 1902, his father died, leaving him shattered and desolate. Shortly after, on January 6, 1903, he married Mileva Maric, a Serbian woman who had been a physics student at the university and part of his small group that gathered for conversation. The couple had a son, Hans Albert, in 1904. Though Einstein had an imperfect marriage in which there were frequent conflicts, his life was more stable than it had been for years, and he was finally independent of his relatives' financial help. He did, however, miss a good university library and the stimulation he received from conversations about science with his university friends. At Einstein's urging, Michele Besso took a job at the patent office, and Einstein again had a friend to listen to his theories and question and criticize them. Though his life had taken a definite upturn, both professionally and personally, he remembered the job rejections with a humility that was present in his mind even after he had achieved fame.

THE 1905 PAPERS LEAD TO A PROFESSORSHIP

Einstein continued his work on problems in physics and produced four scientific papers in one year, each of which explained an entirely new theory; these were his famous 1905 papers. Although many scientists did not immediately recognize the significance of these new theories, the German physicist responsible for the publication of *Annalen der Physik,* Max Frank, did. He said, "If Einstein's theory [of special relativity] should prove to be correct, as I expect it will, he will be considered the Copernicus of the twentieth century."[15]

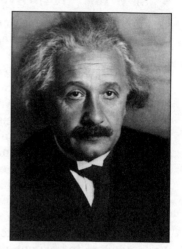

Albert Einstein

After *Annalen der Physik* had published the 1905 papers, Einstein moved forward in his career, but on occasion his personal attitudes hampered him. In 1906, the patent office promoted him from third- to second-class technical expert. Though he liked the job there, he thought more and more about a university job in order to gain access to a good library, but first he had to become a privatdocent to be eligible for a professorship. (A privatdocent learns lecturing skills under the supervision of an experienced lecturer.) Einstein gave lectures at the University of Bern on the science of heat under the direction of a physics professor from the University of Zurich. When Einstein went to class poorly prepared, shabbily dressed, and only two students attended, his supervisor criticized him. Einstein reminded him that he was not demanding to be appointed a professor at Zurich. Nevertheless, Einstein obtained the position as assistant professor, more for his theories than for his performance. He began as a lecturing professor at the University of Zurich in the fall of 1909, when he was thirty years old.

In many ways Einstein was an oddity in the hierarchy of academia. He hated the politicking for position and refused to mix socially or attend meetings with other professors, though he enjoyed discussing scientific ideas with them. He was poor at grinding out lectures, which he referred to as trapeze performances, but good at advising students individually. "If you have a problem, come to me with it. You will never disturb me, since I can interrupt my work at a moment and resume it immediately,"[14] he told them. A humble and unpretentious man, he treated everyone alike—leading university officials, the grocer, and the scrubwoman in the laboratory—much to the consternation of high-ranking professors. As he had done in Bern, Einstein wheeled Hans Albert and now also son Eduard, who had been born in Zurich, through the streets of the city.

Einstein's job in Zurich lasted only two years because, at the urging of German physicist Max Planck, the German University in Prague wanted Einstein as a full professor, knowing that he would add prestige to the school. Einstein, who accepted the position in 1911, enjoyed the school's outstanding library, but found that the duties of a full professor left him little time for his own work, and he longed for the quiet hours at the patent office. Though he realized that he preferred the kind of contemplative life that artists have, he took the trappings of academic life in good humor.

Einstein's reputation among scientists slowly grew. In the fall of 1911, he was one of twenty-one select scientists invited to speak at the prestigious Solvay Congress in Brussels, Belgium. In 1912 he was offered professorships at four universities, one of which was Zurich Polytechnic, where he had been an undergraduate. He had begun working on his general theory of relativity, and by returning to Zurich to teach, he could collaborate with his old friend Marcel Grossman, who was a mathematics professor at Zurich Polytechnic. Because the general theory needed a new kind of mathematics, Grossman's help accelerated Einstein's progress. The men published two papers on their cooperative work.

THE TOP JOB IN EUROPE

Though Einstein had the option of a ten-year contract at Zurich Polytechnic, he stayed only two years because Planck offered him the best position in Europe for a theoretical physicist. The new offer had three parts: the directorship of the Institute of Physics at the Kaiser Wilhelm Institute, a chair (a special position) at the Prussian Academy, and a professorship at the University of Berlin. The honorary titles meant little to Einstein, but he saw the benefits of the comfortable salary and the opportunity to work with the leading European scientists. Best of all, he could teach only if and when he wanted to, leaving him time to work on the general relativity theory. However, Einstein hesitated to return to Germany, where its people had made him uncomfortable as a child. Moreover, Mileva liked Zurich and wanted to stay there, but his relationship with her had deteriorated to the point that he hardly cared what she preferred. In the end, he chose Berlin and moved there with his family in April 1914. He had now reached the top of his profession.

Although this new position made Einstein a director, chair, and professor all within the same job, he was primarily expected to do research. Biographer Anton Reiser describes the academy's purpose:

> The Academy is concerned not with teaching but with investigation. Its regular members are for the most part professors of the University of Berlin or other universities. . . . The Academy is, nevertheless, the highest authority in scholarly circles. It publishes the work of its members, supports important research, arranges for publication of important works, both old and new, and offers prizes. In fact, next to the university, which is concerned with instruction, it is the most important center of learning.[15]

The challenge of the new job made Einstein apprehensive. At a farewell dinner in Zurich, he had described himself as a prize hen, gambled on by the gentlemen of Berlin. He did not know if he would lay another golden egg. In his acceptance speech to the Berlin Academy, he cautioned, "I hope that you will continue to believe in my gratitude and industry even when my efforts appear to yield only poor results."[16]

During the next few years, his private life again changed in significant ways. In the summer of 1914 Mileva and the boys returned to Zurich to visit her family. Before she returned, World War I broke out in August, making it unsafe for her to travel. Einstein hardly cared since their relationship had become so stormy that it interfered with his work. He stayed alone until after Christmas and then lived with his father's cousin, Rudolph Einstein, who had married his mother's sister, and he became reacquainted with their daughter Elsa, now a widow with two teenage daughters, Ilse and Margot.

Einstein tried to keep the war from interfering with his life and work, but it affected his relationship with his German colleagues. He was shocked to see them enthusiastically help with the war by developing chemical weapons; in contrast, the war made Einstein even more committed to pacifism and internationalism. He was not in a position to speak out strongly, however, since the men who financed his job were on the opposite political side. To avoid conflict, he threw himself headlong into his work.

GENERAL RELATIVITY THEORY IS FINALLY COMPLETED

Einstein had worked on general relativity for eight years alone and two years with Marcel Grossman. But now he struggled alone, faced with a set of ten equations that he and Grossman had developed. Einstein hoped to bring all ten equations together, but after trying for two years to do so, he found the summer of 1915 particularly agonizing. Finally, he took a fresh approach. When he discovered it was the correct one, progress went fast, and everything fell into place with beautiful simplicity. He had found a new theory of gravity based on the ten equations. It made four predictions: a measurement of Mercury's orbit, a curvature in the space-time continuum, a red shift indicating that objects are moving away in space, and gravitational waves. When he completed the theory in November 1915, he wrote to a friend, "In all my life I have never before labored so hard. Compared with this problem, the original theory of relativity is child's play."[17]

Late in 1915 Einstein announced to the Prussian Academy of Sciences that he had completed the theory and that the prediction of Mercury's orbit was accurate. This announcement appeared in the academy's 1915 publication, *Proceedings*, and in the spring of 1916 the *Annalen der Physik* published the theory with the title "Foundation of the General Theory of Relativity." German physicist Max Born later described his initial reaction to it:

> The theory appeared to me then, and it still does, the greatest feat of human thinking about nature, the most amazing combination of philosophical penetration, physical intuition, and mathematical skill. But its connections with experience were slender. It appealed to me like a great work of art, to be enjoyed and admired from a distance.[18]

Einstein sent a copy of the journal article to an astronomy professor at the University of Leiden in the Netherlands, who forwarded it to William de Sitter, a foreign corespondent of the Royal Astronomical Society in London, who sent it to Arthur Eddington, the society's secretary. Eddington was the one who introduced Einstein's theory to the non-German-speaking world. The theory had traveled a circuitous route because the war demanded careful communication among scientists who were from countries on opposite sides in the war. After the theory had been published in *Annalen der Physik*, a publisher asked Einstein to write an explanation of special and general relativity that ordinary nonscientists could understand. Einstein limited this book to seventy pages because paper was in short supply during the war; even so, the book went through three printings by 1918.

DIFFICULT TIMES IN EINSTEIN'S PERSONAL LIFE

After Einstein had completed the theory, he experienced significant changes in his personal life during the years between 1917 and 1920. He made several trips to Zurich to negotiate a divorce from Mileva and found the conflicts with her and the worry about his sons stressful. Late in 1917 he became ill with what doctors diagnosed as stomach problems coupled with exhaustion. For three years he had lived alone and worked long hours, eating poorly and sleeping irregularly until the schedule finally took its toll on his health. During his recovery Michele Besso took over negotiations with Mileva, formulating an agreement that gave Mileva the money from the anticipated Nobel Prize. His cousin Elsa cared for his daily needs, and Einstein gradually recovered. On February 14, 1919, his divorce was settled, and on June 2, 1919, he married Elsa, who had taken on the role of organizing undisturbed time and a healthy routine for him. Late in that same year Einstein's mother, Pauline, who was diagnosed with terminal cancer, came to live with Einstein and Elsa until February 1920, when she died. After her death, Einstein felt just as desolate as when his father had died many years earlier. In the meantime, the war had ended in November 1918 with Germany's defeat.

VERIFICATION OF GENERAL RELATIVITY THEORY

After Eddington and the British had announced Einstein's theory outside of Germany, British teams prepared to verify one of the predictions when the next full eclipse of the sun occurred. Astronomers could see if light from a distant star bent around the sun's gravity only during a total eclipse because otherwise the sunlight made the starlight invisible. On May 29, 1919, a full eclipse occurred at two places in the Southern Hemisphere: at Sobral in northern Brazil and at the Principe Island in the Gulf of Guinea, located off the coast of Africa. Teams went to both places and took photographs through telescopes, and both teams found that the photographs confirmed Einstein's predictions. Eddington sent the news to Einstein through physicist Hendrik Lorentz in Holland. When Einstein received the telegram on September 27, 1919, he was meeting with a student and handed her the telegram to read. She asked Einstein what he would have thought had the results not confirmed his theory. Einstein replied, "Then I would have to be sorry for dear God. The theory is correct."[19]

Public announcement of the verification came on November 6, 1919, at a joint meeting of the Royal Society and the Royal Astronomical Society in London. In a tense atmosphere, president J.J. Thomson called Einstein's theory "one of the greatest achievements in the history of human thought. . . . It is not the discovery of an outlying island but of a whole continent of new scientific ideas. It is the greatest discovery in connection with gravitation since Newton enunciated his principles."[20] On November 7, 1919, the London *Times* headline read, "Revolution in Science, . . . Newtonian Ideas Overthrown."[21]

GLOBAL REACTION TO THE RELATIVITY THEORY

Einstein became instantly famous. When streams of reporters sought interviews, he used the opportunity to persuade them to contribute to a benefit fund for starving Viennese children before he allowed photographs to be taken or before he would give statements. Soon sacks of letters arrived with invitations to visit and lecture, with requests that he support causes, and with news that children had been named after him. By 1920 his book explaining relativity had gone through fourteen German editions, totaling sixty-five thousand copies. He had requests from salesmen for a brief summary since some folks thought relativity was about relations between the sexes. Einstein aroused as much attention from common people on the street as from professional scientists, all of them in awe and some near hysteria. Baffled, Einstein wrote to a friend,

> Saying "no" has never been a strong point with me, but in my present distress I am at last gradually learning the art. Since the flood of newspaper articles, I have been so swamped with questions, invitations, challenges, that I dream that I am burning in Hell and that the postman is the Devil eternally roaring at me, throwing new bundles of letters at my head because I have not yet answered the old ones.[22]

He lectured to overflow crowds at numerous universities, each of which usually offered him an honorary degree. By 1921 he had lost count of the number of doctoral degrees he had received, an ironical situation for a man who had had trouble earning his first one.

While the rest of the world praised Einstein, many Germans were hostile toward him and his theory. Right-wing extremists resented him for refusing to work for the war effort and attacked him for his outspoken passion advocating peace and internationalism. They created the Study Group of Natural Philosophers, offering fees to anyone willing to criticize Einstein's theory and publicly defame his character. Philip Lenard, a scientist from Heidelberg, Germany, attacked Einstein's physics, claiming that relativity was a Jewish plot to change and corrupt the world. In June 1922 right-wing extremists killed government minister Walther Rathenau, a Jewish intellectual and friend of Einstein's. One extremist, Rudolph Leibus, who had offered a reward for the murder of Einstein, was eventually charged and convicted of the murder, but he was fined less than twenty dollars as punishment. Einstein considered moving to Leiden, Netherlands, but decided to stay and fight anti-Semitism.

TRAVELS TO AMERICA AND JAPAN

Instead of moving to the Netherlands, Einstein and Elsa temporarily left Germany to make two long trips in 1921–1922: one to America and one to Japan. The American trip was a fund-raising mission to support Zionism, a movement to establish a homeland for Jews in Palestine. Besides raising over one hundred thousand dollars for the movement, Einstein was honored at dinners, shown off on tours, and expected to lecture in New York. Planners had lined up speeches in Chicago, Cleveland, and Boston. In Boston, Einstein told an audience that a man who finds something of beauty in this mysterious universe should not be personally celebrated because he has been sufficiently rewarded with the satisfaction of finding it, but his words were to no avail. The Japan trip was another outpouring of honors, with stops on the way in Colombo, capital of Sri Lanka, and Shanghai, China. Einstein's lecture at Tokyo University lasted six hours, with a break in the middle. For his second lecture, he spoke only three hours, and the crowd took offense because they had received less than the first audience. Japanese officials, who had paid the expenses for the trip, introduced the Einsteins to the emperor and empress, showed them gardens, and took them to festivals. On their return to Germany, the Einsteins stopped in Palestine, where Einstein gave the inaugural address at the newly founded Hebrew University. During this trip, Einstein learned that he had been awarded the Nobel Prize for his photoelectric theory, not his relativity theory, which the Nobel committee felt was still too controversial.

EINSTEIN LENDS SUPPORT TO CAUSES

Einstein disliked all of this celebrity attention, but he felt responsible to use his worldwide fame to promote causes about which he cared deeply. As a Jew, he wanted to help the Zionists who had organized in Basel, Switzerland, in 1897 to establish a homeland in Palestine—later called Israel—where Jews could be safe and protected by public law. Because he had seen prejudice against Jewish students and had received threats on his own life, he believed the Jews needed a place to form a safe community. Moreover, he strongly favored the opportunities that the Hebrew University in Jerusalem offered to young Jews. Yet he realized that the creation of Israel as a political state would displace Palestinians, who, he thought, should be left alone.

World War I heightened Einstein's passion against militarism and nationalism, and he took every opportunity to criticize these topics. He reasoned that nationalism aroused patriotism and a desire for power, which then created a need for a strong military; the combination of nationalism and militarism, he believed, led to war. He criticized his colleagues who worked on war projects and called World War I battles "war crimes." He supported student disarmament groups and conscientious objectors and called for an economic boycott against any country that engaged in warlike activities. Ever since he had watched military parades as a child in Munich, he had hated militarism because it made men act like a herd and have dull thoughts and dull feelings. His harsh criticism antagonized many patriotic Germans, who feared that he belonged to a suspicious political party planning a revolution.

Einstein spoke as vigorously in favor of internationalism and pacifism as he did against nationalism and militarism. He thought world government could prevent fighting among nations by overseeing cooperation; certainly this scheme was superior to the waste and cruelty of war. In May 1922 he joined a committee established to carry out a plan to build a world government, the League of Nations, which had its headquarters in Geneva, Switzerland. Because he spoke bluntly and would not compromise, he resigned from the committee. Three times between 1922 and 1931 he resigned but rejoined again because the committee needed him for the support his fame brought to the concept of world government. He also used other platforms to speak in favor of the League of Nations.

A TEMPORARY RESPITE FROM PUBLIC ATTENTION

After a whirlwind of travels, lectures, and public support for causes, Einstein settled into his Berlin apartment to be a private person. He entertained artists, philosophers, musicians, and other physicists, who offered profound conversations and the give-and-take of thoughts and ideas. In his little sailboat on the lakes around Berlin, Einstein absorbed the quiet beauty of the water and let his thoughts wander about the universe and its laws. In spite of his public role, he despised social pretension. He worked in casual clothes and lectured in a sports suit and sandals. Once, while in Oslo and lacking formal wear, he put on his usual jacket and said he could pin on a note announcing that the suit had just been brushed. Einstein was not merely careless or stubborn; he genuinely believed that dressing up reflected a desire to be high class and disguised the true self. Likewise, he despised professional hypocrites—those who took easy questions and tried to make trivial scientific problems look complicated. Of one physicist who took the easy way, Einstein said, "He strikes me as a man who looks for the thinnest spot in a board and then bores as many holes as possible through it."[23] Because he liked scholars who chose hard problems, even if they could not solve them, Einstein advised few students since the problems he approved for research were too difficult for most of them.

After he had finished his work on the general relativity theory, he focused on three physics topics. His 1905 paper on light quanta had opened up a new field of research called quantum mechanics, which was designed to study atoms and how they work. Though Einstein was not involved directly in this research, he followed the physicists who were and discussed their findings with them. Among the most active were Niels Bohr from Denmark, Louis de Broglie from France, Erwin Schrodinger from Austria, and Max Born and Werner Heisenberg from Germany. These men found that the movement of an electron in an atom is random, and the only way to measure its orbit is statistically, as one predicts coin tosses and rolls of dice. Einstein respected their work, but he disagreed with their conclusions. With his firm belief in an ordered universe, he thought their findings were a temporary conclusion; he repeated many times that God does not throw dice.

Einstein devoted most of his attention for the next decades to finding a unified field theory; he wanted to find equations that incorporated the properties of the gravitational and electromagnetic fields into one theory. He came up with approaches in 1923 and 1929, but neither was correct. Because he worked so long without success, some scientists thought he should have accepted the conclusions of quantum mechanics and worked on more solvable problems.

Einstein's third interest was the philosophy of science, seeing how science and reality relate, how science and religion coexist, and how creativity, imagination, and intuition contribute to scientific theory. He wanted to know how the mind and spirit work together. He said, "Science without religion is lame, religion without science is blind."[24]

Einstein's fiftieth birthday on March 14, 1929, turned into another world event. To escape reporters, Einstein hid in the gardener's cottage at the lake home of his doctor Jonos Plesh, and kept his whereabouts a secret, except from his family. Enough birthday cards came from physicists, philosophers, pacifists, Zionists, and ordinary people to fill several wash baskets. He received a sailboat from a Berlin bank, a plot of land in Palestine already planted with trees named "Einstein's Grove," and a small package of tobacco from an unemployed man who had saved nickels to buy the present. His note apologized for the small amount but assured Einstein that the quality was good. Einstein answered his note first.

TEACHING IN AMERICA AND TROUBLE IN GERMANY

As the 1930s began, Einstein's life was interrupted by teaching in California and by the Nazis and Adolf Hitler in Germany. He had contracts to teach during the winter terms at the California Technological Institute in Pasadena in 1931, 1932, and 1933. He returned to Germany in the spring to find the Nazi threat had increased. The Nazis rose to power under Hitler's leadership and a campaign of hate. Hitler attacked Jews and Communists, hated the "injustice" of the World War I treaty, and believed that the German army had not been defeated but had been betrayed by pacifists and Jews who had refused to help with the war.

When Einstein and Elsa left their lake home for the third

Pasadena term, Einstein had a hunch that he would never see it again. While in Pasadena, Hitler was voted into office on January 30, 1933. At the New York harbor on the way back to Germany, when Einstein spoke publicly about the dangers of Hitler, he was warned (unofficially) by the German consul that returning was too dangerous. He and Elsa stopped in Belgium and stayed in an obscure coastal village. From there he resigned from the Berlin Academy, renounced his German citizenship, turned in his German passport, and withdrew from the Bavarian Academy. His letter said that he "did not wish to live in a country where the individual does not enjoy equality before the law, and freedom of speech and teaching."[25] A Berlin newspaper headline read, "Good News from Einstein—He's Not Coming Back."[26] For the second time Einstein had given up his German citizenship, but this time he was also without a home.

On April 1, 1933, Hitler began to purge Germany of Jews and took severe measures against Einstein. Hitler's officers seized Einstein's bank account and all securities, closed and locked his apartment, seized his lake home, published a book that listed one hundred professors against Einstein, offered a five-thousand-dollar reward to the person who would kill Einstein, and denounced his relativity theory in the Nazi newspaper *Volkische Boebachter.* In the May issue, Heidelberg scientist Philip Lenard called relativity Einstein's "botched-up theories consisting of some ancient knowledge and a few arbitrary additions."[27] On April 12, Einstein's stepdaughters, his assistant, and his doctor fled Germany and got to France safely. On May 10, forty thousand people cheered as they watched a pile of two thousand books burn, and Nazi plans were under way for the extermination of non-Aryans, or Jews.

THE EINSTEINS MOVE TO AMERICA

The summer of 1933 was chaotic: Einstein and Elsa had found a safe temporary hiding place in England but needed to find a safe permanent home. Einstein had job offers from England, Belgium, Spain, France, Jerusalem, Pasadena, and Princeton, New Jersey. He told a friend that he had more offers for professorial positions than he had reasonable ideas in his head. He chose the offer from the Institute for Advanced Study in Princeton, New Jersey, where he could gather with outstanding intellectuals, exchange ideas, and work on his own research without teaching obligations. On October 7, 1933, Einstein left England with his wife; his assistant, Dr. Meyer; and his secretary, Helen Dukas. He chose America to be his new home for its promising intellectual climate and its many institutions awarding doctoral degrees in physics. America was especially rich in scientific talent from Europe since many Jewish scholars, purged from German and Austrian universities, had settled in America.

In Princeton, Einstein lived with Elsa at 112 Mercer Street, worked regularly at the institute during the school year, and often welcomed refugees coming from Germany. Elsa's daughter Ilse had died, but her husband, Rudolf Kayser, came with Elsa's daughter Margot and her husband, Einstein's son Hans Albert, and Einstein's sister, Maja. Einstein helped a German violinist find work playing concerts and a physicist obtain a contract as his assistant. He spent summers sailing at the cottage of his long-standing friend Peter Bucky.

From the time of his arrival in America, he was deluged with invitations for social visits and requests for interviews and appearances, which his secretary screened and answered herself, except for those she thought he might want to accept. For example, he and Elsa visited President Franklin D. Roosevelt and his wife, Eleanor, at the White House. Einstein especially enjoyed the president because he spoke German. Einstein also wrote a message for the time capsule at the New York World's Fair in which he admonished future generations to work for peace and rationality.

Elsa's death in 1936 began a series of changes in Einstein's life. Early in the year she became very ill with a heart and kidney ailment, but she recovered enough to spend the summer with Einstein at a lake in upstate New York. In the fall they returned to Mercer Street, but Elsa's health continued to deteriorate until she died on December 21. Filled with grief, Einstein was unable to concentrate, but, as with past sadnesses, he found the best recovery from his sorrow was to work. His divorced stepdaughter Margot and his secretary, Helen Dukas, moved in and managed the home. Three years later Maja joined them. Realizing he would never return to Europe, Einstein, along with Margot and Dukas, took the exam to become American citizens, and on October 1, 1940, the three of them were sworn in.

Late in the 1930s as an American citizen, Einstein still supported causes, but he changed his views on pacifism when he realized that there were no good choices. Pacifism created a vacuum that had allowed Hitler to believe he could gain control; either choose pacifism and allow Hitler's evil power to prevail or use force and violence to stop Hitler's power. Einstein decided that the second was the better choice. These thoughts prompted him to warn President Roosevelt about German research into an atomic bomb. Fearing that Hitler might gain access to the bomb first, Einstein recommended to Roosevelt that the Americans begin research. Once the bomb was developed, Einstein sent another letter urging the Americans to refrain from dropping it on Japanese citizens.

STILL A CELEBRITY IN RETIREMENT AND OLD AGE

Einstein continued to work and speak even though he had formally retired in April 1945. He focused on peace and his concern about atomic energy. He received additional honors and new invitations to head scientific organizations. In 1949, when he turned seventy, the Institute for Advanced Studies organized a conference at which selected scientists read papers. Eleanor Roosevelt also invited Einstein to contribute to her television program on the hydrogen bomb. In 1952 he was invited to be president of Israel, the Jewish state established in 1948, but he declined, claiming that he was too old and too bad at politics. He preferred his life on Mercer Street surrounded by the women who cared for him and his cat.

But Einstein never became a mellow old man and never forgave the Germans. After the German defeat in World War II, he was asked to renew his ties with the Kaiser Wilhelm Institute. He refused in a stinging letter:

> The crime of the Germans is truly the most abominable ever to be recorded in the history of the so-called civilized nations. The conduct of German intellectuals—seen as a group—was no better than that of a mob. And even now there is no indication of any regret or any real desire to repair whatever little may be left to restore after the gigantic murders. In the view of these circumstances I feel an irrepressible aversion to participating in anything that represents any aspect of public life in Germany.[28]

Einstein received many other invitations from Germans, but he never relented. He spoke his mind on the usual topics, but he recognized that his words on peace and internationalism had little effect. He joked that he still lost his temper dutifully about politics, but he said he no longer flapped his wings—only ruffled his feathers.

DEATH COMES QUICKLY

In April 1955 Einstein's health began to fail. On Wednesday, April 13, he was struck with severe pain; when the doctor came the next day, Einstein asked him how long death would take. Friday passed at home, but on Saturday the pain was so severe that Einstein agreed to go to the hospital. On Sunday the pain had lifted, and Margot and Hans Albert came to be with him. In the afternoon, Einstein asked for his papers and calculations, hoping to work on the unified field theory on Monday. Shortly after midnight, however, his breathing changed, and the nurse raised his bed. He quietly spoke words in German, but the nurse understood only English. Then he died. In the morning reporters cabled millions of words out of Princeton, and in Germany an opera was being written about his life, soon to be presented in East Berlin. The man of the century was gone, but not his legacy.

NOTES

1. Albert Einstein, *Autobiographical Notes*. Trans. and ed. Paul Arthur Schilpp. 1949. Reprint. La Salle, IL: Open Court, 1979, p. 9.
2. Quoted in Phillip Frank, *Einstein: His Life and Times*. Trans. George Rosen. Ed. and rev. Shuichi Kusaka. New York: Alfred A. Knopf, 1953, p. 8.
3. Einstein, *Autobiographical Notes*, pp. 9, 11.
4. Quoted in Banesh Hoffmann, in collaboration with Helen Dukas, *Albert Einstein: Creator and Rebel*. New York: Penguin, 1972, p. 24.
5. Quoted in Hoffmann, *Albert Einstein*, p. 20.
6. Einstein, *Autobiographical Notes*, p. 5.
7. Einstein, *Autobiographical Notes*, p. 5.
8. Quoted in Hoffmann, *Albert Einstein*, p. 25.
9. Anton Reiser, *Albert Einstein: A Biographical Portrait*. New York: Albert and Charles Boni, 1930, p. 49.
10. Quoted in Hoffmann, *Albert Einstein*, p. 32.
11. Hoffmann, *Albert Einstein*, p. 34.
12. Ronald W. Clark, *Einstein: The Life and Times*. New York: World, 1971, p. 86.
13. Quoted in Frank, *Einstein*, p. 101.
14. Quoted in Frank, *Einstein*, p. 118.
15. Reiser, *Albert Einstein*, pp. 124–25.
16. Quoted in Clark, *Einstein*, p. 174.

17. Quoted in Timothy Ferris, *Coming of Age in the Milky Way.* New York: William Morrow, 1988, p. 200.

18. Quoted in Clark, *Einstein,* p. 200.

19. Quoted in Clark, *Einstein,* p. 230.

20. Quoted in Clark, *Einstein,* p. 232.

21. Quoted in Frank, *Einstein,* p. 140.

22. Quoted in Clark, *Einstein,* p. 246.

23. Quoted in Frank, *Einstein,* p. 117.

24. Albert Einstein, *Ideas and Opinions.* Ed. Carl Seelig. New York: Crown, 1954, p. 46.

25. Einstein, *Ideas and Opinions,* pp. 206–207.

26. Quoted in Clark, *Einstein,* p. 463.

27. Quoted in Frank, *Einstein,* p. 232.

28. Quoted in Hoffmann, *Albert Einstein,* p. 237.

CHAPTER 1

MAJOR INFLUENCES ON EINSTEIN'S DEVELOPMENT AS A SCIENTIST

Boyhood Influences

Ronald W. Clark

Ronald W. Clark cites experiences from Einstein's boyhood that affected his career. A gift of a compass from his father and algebra stories from his uncle aroused Einstein's interest in science and mathematics, and books from a family friend introduced him to physics, higher mathematics, and philosophy. According to Clark, the Luitpold Gymnasium was where Einstein developed a skeptical attitude, a benefit for one who would someday be on the cutting edge of science. Einstein's own reading and thinking led him to reconcile science and church teachings into a unified religious attitude. Ronald W. Clark, a writer, is the author of *The Huxley's, The Birth of the Bomb, The Victorian Mountaineer,* and several others.

[Einstein's] boyhood was straightforward enough. From the age of five until the age of ten he attended a Catholic school near his home, and at ten was transferred to the Luitpold Gymnasium, where the children of the middle classes had drummed into them the rudiments of Latin and Greek, of history and geography, as well as of simple mathematics. The choice of a Catholic school was not as curious as it seems. Elementary education in Bavaria was run on a denominational basis. The nearest Jewish school was some distance from the Einstein home and its fees were high. To a family of little religious feeling the dangers of Catholic orientation were outweighed by the sound general instruction which the school gave. . . .

THE INFLUENCE OF PARENTS AND UNCLES

Before he left his Catholic elementary school for the very different Luitpold Gymnasium he received what appears to have been the first genuine shock to his intellectual system. The "appears" is necessary. For this was the famous incident of the pocket compass and while he confirmed that it actually happened he was also to put a gloss on its significance.

The story is simply that when the boy was five, ill in bed, his father showed him a pocket compass. What impressed the child was that since the iron needle always pointed in the same direction, whichever way the case was turned, it must be acted upon by something that existed in space—the space that had always been considered empty. The incident, so redolent of "famous childhoods," is reported persistently in the accounts of Einstein's youth that began to be printed after he achieved popular fame at the end of the First World War. Whether it always had its later significance is another matter. Einstein himself, answering questions in 1953 at the time of his seventy-fourth birthday, gave it perspective by his assessment of how it had—or might have—affected him. Did the compass, and the book on Euclidean geometry which he read a few years later, really influence him, he was asked. "I myself think so, and I believe that these outside influences had a considerable influence on my development," he replied with some caution. "But a man has little insight into what goes on within him. When a young puppy sees a compass for the first time it may have no similar influence, nor on many a child. What does, in fact, determine the particular reaction of an individual? One can postulate more or less plausible theories on this subject, but one never really finds the answer."

Soon afterwards another influence entered Einstein's life. From the age of six he began to learn the violin. The enthusiasm this evoked did not come quickly. He was taught by rote rather than inspiration, and seven years passed before he was aroused by Mozart into an awareness of the mathematical structure of music. Yet his delight in the instrument grew steadily and became a psychological safety valve; it was never quite matched by performance. In later years the violin became the hallmark of the world's most famous scientist; but Einstein's supreme and obvious enjoyment in performance was the thing. Amateur, gifted or not, remained amateur.

Hermann Einstein with his compass and Pauline Einstein with her insistence on music lessons brought two influences to bear on their son. A third was provided by his uncle Jakob, the sound engineer without whom Hermann would have foundered even faster in the sea of good intentions.

Jakob Einstein is a relatively shadowy figure, and his memorial is a single anecdote, remembered over more than thirty years and recalled by Einstein to his early biographers. "Algebra is a merry science," Uncle Jakob would say. "We go hunting for a little animal whose name we don't know, so we call it x. When we bag our game we pounce on it and give it its right name." Uncle Jakob may or may not have played a significant part in making mathematics appear attractive, but his influence seems to have been long-lasting. In many of Einstein's later attempts to present the theory of relativity to nonmathematicians, there is recourse to something not so very different; to analogies with elevators, trains, and ships that suggest a memory of the stone house at Sendling and Uncle Jakob's "little animal whose name we don't know."

However, the Einstein family included an in-law more important than Father, Mother, or Uncle Jakob. This was Cäsar Koch, Pauline Koch's brother, who lived in Stuttgart and whose visits to the Einstein family were long remembered. "You have always been my best-loved uncle," Einstein wrote to him as a man of forty-five. "You have always been one of the few who have warmed my heart whenever I thought of you, and when I was young your visit was always a great occasion." In January, 1885, Cäsar Koch returned to Germany from Russia, where part of his family was living. With him he brought as a present for Albert a model steam engine, handed over during a visit to Munich that year, and drawn from memory by his nephew thirty years later. Soon afterwards Cäsar married and moved to Antwerp—where the young Albert was subsequently taken on a conducted tour of the Bourse [a stock exchange]. A well-to-do grain merchant, Cäsar Koch appears to have had few intellectual pretensions. But some confidence was sparked up between uncle and nephew and it was to Cäsar that Einstein was to send, as a boy of sixteen, an outline of the imaginative ideas later developed into the Special Theory of Relativity.

EINSTEIN LEARNS SKEPTICISM AT THE LUITPOLD GYMNASIUM

However, nothing so precocious appeared likely when Einstein in 1889 made his first appearance at the Luitpold Gymnasium. Still slightly backward, introspective, keeping to himself the vague stirrings of interest which he felt for the world about him, he had so far given no indication that he was in any way different from the common run of children. The next six years at the Gymnasium were to alter that, although hardly in the way his parents can have hoped.

Within the climate of the time, the Luitpold Gymnasium seems to have been no better and no worse than most establishments of its kind. It is true that it put as great a premium on a thick skin as any British public school but there is no reason to suppose that it was particularly ogreish. Behind what might be regarded as no more than normal discipline it held, in reserve, the ultimate weapon of appeal to the unquestionable Prussian god of authority. Yet boys, and even sensitive boys, have survived as much; some have even survived Eton.

The Gymnasium was to have a critical effect on Einstein in separate ways. The first was that its discipline created in him a deep suspicion of authority in general and of educational authority in particular. This feeling lasted all his life, without qualification. "The teachers in the elementary school appeared to me like sergeants and in the Gymnasium the teachers were like lieutenants," he remembered. More than forty years later, speaking to the seventy-second Convocation of the State University of New York, he noted that to him, "the worst thing seems to be for a school principally to work with methods of fear, force, and artificial authority. Such treatment destroys the healthy feelings, the integrity, and self-confidence of the pupils. All that it produces is a servile helot." And years later, replying to a young girl who had sent him a manuscript, he wrote, "Keep your manuscript for your sons and daughters, in order that they may derive consolation from it and—not give a damn for what their teachers tell them or think of them."

Not giving a damn about accepted beliefs was an attitude which certainly developed at the Gymnasium The teaching may or may not have justified the principle, but the outcome was singularly fortunate as far as Einstein was concerned. It taught him the virtues of scepticism. It encouraged him to question and to doubt, always valuable qualities in a scientist and particularly so at this period in the history of physics. Here the advance of technology was bringing to light curious new phenomena which, however hard men might try, could not be fitted into the existing order of things. Yet innate conservatism presented a formidable barrier to discussion, let alone acceptance, of new ideas. If Einstein had not been pushed by the Luitpold Gymnasium into the stance of opposition he was to retain all his life, then he might not have questioned so quickly so many assumptions that most men took for granted, nor have arrived at such an early age at the Special Theory of Relativity.

A third effect was of a very different kind. There is no doubt that he despised educational discipline and that this in turn nourished the radical inquiring attitude that is essential to the scientist. Yet it was only years later, as he looked back from middle life to childhood, that he expressed his dislike of the Gymnasium so vehemently. Until then, according to one percipient biographer who came to know him well, "he could not even say that he hated it. According to family legend, this taciturn child, who was not given to complaining, did not even seem very miserable. Only long afterwards did he identify the tone and atmosphere of his schooldays with that of barracks, the negation, in his opinion, of the human being."

THE GYMNASIUM COLORS EINSTEIN'S ATTITUDE TOWARD GERMANS

Yet by the end of the First World War this school environment had become a symbol in an equation whose validity Einstein never doubted. The Luitpold Gymnasium as he looked back on it equaled ruthless discipline, and the Luitpold Gymnasium was German. Thus the boyhood hardships became transformed into the symbol of all that was worst in the German character—a transformation that was to produce dire and ironic consequences. With the stench of Belsen [the site of a Nazi concentration camp during World War II] still in the nostrils after twenty-five years it is easy enough to understand the near paranoia that affected Einstein when in later life he regarded his own countrymen. It is easy enough to understand his reply when, at the age of sixty-nine, he was asked: "Is there any German person towards whom you feel an estimation, and who was your very personal friend among the German-born?" "Respect for Planck," Einstein had replied. "No friendship for any real German. [Physicist] Max van Laue was the closest to me." All this is understandable. Yet Germans were among the first to die in the concentration camps, and it is remarkable to find in Einstein, normally the most compassionate of men, an echo of the cry that the only good German is a dead one.

Thus the Luitpold Gymnasium, transmogrified by memory, has a lot to answer for; it convinced Einstein that the Prussians had been handed out a double dose of original sin. Later experiences tended to confirm the belief.

At the Gymnasium there appears to have been, as there frequently is in such schools, one master who stood apart, the odd man out going his nonconformist way. His name was Reuss. He tried to make his pupils think for themselves while most of his colleagues did little more—in Einstein's later opinion—than encourage an academic *Kadavergehorsamkeit* ("the obedience of the corpse") that was required among troops of the Imperial Prussian army. In later life Einstein would recall how Reuss had tried to spark alive a real interest in ancient civilizations and their influences which still could be seen in the contemporary life of southern Germany. There was to be an unexpected footnote to Einstein's memory. For after his first work had begun to pass a disturbing electric shock through the framework of science, he himself visited Munich and called on his old teacher, then living in retirement. But the worn suit and baggy trousers which had already become the Einstein hallmark among his colleagues merely suggested poverty. Reuss had no recollection of Einstein's name and it became clear that he thought his caller was on a begging errand. Einstein left hurriedly.

MAX TALMEY STEERS EINSTEIN TO PHYSICS, MATH, AND PHILOSOPHY

The influence that initially led Einstein on to his chosen path did not come from the Luitpold Gymnasium but from Max Talmey, a young Jewish medical student who in 1889 matriculated at Munich University. Talmey's elder brother, a practicing doctor, already knew the Einstein family, and quickly introduced him to what Max called "the happy, comfortable, and cheerful Einstein home, where I received the same generous consideration as he did." In later life Talmey was seized with the idea for a universal language, an Esperanto which he felt would be particularly valuable for science. He tried to enlist Einstein's support, became interested in relativity, and then, like so many others, attempted to explain the theory. More important was the inclusion in his little-known book on the subject of his own impressions of Einstein at the age of twelve, the only reliable first-hand account that exists.

"He was a pretty, dark-haired boy . . . a good illustration . . . against the theory of Houston Stewart Chamberlain and others who try to prove that only the blond races produce geniuses," Talmey wrote.

> He showed a particular inclination toward physics and took pleasure in conversing on physical phenomena. I gave him therefore as reading matter A. Bernstein's *Popular Books on Physical Science* and L. Buchner's *Force and Matter,* two works that were then quite popular in Germany. The boy was profoundly impressed by them. Bernstein's work especially, which describes physical phenomena lucidly and engagingly, had a great influence on Albert, and enhanced considerably his interest in physical science.

Soon afterwards he began to show keenness for mathematics, and Talmey gave him a copy of Spieker's *Lehrbuch der ebenen Geometrie,* a popular textbook. Thereafter, whenever the young medical student arrived for the midday meal on Thursdays, he would be shown the problems solved by Einstein during the previous week.

> After a short time, a few months, he had worked through the whole book of Spieker. He thereupon devoted himself to higher mathematics, studying all by himself Lubsen's excellent works on the subject. These, too, I had recommended to him if memory serves me right. Soon the flight of his mathematical genius was so high that I could no longer follow. Thereafter philosophy was often a subject of our conversations. I recommended to him the reading of Kant. At that time he was still a child, only thirteen years old, yet Kant's works, incomprehensible to ordinary mortals, seemed to be clear to him. Kant became Albert's favorite philosopher after he had read through his *Critique of Pure Reason* and the works of other philosophers.

EINSTEIN DEVELOPS A RELIGIOUS ATTITUDE

. . . By the time he was twelve Einstein had attained, in his own words, "a deep religiosity." His approval of this translation of the German in his autobiographical notes is significant; for religiosity, the "affected or excessive religiousness" of the dictionary, appears to describe accurately the results of what he called "the traditional education-machine." Always sensitive to beauty, abnormally sensitive to music, Einstein had no doubt been deeply impressed by the splendid trappings in which Bavarian Catholicism of those days was decked out. But if his emotions were won over, his mind remained free—with considerable results. "Through the reading of popular scientific books I soon reached the conviction that much of the stories in the Bible could not be true," he wrote.

> The consequence was a positively fanatic [orgy of] free-thinking coupled with the impression that youth is intentionally being deceived by the state through lies; it was a crushing impression. Suspicion against every kind of authority grew out of this experience, a sceptical attitude towards the convictions which were alive in any specific social environment—an attitude which has never again left me, even though later on, because of a better insight into the causal connections, it lost some of its original poignancy.

This is important not because the change of heart itself was unusual but because of Einstein's future history. For centuries young people have abandoned revealed religion at the impressionable age and turned to the laws of nature as a substitute. The process is hardly one for wide-eyed wonder. What was different with Einstein was that the common act should have such uncommon results.

His need of something to fill the void, the desperate need to find order in a chaotic world may possibly have been a particularly Jewish need. Certainly Abba Eban, in 1955 Israeli ambassador to the United States, noted after Einstein's death how "the Hebrew mind has been obsessed for centuries by a concept of order and harmony in the universal design. The search for laws hitherto unknown which govern cosmic forces; the doctrine of a relative harmony in nature; the idea of a calculable relationship between matter and energy—these are all more likely to emerge from a basic Hebrew philosophy and turn of mind than from many others." This may sound like hindsight plus special pleading; yet the long line of Jewish physicists from the nineteenth century, and the even longer list of those who later sought the underlying unifications of the subatomic world, give it a plausibility which cannot easily be contested.

If there were no order or logic in the man-made conceptions of the world based on revealed religion, surely order and logic could be discovered in the huge world which, Einstein wrote, "exists independently of us human beings and which stands before us like a great eternal riddle, at least partially accessible to our inspection and thinking. The contemplation of this world beckoned like a liberation, and I soon noticed that many a man who I had learned to esteem and to admire had found inner freedom and security in devoted occupation with it." The young Einstein, like many a

Victorian ecclesiastic who wished "to penetrate into the *ar-cana* [secret, mystery] of nature, so as to discern 'the law within the law,'" picked up science where religion appeared to leave off. Later he was to see both as different sides of the same coin, as complementary as the wave and corpuscle conceptions of light, and both just as necessary if one were to see reality in the round. All this, however, developed in the decades after conversion.

From Experience to Thinking to Worldview

Albert Einstein

In his autobiographical reflections written at the age of sixty-seven, Albert Einstein identifies earlier experiences that influenced his worldview. When at twelve he rejected a "religious paradise" as a way of satisfying the thinking and feeling part of his being, he envisioned a great outside world filled with riddles, a world to which men he admired had devoted themselves. Einstein elaborates on thinking: what thought is and is not, how thinking is connected to wonder, and how two childhood experiences contributed to his sense of wonder and, consequently, to his thought. In addition to his scientific works, Albert Einstein published numerous essays on politics, religion, Zionism, freedom, and education.

Even when I was a fairly precocious young man the nothingness of the hopes and strivings which chases most men restlessly through life came to my consciousness with considerable vitality. Moreover, I soon discovered the cruelty of that chase, which in those years was much more carefully covered up by hypocrisy and glittering words than is the case today. By the mere existence of his stomach everyone was condemned to participate in that chase. Moreover, it was possible to satisfy the stomach by such participation, but not man in so far as he is a thinking and feeling being. As the first way out there was religion, which is implanted into every child by way of the traditional education-machine. Thus I came—despite the fact that I was the son of entirely irreligious (Jewish) parents—to a deep religiosity, which, however, found an abrupt ending at the age of 12. Through the reading of popular scientific books I soon reached the conviction that much in the stories of the Bible could not be true. The consequence was a positively fanatic [orgy of] freethinking coupled with the impression that youth is intentionally being deceived by the state through lies; it was a crushing impression. Suspicion against every kind of authority grew out of this experience, a skeptical attitude towards the convictions which were alive in any specific social environment—an attitude which has never again left me, even though later on, because of a better insight into the causal connections, it lost some of its original poignancy.

LOSING RELIGIOUS PARADISE, EINSTEIN TURNS TO THE GREAT EXTRA-PERSONAL WORLD

It is quite clear to me that the religious paradise of youth, which was thus lost, was a first attempt to free myself from the chains of the "merely-personal," from an existence which is dominated by wishes, hopes and primitive feelings. Out yonder there was this huge world, which exists independently of us human beings and which stands before us like a great, eternal riddle, at least partially accessible to our inspection and thinking. The contemplation of this world beckoned like a liberation, and I soon noticed that many a man whom I had learned to esteem and to admire had found inner freedom and security in devoted occupation with it. The mental grasp of this extra-personal world within the frame of the given possibilities swam as highest aim half consciously and half unconsciously before my mind's eye. Similarly motivated men of the present and of the past, as well as the insights which they had achieved, were the friends which could not be lost. The road to this paradise was not as comfortable and alluring as the road to the religious paradise; but it has proved itself as trustworthy, and I have never regretted having chosen it.

What I have here said is true only within a certain sense, just as a drawing consisting of a few strokes can do justice to a complicated object, full of perplexing details, only in a very limited sense. If an individual enjoys well-ordered thoughts, it is quite possible that this side of his nature may grow more pronounced at the cost of other sides and thus may determine his mentality in increasing degree. In this case it is well possible that such an individual in retrospect sees a uniformly systematic development, whereas the actual experience takes place in kaleidoscopic particular situations. The manifoldness of the external situations and the narrowness of the momentary content of consciousness bring about a sort of atomizing of the life of every human being. In a man of my type the turning-point of the development lies in the fact that gradually the major interest disengages itself to a far-reaching degree from the momentary and the merely personal and turns towards the striving for a mental grasp of things. Looked at from this point of view the above schematic remarks contain as much truth as can be uttered in such brevity.

EINSTEIN DELIMITS THINKING

What, precisely, is "thinking"? When, at the reception of sense-impressions, memory-pictures emerge, this is not yet "thinking." And when such pictures form series, each member of which calls forth another, this too is not yet "thinking." When, however, a certain picture turns up in many such series, then—precisely through such return—it becomes an ordering element for such series, in that it connects series which in themselves are unconnected. Such an element becomes an instrument, a concept. I think that the transition from free association or "dreaming" to thinking is characterized by the more or less dominating rôle which the "concept" plays in it. It is by no means necessary that a concept must be connected with a sensorily cognizable and reproducible sign (word); but when this is the case thinking becomes by means of that fact communicable.

With what right—the reader will ask—does this man operate so carelessly and primitively with ideas in such a problematic realm without making even the least effort to prove anything? My defense: all our thinking is of this nature of a free play with concepts; the justification for this play lies in the measure of survey over the experience of the senses which we are able to achieve with its aid. The concept of "truth" can not yet be applied to such a structure; to my thinking this concept can come in question only when a far-reaching agreement (*convention*) concerning the elements and rules of the game is already at hand.

WONDER LEADS TO THOUGHT

For me it is not dubious that our thinking goes on for the most part without use of signs (words) and beyond that to a considerable degree unconsciously. For how, otherwise, should it happen that sometimes we "wonder" quite spontaneously about some experience? This "wondering" seems to occur when an experience comes into conflict with a world of concepts which is already sufficiently fixed in us. Whenever such a conflict is experienced hard and intensively it reacts back upon our thought world in a decisive way. The development of this thought world is in a certain sense a continuous flight from "wonder."

A wonder of such nature I experienced as a child of 4 or 5 years, when my father showed me a compass. That this needle behaved in such a determined way did not at all fit into the nature of events, which could find a place in the unconscious world of concepts (effect connected with direct "touch"). I can still remember—or at least believe I can remember—that this experience made a deep and lasting impression upon me. Something deeply hidden had to be behind things. What man sees before him from infancy causes no reaction of this kind; he is not surprised over the falling of bodies, concerning wind and rain, nor concerning the moon or about the fact that the moon does not fall down, nor concerning the differences between living and non-living matter.

At the age of 12 I experienced a second wonder of a totally different nature: in a little book dealing with Euclidian plane geometry, which came into my hands at the beginning of a schoolyear. Here were assertions, as for example the intersection of the three altitudes of a triangle in one point, which—though by no means evident—could nevertheless be proved with such certainty that any doubt appeared to be out of the question. This lucidity and certainty made an indescribable impression upon me. That the axiom had to be accepted unproved did not disturb me. In any case it was quite sufficient for me if I could peg proofs upon propositions the validity of which did not seem to me to be dubious. For example I remember that an uncle told me the Pythagorean theorem before the holy geometry booklet had come into my hands. After much effort I succeeded in "proving" this theorem on the basis of the similarity of triangles; in doing so it seemed to me "evident" that the relations of the sides of the right-angled triangles would have to be completely determined by one of the acute angles. Only something which did not in similar fashion seem to be "evident" appeared to me to be in need of any proof at all. Also, the objects with which geometry deals seemed to be of no different type than the objects of sensory perception, "which can be seen and touched." This primitive idea, which probably also lies at the bottom of the well known Kantian problematic concerning the possibility of "synthetic judgments *a priori* [made before or without examination]," rests obviously upon the fact that the relation of geometrical concepts to objects of direct experience (rigid rod, finite interval, etc.) was unconsciously present.

If thus it appeared that it was possible to get certain knowledge of the objects of experience by means of pure thinking, this "wonder" rested upon an error. Nevertheless, for anyone who experiences it for the first time, it is marvellous enough that man is capable at all to reach such a degree of certainty and purity in pure thinking as the Greeks showed us for the first time to be possible in geometry.

A Friend Helps Einstein Advance His Career

Banesh Hoffmann and Helen Dukas

Banesh Hoffmann explains that Marcel Grossmann helped Einstein obtain his university degree and his first full-time job. Einstein, who had neglected his studies, was able to pass his examinations because Grossmann let Einstein study his notes. Two years later, when Einstein had failed to obtain a university assistantship, Grossmann and his father helped Einstein obtain a job at the patent office in Bern, Switzerland. For both favors, Einstein was forever grateful. Banesh Hoffmann taught mathematics at Queens College of the City University of New York. He is the author of several books, including *The Strange Story of Quantum, The Tyranny of Testing,* and *Albert Einstein: The Human Side.* Helen Dukas was Einstein's secretary from 1928 to 1955.

After an unexpectedly pleasant year in Aarau [Switzerland], Einstein obtained his diploma. With the age requirement waived, it made him eligible for admission to the Zurich Polytechnic. He entered in the fall of 1896, though no longer intending to become an engineer. With Just Winteler[1] as a shining example, Einstein now looked on teaching as a preferable way of earning a living. Accordingly, he enrolled in the course for training specialist teachers of mathematics and science. Uncles in Genoa resolved his immediate financial problems by giving him an allowance of a hundred francs a month, and at last his career seemed safely on its way.

EINSTEIN NEGLECTS STUDIES AND NEEDS HELP

But freedom once tasted is rarely forgotten. And a youth whom playmates had once called *Biedermeier*[2] does not

1. the teacher at Aarau who provided lodging for Einstein   2. a nickname meaning Honest John

Excerpted from "The Child and the Young Man," in *Albert Einstein: Creator and Rebel,* by Banesh Hoffmann and Helen Dukas. Copyright © 1972 by Helen Dukas and Banesh Hoffmann. Reprinted with permission of Dutton, a division of Penguin Putnam Inc.

readily acquire tact. At the Zurich Polytechnic, Einstein could not easily bring himself to study what did not interest him. Most of his time he spent on his own in joyful exploration of the wonderland of science, performing experiments and studying at first hand the works of great pioneers in science and philosophy. Some of these works he read with his Serbian classmate Mileva Maric, whom he later married.

As for the lectures, they were for him an intrusion. He attended them only fitfully, and for the most part with little enthusiasm.

By now he knew that his true interests lay not in mathematics but in physics; yet even the physics lectures did not attract him. Unfortunately, in the four-year course two major examinations had to be passed. Again disaster threatened, and again it was narrowly averted. His classmate Marcel Grossmann, a brilliant mathematician, had quickly recognized Einstein's quality. The two became friends. Grossmann was meticulous in attending the lectures, and meticulous, too, in taking notes that were models of detail and clarity. He gladly let Einstein study these notes, and without them to cram from, Einstein might well have failed the examinations. He graduated in 1900.

Grossmann's notes had given Einstein freedom to pursue his own studies. Among the fields he mastered was what is known as Maxwell's theory of electromagnetism, an important theory that, to Einstein's disappointment, had not been taken up in the lectures of Heinrich Weber. . . .

In Zurich, Einstein lived frugally. Not that his allowance was inadequate. From the start he had deliberately set aside a fifth of it, saving up to be able later to pay the fees for acquiring Swiss citizenship. With his father's help he applied for it in October of 1899, and after the majestic unrolling of red tape he became in February of 1901 a citizen of the city of Zurich and thereby of the canton of Zurich and of Switzerland itself. He retained his Swiss citizenship through all vicissitudes for the rest of his life.

The four years at the Poly had not been altogether pleasant. As he wrote in his "Autobiographical Notes":

> One had to cram all this stuff into one's mind for the examinations, whether one liked it or not. This coercion had such a deterring effect on me that, after I passed the final examination, I found the consideration of any scientific problems distasteful to me for an entire year.

PROBLEMS FINDING A JOB

With graduation came bitter times for Einstein. Everything went wrong. His beloved science had lost its appeal. By his forthrightness and his distrust of authority he had alienated his professors, among them Heinrich Weber, who apparently conceived a particular dislike of him. This was the same Heinrich Weber who, five years before, had generously gone out of his way to encourage the youth who had failed the entrance examinations. The relationship had since deteriorated, Weber on one occasion saying to Einstein with probably justified exasperation, "You're a clever fellow! But you have one fault. You won't let anyone tell you a thing. You won't let anyone tell you a thing."

With the end of the course Einstein's allowance had stopped and he had to look desperately for a job. He was now twenty-one. When he sought university positions, he was rebuffed. Writing in 1901, he said, "From what people tell me, I am not in the good graces of any of my former teachers," and, "I would long ago have found [a position as assistant in a university] had not Weber intrigued against me."

Einstein managed to keep body and soul together by finding temporary jobs—performing calculations, teaching in

---

EINSTEIN THANKS GROSSMANN

Marcel Grossmann asked his father to help Einstein get a job at the patent office in Bern. Thanking his friend, Einstein wrote the following letter, printed in Ronald W. Clark's Einstein: The Life and Times.

Dear Marcel,

When I found your letter yesterday I was deeply moved by your devotion and compassion which do not let you forget an old, unlucky friend. I could hardly find better friends than you and Ehrat. Needless to say, I would be delighted to get the job. I would spare no effort to live up to your recommendation. I have spent three weeks at my parents' home looking for a position of assistant lecturer at some university. I am sure I would have found one long ago were it not for Weber's intrigues against me. In spite of all this, I don't let a single opportunity pass unheeded, nor have I lost my sense of humor. . . . When God created the ass he gave him a thick skin.

Ronald W. Clark, *Einstein: The Life and Times.* New York: Avon, 1971.

school, and tutoring. Yet even here his independence and unworldliness caused difficulties.

However, his love of science gradually returned, and, while tutoring in Zurich, he wrote a research article on capillarity that was published in 1901 in the important scientific journal *Annalen der Physik.* Later in life Einstein dismissed this article as "worthless," but by then he was judging it by unusual standards.

Actually, young Einstein pinned high hopes on this paper on capillarity. In Germany, especially in those days, a Professor was an Exalted Personage, almost unapproachable by lesser men. And the Professors, well aware of their prestige and power, tended to be autocrats. It took the courage of desperation for Einstein, a struggling nobody, to write the following letter to the great physical chemist at the University of Leipzig, Professor Wilhelm Ostwald, who later won the Nobel Prize:

> Since I was inspired by your book on general chemistry to write the enclosed article [on capillarity], I am taking the liberty of sending you a copy. On this occasion I venture also to ask you whether perhaps you might have use for a mathematical physicist who is familiar with absolute measurements. I am taking the liberty of making such a request only because I am without means and only such a position would give me the possibility of further education.

The letter was sent on 19 March 1901. As the days passed and the postman brought no response, Einstein's high hopes began to fade. On 3 April he followed up his letter with a postcard saying how important the decision would be for him and—perhaps as a pretext for writing the postcard—wondering whether he had given his Milan address in the letter, which in fact he had.

Still there was no response. On 17 April Einstein tried elsewhere, writing a brief note to Professor Heike Kamerlingh-Onnes in Leiden, Netherlands, again enclosing a reprint of his paper on capillarity. In those days it was his main tangible asset. Nothing came of this application. Meanwhile there had occurred a beautiful event in Einstein's life of which he knew nothing. It reveals his father's love for him and reveals too the aspirations and heartbreaks of Albert Einstein at this bitter time. On 13 April 1901 Hermann Einstein, the unsuccessful merchant, in ill health and a stranger to the academic community, took it upon himself to write to Professor Ostwald. Here is his letter:

I beg you to excuse a father who dares to approach you, dear Professor, in the interests of his son.

I wish to mention first that my son Albert Einstein is 22 years old, has studied for four years at the Zurich Polytechnic and last summer brilliantly passed his diploma examinations in mathematics and physics. Since then he has tried unsuccessfully to find a position as assistant, which would enable him to continue his education in theoretical and experimental physics. Everybody who is able to judge praises his talent, and in any case I can assure you that he is exceedingly assiduous and industrious and is attached to his science with a great love.

My son is profoundly unhappy about his present joblessness, and every day the idea becomes more firmly implanted in him that he is a failure in his career and will not be able to find the way back again. And on top of this he is depressed by the thought that he is a burden on us since we are not very well-to-do people.

Because, dear Professor, my son honors and reveres you the most among all the great physicists of our time, I permit myself to apply to you with the plea that you will read his article published in the *Annalen der Physik* and, hopefully, that you will write him a few lines of encouragement so that he may regain his joy in his life and his work.

If, in addition, it should be possible for you to obtain for him a position as assistant, now or in the fall, my gratitude would be boundless.

I beg again your forgiveness for my audacity in sending you this letter and I want to add that my son has no idea of this extraordinary step of mine.

Whether as a result of this letter Professor Ostwald wrote to Albert Einstein is not known. What is known is that Einstein did not receive an assistantship, and that the seeds of a great irony were thus planted.

GROSSMANN RECOMMENDS EINSTEIN FOR JOB AT THE PATENT OFFICE

Throughout the black days of 1901 Einstein could still find consolation and escape in his music. And, more important, exciting scientific ideas and speculations once more came crowding into his mind. Yet even as his mind soared, he felt himself sinking helplessly in the quagmire of a world that had no place for him. Rescue, however, was on its way. It came just in time—and once more from his friend Marcel Grossmann, whose meticulous lecture notes had proved invaluable at the Poly. Grossmann could not offer Einstein an assistantship. He was still only an assistant himself. But early in 1901 he had spoken earnestly to his father about Einstein's troubles, and the father had strongly recommended Einstein to his friend Friedrich Haller, the Director of the Swiss Patent Office in Bern.

Haller called Einstein for an interview, which quickly revealed Einstein's lack of relevant technical qualifications. But as it continued its grueling two-hour course, Haller began to realize that there was something about the young man that transcended technicalities. There are strong reasons to believe that it was Einstein's rare mastery of Maxwell's electromagnetic theory that ultimately prompted Haller to offer Einstein a provisional job in the Patent Office. Since there was no immediate opening, and since the law required that all openings be advertised, this meant delay.

While waiting, Einstein supported himself precariously by teaching and private tutoring. From May to July 1901 he had a temporary job as a substitute teacher of mathematics in the Technical School in Winterthur, and while there he completed a research article on thermodynamics. This he submitted in November to the University of Zurich in order to obtain a doctoral degree. Einstein's article was ultimately accepted for publication by *Annalen der Physik.* But this was after Professor Kleiner had rejected it as a Ph.D. thesis.

The outcome of his doctoral attempt was still in doubt when, on 11 December 1901, a vacancy at the Patent Office was advertised in the federal gazette. Einstein immediately applied for the position: Engineer, Second Class.

In February 1902 he went to live in Bern, supporting himself there as best he could by private tutoring. On 14 March he became twenty-three, and a week later, according to the official calendar, winter gave way to spring. The tutoring continued.

April came, and May, and June. And at long last, on 23 June 1902, almost simultaneously with the advent of summer, Einstein started work at the Swiss Patent Office: a probationary Technical Expert, Third Class, with a modest salary of 3500 francs a year.

At last Einstein had a steady job. He quickly became adept at the work. He was well content to be free of the hostile academic world that had brought him repeated heartache. Through his friend Marcel Grossmann he had found a haven in which, in his spare time, he could work serenely, with growing excitement, on his burgeoning ideas. And in this unlikely conservatory his genius matured.

In the last year of his life he wrote of the recommendation to Haller at the Patent Office as "the greatest thing Marcel Grossmann did for me as a friend." Not that Grossmann now vanishes from our story. On the contrary, the destinies of the two men were intertwined in a way that strains credulity, and we shall see Grossmann do yet more for Einstein. When, in 1936, after a long, crippling illness, Grossmann died of multiple sclerosis, Einstein wrote a heartfelt letter of condolence to Grossmann's widow. Trying to convey to her how much Grossmann had meant to him, he wrote:

> . . . our student days together [at the Polytechnic] come back to me. He a model student; I untidy and a daydreamer. He on excellent terms with the teachers and grasping everything easily; I aloof and discontented, not very popular. But we were good friends and our conversations over iced coffee at the Metropol every few weeks belong among my nicest memories. Then the end of the studies . . . I suddenly abandoned by everyone, facing life not knowing which way to turn. But he stood by me and through him and his father I came to Haller in the Patent Office a few years later. In a way, this saved my life; not that I would have died without it, but I would have been intellectually stunted.

CHAPTER 2

EINSTEIN'S WORK IN PHYSICS

ALBERT EINSTEIN

Einstein's 1905 Papers

Heinz R. Pagels

Heinz R. Pagels explains each of Einstein's four 1905 scientific papers, what ideas each paper overturned, and how the ideas in each paper were tested and validated. The first paper proved the existence of atoms, the second that light is composed of particles, the third that space and time are relative and can be measured by comparison with the constant speed of light, and the fourth that mass and energy are two manifestations of the same thing. According to Pagels, these theories launched twentieth-century physics. Heinz R. Pagels, who has taught theoretical physics at Rockefeller University in New York, is the author of *Perfect Symmetry*.

In 1905, the year he received his doctorate in Zurich, Einstein published three papers in volume 17 of *Annalen der Physik*, altering the course of scientific history. The volume is now a collector's item. Each of the three papers is a scientific masterpiece reflecting one of Einstein's three major interests: statistical mechanics, the quantum theory, and relativity. These papers began the physics revolution of the twentieth century. It would be decades before a new consensus on the nature of physical reality could be formed.

PROVING THE EXISTENCE OF ATOMS

The first paper was on statistical mechanics, a theory of gases invented by [Scottish physicist] James Clerk Maxwell, the Austrian physicist Ludwig Boltzmann and the American, J. Willard Gibbs. According to statistical mechanics, a gas like air consists of lots of molecules or atoms bouncing off each other in rapid random motion like a room filled with flying tennis balls. The tennis balls hit the walls, each other, and anything in the room. This model imitates the properties of a gas. But the atomic hypothesis that a gas actually consists of tiny atoms and molecules too small to see all flying around seems to be incapable of direct test. . . .

The problem Einstein addressed was how to prove the existence of atoms. How could he do that when atoms were too small to be seen? Suppose you put a basketball into the room full of flying tennis balls. The big basketball gets bombarded from all sides by the tennis balls, and it begins to move in a random way. Assuming the randomness of the bombardment by the tennis balls, the features of the movements of the basketball can be determined. It jumps and bounces around because of the balls hitting it.

Einstein's paper made use of a similar idea to furnish the first convincing proof of the existence of atoms. He recognized that if you put into a gas or liquid relatively large grains of pollen—which could be seen under a powerful microscope—you could see them move around. The English botanist Robert Brown had observed this movement of pollen grains long before Einstein wrote his paper, but he had no explanation for his observation. Einstein explained that this Brownian movement of the pollen grains is due to atoms hitting the grains. The pollen grains are so small they get bounced and jiggled by the atoms hitting them just as would be a basketball being hit by tennis balls. [Jean Baptiste] Perrin, the French experimentalist, did some remarkable experiments that confirmed Einstein's quantitative predictions for the motion of the pollen grains. Many physicists then accepted the atomic hypothesis. [Wilhelm Friedrich] Ostwald, the chemist, who didn't believe in atoms for reasons of his own, was converted to atomism by Einstein's analysis and Perrin's experiments. [Philosopher-physicist] Ernst Mach, the strict positivist[1], was, however, never convinced of the existence of atoms, maintaining his "incorruptible skepticism" to his death. Physicists today recognize the paper of the patent examiner Einstein as proposing the first convincing test for the existence of atoms. That single paper alone would have made his scientific reputation.

PROVING THAT LIGHT IS MADE OF PARTICLES

The second bombshell paper of 1905 was Einstein's paper on the photoelectric effect. If a beam of light shines on a

1. one who believes that sense perceptions are the only admissible basis of human knowledge and precise thought; the "seeing is believing" approach to physics

metal surface, electrically charged particles, electrons, are emitted by the metal, causing an electric current to flow. This is the photoelectric effect—light produces an electric current. The photoelectric effect is used in automatic elevator doors. A beam of light crossing the elevator door hits a metal surface, causing an electric current to flow. If the current flows, the door will close. But if the beam of light is interrupted by a person walking through the door, the current stops and the door stays open.

In 1905, little was known about the photoelectric effect. It is characteristic of Einstein's genius that he was able to see in this obscure physical effect a deep clue about the nature of light and physical reality. The creative movement in science moves from the specific—like the photoelectric effect—to the general—the nature of light. In a grain of sand one may see the universe.

Einstein, in his paper on the photoelectric effect, used Planck's quantum hypothesis.[2] He went beyond Planck to make the radical assumption that light itself was quantized into particles. Most physicists, including Planck, thought that light was a wavelike phenomenon in accord with the view of nature as a continuum. Einstein's hypothesis implied that actually light was a rain of particles consisting of the light quanta later called photons—little packets of definite energy. Using his idea of light quanta, Einstein deduced an equation to describe the photoelectric effect.

Of the three 1905 papers, Einstein referred only to the paper on the photoelectric effect as "truly revolutionary," and indeed it was. One thing physicists had thought they understood was light; they understood it as a continuous electromagnetic wave. Einstein's work seemed to deny this, to claim instead that light was a particle. This is one reason why other physicists resisted his revolutionary idea. Another reason was that, unlike Planck's formula for black-body radiation, which was immediately checked experimentally, there was simply no way to confirm Einstein's photoelectric equation experimentally—and there wouldn't be until 1915. His introduction of the light quantum seemed gratuitous.

Einstein stood alone for more than a decade on the question of energy quantization of light. When he was recom-

2. German physicist Max Planck proved that matter is composed of discrete, or separate, atoms not composed of one continuous substance.

mended for membership in the Prussian Academy of Sciences in 1913, the letter read, "In sum, one can hardly say that there is not one among the great problems, in which modern physics is so rich, to which Einstein has not made a remarkable contribution. That he may have missed the target in his speculations, as, for example, in his hypothesis of the light quanta, cannot really be held too much against him, for it is not possible to introduce really new ideas even in the exact sciences without taking a risk." [Robert A.] Millikan, the American experimentalist, spent years working on the photoelectric effect, devising precise measurements to test Einstein's photoelectric equation. In 1915 he said, "Despite . . . the apparent complete success of the Einstein equation, the physical theory of which it was designed to be the symbolic expression is found so untenable that Einstein himself, I believe, no longer holds to it." Einstein held to it. But it was clear that even after his photoelectric equation was experimentally confirmed, other physicists resisted the idea that light is a particle. The "truly revolutionary" idea of the photon, the light particle, needed further experimental confirmation before it could be accepted.

The final confirmation of the photon came in 1923–24. Assuming that light consisted of true particles that had a definite energy and directed momentum like little bullets, [Arthur A.] Compton, one of the first American atomic physicists, and [Peter J.] Debye, a Dutch physicist, independently made theoretical predictions for the scattering of photons from another particle, the electron. Compton performed the scattering experiments, and the predictions based on the light particle assumption were confirmed. Opposition to the photon concept fell rapidly after that. Einstein's Nobel Prize was for his light quantum hypothesis, not for his greatest work, the relativity theory.

PROVING THAT SPACE AND TIME ARE RELATIVE

Einstein's third 1905 article was on the special theory of relativity. This article changed forever the way we think about space and time. Max Planck said in 1910 of this paper, "if [it] . . . should prove to be correct, as I expect it will, he will be considered the Copernicus of the twentieth century." Planck was right.

The special theory of relativity—as the topic of his 1905 paper was later called—dealt with space and time concepts that philosophers and scientists had devoted much thought to over the ages. Some thought that space was a substance—the ether—which pervaded everything. Others evoked images of the flow of time like a river or sand falling in an hourglass. While such images appeal to our feelings, they have little to do with the concept of time in physics. Understanding space and time in physics requires that we distinguish our subjective experience of space and time from what we can actually measure about them. Einstein said it very simply: Space is what we measure with a measuring rod and time is what we measure with a clock. The clarity of these definitions reveals a mind intent on great purpose.

Armed with these definitions, Einstein asked how the measurement of space and time changes between two observers moving at a constant velocity relative to one another. Suppose one observer is riding on a moving train with his measuring rod and clock and his friend is on the station platform with his rod and clock. The person on the train measures the length of the window on the side of his car. Likewise, the person on the platform measures the length of the same window as it moves by. How do the measurements of the two observers compare? Naively, we would think they must agree—after all, it is the same window that is being measured. But this is incorrect, as Einstein showed by a careful analysis of the measurement process. The person standing on the platform with his measuring rod must "see" the window moving past him. In other words, light which bears information about the length of the moving window must be transmitted to the person standing on the platform, otherwise it can't be measured at all. The properties of light have entered our comparison of the two measurements, and we must first examine what light does.

THE SPEED OF LIGHT IS NECESSARY FOR MEASURING SPACE AND TIME

Even before Einstein, physicists knew the speed of light was finite but very fast, about 180,000 miles per second. But Einstein thought there was something special about the speed of light—that the speed of light is an absolute constant. No matter how fast you move, the speed of light is always the same—you can never catch up to a light ray. To appreciate how odd this really is, imagine that a gun fires a bullet at some high speed. But the speed of a bullet is not an absolute constant, so that if we take off after the bullet in a rocket we can catch up to it and it appears to be at rest. There is no absolute meaning to the speed of the bullet because it is always relative to our speed. But not so with light; its speed is absolute—always the same, completely independent of our own velocity. That is the odd property of light that makes its speed qualitatively different from the speed of anything else.

The assumption of the absolute constancy of the speed of light was the second postulate of the special theory of relativity. The first postulate Einstein made was that it is impossible to determine absolute uniform motion. Uniform motion proceeds in a fixed direction at a constant speed—basically coasting. Einstein's postulate is that you cannot determine if you are coasting unless you compare your motion relative to another object. The two observers, one on the train, the other on the platform, illustrate this postulate. For the person on the platform it is the train that is moving. But the person in the train can just as well suppose he is standing still and the platform and the whole earth with it are moving past him. Uniform motion is only relative—you can only say you are moving relative to something else.

From these two postulates, the constancy of the speed of light and the relativity of motion, the entire logical structure of special relativity followed. But, as Paul Ehrenfest, a physicist and a friend of Einstein's, emphasized, there is implicit a third postulate which states that the first two are not in contradiction. Superficially, it seems that they are. All uniform motions are relative to one another, says one postulate. Except the motion of light, which is absolute, says the other postulate. It is the interplay between the relativity of motion for all material objects and the absoluteness of the speed of light which is at the root of all the unfamiliar features of the world according to special relativity.

Using these postulates, Einstein mathematically deduced the laws that related space and time measurements made by one observer to the same measurements made by another observer moving uniformly relative to the first. He showed that the person on the platform would actually find the length of the window on the moving train is shorter than the person on the train. As the train speeds up, the length of the window would be measured to be shorter and shorter by the person on the platform, until, as the imaginary train approached the speed of light, the length of the window would shrink to zero.

Because in our familiar world the speed of most objects, like real trains, is so small compared to the speed of light, we never see such length contractions, which become dramatic only at speeds near that of light.

MOVING CLOCKS SLOW DOWN

Einstein's theory of relativity linked space and time. Einstein showed that a moving clock marked time more slowly than one at rest. For the person on the platform, the watch on the wrist of the train's passenger actually moves more slowly— time slows down. If the train was moving near light velocity, time changes would actually slow down to close to zero. Likewise, the person on the train will see the watch of the person on the platform move more slowly. Absolute time is abolished. Time is measured differently for persons moving relative to one another.

It seems as if the relativity of time poses a paradox—for how can both the passenger on the train and the person on the platform *both* see each other's watches slow down? What happens if now these people meet and compare the time; whose watch has really slowed down? To emphasize this paradox (often called the twin paradox), imagine twins who each set their watches before one of them gets on the train. The train speeds up to nearly the speed of light—at which point each twin will see the other's watch running slower— and then the train slows down and returns to the station. Which twin is older? From the point of view of the twin on the platform, the one on the train has made a round-trip journey, while for the twin on the train, the twin on the platform is the one who has made the round trip. It seems as if the motion of each twin is simply relative to the other's motion. But there is in fact an asymmetry in the motion of the twins, and that is the clue for resolving the paradox. While the train is speeding up it is no longer in uniform motion but is accelerating, and later in the trip it is decelerating. The twin on the platform never experiences such acceleration and deceleration so there is an absolute distinction between the twins' motion. Einstein's special theory of relativity applies only to uniform motions, and the motion of the train is not always uniform. By using Einstein's general theory of relativity, which applies to nonuniform motions like that of the train, one can demonstrate that the twin on the train has actually aged less.

The relativity of space and time disturbs us because it contradicts our intuition. In everyday experience, space and time do not appear to shrink. We might want to think that these odd effects of space and time are merely a mathematical fiction. The French mathematician [Jules Henri] Poincaré independently discovered the same space-time transformation laws in 1905, but he thought of them as postulates [assertions of truth], without physical significance. Einstein was the first to understand the physical implications of those laws; for this reason he is considered the inventor of relativity. He took the physics seriously: clocks really slow down when they move. . . .

The consequences of special relativity seem paradoxical compared to our everyday experience. The unfamiliar world of special relativity becomes apparent only when speeds approach that of light; the speeds we encounter in everyday life are not near that. But special relativity is a logically consistent and coherent theory; there are no paradoxes.

PROVING THAT MASS AND ENERGY ARE DIFFERENT FORMS OF THE SAME THING

Einstein wrote a final, fourth short paper in 1905, the full consequences of which were not developed until 1907. By an analysis of the energy of motion E, of a relativistic particle of mass m, he showed that the particle had an energy given by $E = mc^2$. The constant c is the speed of light.

Before Einstein, physicists thought of energy and mass as distinct. This seems evident from our experience. What does the energy we expend by lifting a stone have to do with the mass of the stone? Mass conveys the impression of a material presence, while energy does not.

Mass and energy were also quantities that seemed to be separately conserved. In the nineteenth century, physicists discovered the law of conservation of energy—it can neither be created nor destroyed. If you lift a stone, energy has been expended but not lost. The stone has potential energy that is released if the stone is dropped. There was also a separate conservation law for mass—mass could neither be created nor destroyed. If a stone is broken up, the pieces have the same total mass as the original stone. The distinction of energy and mass and their separate conservation was deeply embedded in the thinking of physicists in 1905, because it had enormous experimental support. With that background of thought, the novelty of Einstein's insight may be contrasted.

Einstein discovered that the postulates of relativity theory implied that the distinction between energy and mass and the notion of their separate conservation had to be abandoned. This shattering discovery is what is summarized in his equation $E = mc^2$. Mass and energy are simply different manifestations of the same thing. All the mass you see about you is a form of bound energy. If even a small part of this bound energy were ever released, the result would be a catastrophic explosion like that of a nuclear bomb. Of course, the matter around us is not about to convert itself into energy—it takes very special physical conditions to accomplish that. But at the beginning of time during the big bang that created the universe, mass and energy were freely converting into one another. Today energy and matter only appear distinct, and someday in the far future the matter we see about us may again be freely converting into energy.

THE 1905 THEORIES ARE TESTED AND PROVED

How well tested is the theory of special relativity? Today there is a whole technology that depends on the correctness of the theory—practical devices that simply would not work if special relativity were wrong. The electron microscope is one such device. The focusing of the electron microscope takes into account effects of relativity theory. The principles of relativity theory are also incorporated into the design of klystrons, electronic tubes that supply microwave power to radar systems. Perhaps the best evidence that special relativity theory works is the operation of the huge particle accelerators that accelerate subatomic particles like electrons and protons nearly to light velocity. The two-mile-long electron accelerator near Stanford University in California accelerates electrons until their mass increases as predicted by relativity by a factor of forty thousand at the end of their two-mile journey.

One of the oddest predictions of relativity theory is the slowing down of moving clocks. Interestingly, this is one of the most precisely tested predictions of the theory. While we can't accelerate real clocks up to the speed of light, there does exist a tiny subatomic particle, the moun, that behaves just like a tiny clock. After a fraction of a second, the moun disintegrates into other particles. The time it takes the moun to disintegrate may be thought of as a single tick of this tiny clock. By comparing the lifetime of a moun at rest with one that is rapidly moving, we can know how much this tiny clock has slowed down. This was done at CERN [European Organization for Nuclear Research], a nuclear laboratory near Geneva, Switzerland, by putting the rapidly moving mouns into a storage ring and precisely measuring their lifetime. The observed increase in their lifetime was a precise confirmation of the slowing of moving clocks predicted by special relativity.

These and many other tests confirm the correctness of the early work of Einstein. The young Einstein was a bohemian and a rebel who identified himself with the highest and best in human thought. During his period of intense creativity from 1905 to 1925 he seemed to have a hotline to "the old One"—his term for the Creator or Intelligence of nature. His gift was an ability to go to the heart of the matter with simple and compelling arguments. Separate from the community of physicists but in touch with the perennial problems of his science, Einstein realized a new vision of the universe.

Einstein's papers of 1905 and Planck's paper of 1900 ushered in the physics of the twentieth century. They transformed the physics that went before. Planck's idea of the quantum, further developed by Einstein as a photon, the particle of light, implied that the continuous view of nature could not be maintained. Matter was shown to be composed of discrete atoms. The ideas of space and time held since the age of [Isaac] Newton were overthrown. Yet in spite of these advances, the idea of determinism—that every detail of the universe was subject to physical law—remained entrenched in Einstein and his entire generation of physicists. Nothing in these discoveries challenged determinism.

Einstein's great strength lay not in mathematical technique but in a depth of understanding and a steadfast commitment to principles. That commitment to the principles of classical physics and determinism now moved him from his work on special relativity toward his greatest work, the general theory of relativity.

The Meaning of Relativity: Space-Time and Curved Space

Fritjof Capra

Fritjof Capra clarifies the meaning of space-time by comparing the Western view that space and time are real entities with the Eastern view that space and time are constructs of the human mind. Einstein's special relativity theory is a construct of the mind, and holds that measurements of space and time depend on the observer and can only be measured relative to one another, thus creating the fourth dimension of space-time. According to Capra, Einstein shows in general relativity theory that space-time is curved by gravitational fields surrounding large bodies, such as the sun and planets. Both concepts—space-time and curved space—are difficult to imagine. Fritjof Capra, who has done physics research in European and American universities, is the author of *The Turning Point* and *The Web of Life*.

Modern physics has confirmed most dramatically one of the basic ideas of Eastern mysticism; that all the concepts we use to describe nature are limited, that they are not features of reality, as we tend to believe, but creations of the mind; parts of the map, not of the territory. Whenever we expand the realm of our experience, the limitations of our rational mind become apparent and we have to modify, or even abandon, some of our concepts.

Our notions of space and time figure prominently on our map of reality. They serve to order things and events in our environment and are therefore of paramount importance not only in our everyday life, but also in our attempts to understand nature through science and philosophy. There is no law of physics which does not require the concepts of space and time for its formulation. The profound modification of these basic concepts brought about by relativity theory was therefore one of the greatest revolutions in the history of science.

CLASSICAL PHYSICS WAS BASED ON EUCLIDEAN GEOMETRY AND A SEPARATE MEASURE OF TIME

Classical physics was based on the notion both of an absolute, three-dimensional space, independent of the material objects it contains, and obeying the laws of Euclidean geometry, and of time as a separate dimension which again is absolute and flows at an even rate, independent of the material world. In the West, these notions of space and time were so deeply rooted in the minds of philosophers and scientists that they were taken as true and unquestioned properties of nature.

The belief that geometry is inherent in nature, rather than part of the framework we use to describe nature, has its origin in Greek thought. Demonstrative geometry was the central feature of Greek mathematics and had a profound influence on Greek philosophy. Its method of starting from unquestioned axioms, and deriving theorems from these by deductive reasoning, became characteristic of Greek philosophical thought; geometry was therefore at the very centre of all intellectual activities and formed the basis of philosophical training. The gate of [Greek philosopher] Plato's Academy in Athens is said to have borne the inscription, 'You are not allowed to enter here, unless you know geometry.' The Greeks believed that their mathematical theorems were expressions of eternal and exact truths about the real world, and that geometrical shapes were manifestations of absolute beauty. Geometry was considered to be the perfect combination of logic and beauty and was thus believed to be of divine origin. Hence Plato's dictum, 'God is a geometer'. . . .

In subsequent centuries, Greek geometry continued to exert a strong influence on Western philosophy and science. Euclid's *Elements* was a standard textbook in European schools until the beginning of this century, and Euclidean geometry was taken to be the true nature of space for more than two thousand years. It took an Einstein to make scientists and philosophers realize that geometry is not inherent in nature, but is imposed upon it by the mind. In the words of [physicist] Henry Margenau,

The central recognition of the theory of relativity is that geometry . . . is a construct of the intellect. Only when this discovery is accepted can the mind feel free to tamper with the time-honoured notions of space and time, to survey the range of possibilities available for defining them, and to select that formulation which agrees with observation.

EASTERN PHILOSOPHERS' VIEW OF SPACE AND TIME

Eastern philosophy, unlike that of the Greeks, has always maintained that space and time are constructs of the mind. The Eastern mystics treated them like all other intellectual concepts; as relative, limited, and illusory. In a Buddhist text, for example, we find the words,

It was taught by the Buddha, oh Monks, that . . . the past, the future, physical space, . . . and individuals are nothing but names, forms of thought, words of common usage, merely superficial realities.

. . . Thus the ancient Eastern philosophers and scientists already had the attitude which is so basic to relativity theory—that our notions of geometry are not absolute and unchangeable properties of nature, but intellectual constructions. In the words of [first-century Buddhist patriarch] Ashvaghosha,

Be it clearly understood that space is nothing but a mode of particularisation and that it has no real existence of its own . . . Space exists only in relation to our particularising consciousness.

The same applies to our idea of time. The Eastern mystics link the notions of both space and time to particular states of consciousness. Being able to go beyond the ordinary state through meditation, they have realized that the conventional notions of space and time are not the ultimate truth. The refined notions of space and time resulting from their mystical experiences appear to be in many ways similar to the notions of modern physics, as exemplified by the theory of relativity.

THE VIEW OF SPACE AND TIME IN RELATIVITY THEORY

What, then, is this new view of space and time which emerged from relativity theory? It is based on the discovery that all space and time measurements are relative. The relativity of spatial specifications was, of course, nothing new. It was well known before Einstein that the position of an object in space can only be defined relative to some other object. This is usually done with the help of three coordinates and the point from which the coordinates are measured may be called the location of the 'observer'.

To illustrate the relativity of such coordinates, imagine two observers floating in space and observing an umbrella, as drawn opposite. Observer A sees the umbrella to his left and slightly inclined, so that the upper end is nearer to him. Observer B, on the other hand, sees the umbrella to his right and in such a way that the upper end is farther away. By extending this two-dimensional example to three dimensions, it becomes clear that all spatial specifications—such as 'left', 'right', 'up', 'down', 'oblique', etc.—depend on the position of the observer and are thus relative. This was known long before relativity theory. As far as time is concerned, however, the situation in classical physics was entirely different. The temporal order of two events was assumed to be independent of any observer. Specifications referring to time—such

---

RELATIVITY REQUIRES NEW THINKING

In A Brief History of Time *Stephen Hawking emphasizes the necessity to reject the idea that space and time are fixed; he confirms the idea that space and time are dynamic, relative quantities.*

In the theory of relativity there is no unique absolute time, but instead each individual has his own personal measure of time that depends on where he is and how he is moving.

Before 1915, space and time were thought of as a fixed arena in which events took place, but which was not affected by what happened in it. This was true even of the special theory of relativity. Bodies moved, forces attracted and repelled, but time and space simply continued, unaffected. It was natural to think that space and time went on forever.

The situation, however, is quite different in the general theory of relativity. Space and time are now dynamic quantities: when a body moves, or a force acts, it affects the curvature of space and time—and in turn the structure of space-time affects the way in which bodies move and forces act. Space and time not only affect but also are affected by everything that happens in the universe. Just as one cannot talk about events in the universe without the notions of space and time, so in general relativity it became meaningless to talk about space and time outside the limits of the universe.

Stephen W. Hawking, *A Brief History of Time: From the Big Bang to Black Holes.* Introduction by Carl Sagan. Illustrated by Ron Miller. New York: Bantam, 1988.

as 'before', 'after' or 'simultaneous'—were thought to have an absolute meaning independent of any coordinate system.

Einstein recognized that temporal specifications, too, are relative and depend on the observer. In everyday life, the impression that we can arrange the events around us in a unique time sequence is created by the fact that the velocity of light—186,000 miles per second—is so high, compared to any other velocity we experience, that we can assume we are observing events at the instant they are occurring. This, however, is incorrect. Light needs some time to travel from the event to the observer. Normally, this time is so short that the propagation of light can be considered to be instantaneous; but when the observer moves with a high velocity with respect to the observed phenomena, the time span between the occurrence of an event and its observation plays a crucial role in establishing a sequence of events. Einstein realized that in such a case, observers moving at different velocities will order events differently in time. Two events which are seen as occurring simultaneously by one observer may occur in different temporal sequences for others. For ordinary velocities, the differences are so small that they cannot be detected, but when the velocities approach the speed of light, they give rise to measurable effects. In high energy physics, where the events are interactions between particles moving almost at the speed of light, the relativity of time is well established and has been confirmed by countless experiments.

The relativity of time also forces us to abandon the Newtonian concept of an absolute space. Such a space was seen as containing a definite configuration of matter at every instant; but now that simultaneity is seen to be a relative concept, depending on the state of motion of the observer, it is no longer possible to define such a definite instant for the whole universe. A distant event which takes place at some particular instant for one observer may happen earlier or later for another observer. It is therefore not possible to speak about 'the universe at a given instant' in an absolute way; there is no absolute space independent of the observer.

Relativity theory has thus shown that all measurements involving space and time lose their absolute significance and has forced us to abandon the classical concepts of an absolute space and an absolute time. The fundamental importance of this development has been clearly expressed by [physicist] Mendel Sachs in the following words:

> The real revolution that came with Einstein's theory . . . was the abandonment of the idea that the space-time coordinate system has objective significance as a separate physical entity. Instead of this idea, relativity theory implies that the space and time coordinates are only the elements of a language that is used by an observer to describe his environment.

This statement from a contemporary physicist shows the close affinity between the notions of space and time in modern physics and those held by the Eastern mystics who say, as quoted before, that space and time 'are nothing but names, forms of thought, words of common usage'. . . .

MEASURING LENGTH AND TIME ACCORDING TO RELATIVITY THEORY

In classical physics it was always assumed that rods in motion and at rest have the same length. Relativity theory has shown that this is not true. The length of an object depends on its motion relative to the observer and it changes with the velocity of that motion. The change is such that the object contracts in the direction of its motion. A rod has its maximum length in a frame of reference where it is at rest, and it becomes shorter with increasing velocity relative to the observer. In the 'scattering' experiments of high-energy physics, where particles collide with extremely high velocities, the relativistic contraction is so extreme that spherical particles are reduced to 'pancake' shapes.

It is important to realize that it makes no sense to ask which is the 'real' length of an object, just as it makes no sense in our everyday life to ask for the real length of somebody's shadow. The shadow is a projection of points in three-dimensional space on to a two-dimensional plane, and its length will be different for different angles of projection. Similarly, the length of a moving object is the projection of points in four-dimensional space-time on to three-dimensional space, and its length is different in different frames of reference.

What is true for lengths is also true for time intervals. They, too, depend on the frame of reference, but contrary to spatial distances they become longer as the velocity relative to the observer increases. This means that clocks in motion run slower; time slows down. These clocks can be of varying types: mechanical clocks, atomic clocks, or even a human heartbeat. If one of two twins went on a fast round-trip into outer space, he would be younger than his brother when he came back home, because all his 'clocks'—his heartbeat, bloodflow, brainwaves, etc.—would slow down during the journey, from the point of view of the man on the ground. The traveller himself, of course, would not notice anything unusual, but on his return he would suddenly realize that his twin brother was now much older. This 'twin paradox' is perhaps the most famous paradox of modern physics. It has provoked heated discussions in scientific journals, some of which are still going on; an eloquent proof of the fact that the reality described by relativity theory cannot easily be grasped by our ordinary understanding. . . .

All these relativistic effects only seem strange because we cannot experience the four-dimensional space-time world with our senses, but can only observe its three-dimensional 'images'. These images have different aspects in different frames of reference; moving objects look different from objects at rest, and moving clocks run at a different rate. These effects will seem paradoxical if we do not realize that they are only the projections of four-dimensional phenomena, just as shadows are projections of three-dimensional objects. If we could visualize the four-dimensional space-time reality, there would be nothing paradoxical at all. . . .

The theory of relativity discussed so far is known as the 'special theory of relativity'. It provides a common framework for the description of the phenomena associated with moving bodies and with electricity and magnetism, the basic features of this framework being the relativity of space and time and their unification into four-dimensional space-time.

In General Relativity Space-Time Is Curved

In the 'general theory of relativity', the framework of the special theory is extended to include gravity. The effect of gravity, according to general relativity, is to make space-time curved. This, again, is extremely hard to imagine. We can easily imagine a two-dimensional curved surface, such as the surface of an egg, because we can see such curved surfaces lying in three-dimensional space. The meaning of the word curvature for two-dimensional curved surfaces is thus quite clear; but when it comes to three-dimensional space—let alone four-dimensional space-time—our imagination abandons us. Since we cannot look at three-dimensional space 'from outside', we cannot imagine how it can be 'bent in some direction'.

To understand the meaning of curved space-time, we have to use curved two-dimensional surfaces as analogies. Imagine, for example, the surface of a sphere. The crucial fact which makes the analogy to space-time possible is that the curvature is an intrinsic property of that surface and can be measured without going into three-dimensional space. A two-dimensional insect confined to the surface of the sphere and unable to experience three-dimensional space could nevertheless find out that the surface on which he is living is curved, provided that he can make geometrical measurements.

To see how this works, we have to compare the geometry of our bug on the sphere with that of a similar insect living on a flat surface.[1] Suppose the two bugs begin their study of geometry by drawing a straight line, defined as the shortest connection between two points. The result is shown below. We see that the bug on the flat surface drew a very nice straight line; but what did the bug on the sphere do? For him, the line he drew is the shortest connection between the two

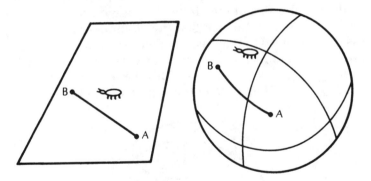

drawing a 'straight line' on a plane and on a sphere

points A and B, since any other line he may draw will be longer; but from our point of view we recognize it as a curve (the arc of a great circle, to be precise). Now suppose that the two bugs study triangles. The bug on the plane will find that the three angles of any triangle add up to two right angles, i.e. to 180°; but the bug on the sphere will discover that the sum of the angles in his triangles is always greater than 180°. For small triangles, the excess is small, but it increases as the tri-

1. The following examples are taken from R.P. Feynman, R.B. Leighton and M. Sands, *The Feynman Lectures on Physics* (Addison-Wesley, Reading, Mass., 1966), vol. II, Ch. 42.

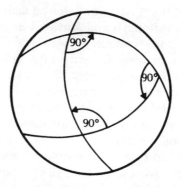

on a sphere a triangle can have three right angles

angles become larger; and as an extreme case, our bug on the sphere will even be able to draw triangles with three right angles. Finally, let the two bugs draw circles and measure their circumference. The bug on the plane will find that the circumference is always equal to 2π times the radius, independent of the size of the circle. The bug on the sphere, on the other hand, will notice that the circumference is always less than 2π times the radius. As can be seen in the figure below, our three-dimensional point of view allows us to see that what the bug calls the radius of his circle is in fact a curve which is always longer than the true radius of the circle.

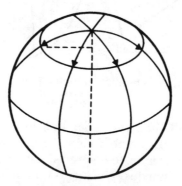

drawing a circle on a sphere

As the two insects continue to study geometry, the one on the plane should discover the axioms and laws of Euclidean geometry, but his colleague on the sphere will discover different laws. The difference will be small for small geometrical figures, but will increase as the figures become larger. The example of the two bugs shows that we can always determine whether a surface is curved or not, just by making geometrical measurements on the surface, and by comparing the results with those predicted by Euclidean geometry. If there is a discrepancy, the surface is curved; and the larger the discrepancy is—for a given size of figures—the stronger the curvature.

GRAVITATIONAL FIELDS CAUSE CURVED SPACE

In the same way, we can define a curved three-dimensional space to be one in which Euclidean geometry is no longer valid. The laws of geometry in such a space will be of a different, 'non-Euclidean' type. Such a non-Euclidean geometry was introduced as a purely abstract mathematical idea in the nineteenth century by the mathematician Georg Riemann, and it was not considered to be more than that, until Einstein made the revolutionary suggestion that the three-dimensional space in which we live is actually curved. According to Einstein's theory, the curvature of space is caused by the gravitational fields of massive bodies. Wherever there is a massive object, the space around it is curved, and the degree of curvature, that is, the degree to which the geometry deviates from that of Euclid, depends on the mass of the object. . . .

In our terrestrial environment, the effects of gravity on space and time are so small that they are insignificant, but in astrophysics, which deals with extremely massive bodies, like planets, stars and galaxies, the curvature of space-time is an important phenomenon. All observations have so far confirmed Einstein's theory and thus force us to believe that space-time is indeed curved. . . .

In the general theory of relativity, the classical concepts of space and time as absolute and independent entities are completely abolished. Not only are all measurements involving space and time relative, depending on the state of motion of the observer, but the whole structure of space-time is inextricably linked to the distribution of matter. Space is curved to different degrees and time flows at different rates in different parts of the universe. We have thus come to apprehend that our notions of a three-dimensional Euclidean space and of linear flowing time are limited to our ordinary experience of the physical world and have to be completely abandoned when we extend this experience.

Einstein Develops General Relativity

Timothy Ferris

Timothy Ferris explains how Einstein invented the
theory of general relativity to account for gravity, a
force not accounted for in special relativity. Einstein
noticed that inertial mass and gravitational mass are
equivalent; looking for the explanation for this phenomenon led him to his theory of general relativity.
General relativity is the geometry of space: Matter
curves space, and planets follow the curved paths
dictated by the sun's mass. The theory has been
tested in several experiments and has proved correct
in each one. Timothy Ferris teaches science writing
and astronomy at the University of California at
Berkeley. He is the author of *The Red Limit, Galaxies, The Mind's Sky,* and *The Whole Shebang.*

For all its protean achievements, special relativity was silent
with regard to gravitation, the other known large-scale force
in the universe. The special theory has to do with *inertial*
mass, the resistance objects offer to change in their state of
motion—their "clout," or "heft," so to speak. Gravitation acts
upon objects according to their *gravitational* mass—i.e.,
their "weight." Inertial mass is what you feel when you slide
a suitcase along a polished floor; gravitational mass is what
you feel when you lift the suitcase. There would appear to be
distinct differences between the two: Gravitational mass
manifests itself only in the presence of gravitational force,
while inertial mass is a permanent property of matter. Take
the suitcase on a spaceship and, once in orbit, it will weigh
nothing (i.e., its gravitational mass will measure zero), but
its inertial mass will remain the same: You'll have to work
just as hard to wrest it around the cabin, and once in motion
it will have the same momentum as if it were sliding across
a floor on Earth.

The Equality of Inertial and Gravitational Mass

Yet for some reason, the inertial and gravitational mass of any given object are equivalent. Put the suitcase on the airport scale and find that it weighs thirty pounds: That is a result of its gravitational mass. Now set it on a sheet of smooth, glazed ice or another relatively friction-free surface, attach a spring scale to the handle, and pull it until you get it accelerating at the same rate at which it would fall (i.e., 16 feet per second, on Earth), and the scale will register, again, thirty pounds: That is a result of its *inertial* mass. Experiments have been performed to a high degree of precision on all sorts of materials, in many different weights, and the gravitational mass of each object repeatedly turns out to be exactly equal to its inertial mass.

The equality of inertial and gravitational mass had been an integral if inconspicuous part of classical physics for centuries. It can be seen, for instance, to explain Galileo's discovery that cannonballs and boccie balls[1] fall at the same velocity despite their differing weight: They do so because the cannonball, though it has greater gravitational mass and ought (naïvely) to fall faster, also has a greater inertial mass, which makes it accelerate more slowly; since these two quantities are equivalent they cancel out, and the cannonball consequently falls no faster than the boccie ball. But in Newtonian mechanics the equivalence principle was treated as a mere coincidence. Einstein was intrigued. Here, he thought, "must lie the key to a deeper understanding of inertia and gravitation." His inquiry set him on his way up the craggy road toward the general theory of relativity.

Thought Experiments Regarding Inertia and Gravity

Einstein's first insight into the question came one day in 1907, in what he later called "the happiest thought of my life." The memory of the moment remained vivid decades later:

> I was sitting in a chair in the patent office at Bern, when all of a sudden a thought occurred to me: "If a person falls freely he will not feel his own weight." I was startled. This simple thought made a deep impression on me. It impelled me toward a theory of gravitation.

To appreciate why this seemingly straightforward picture should have so excited Einstein, imagine that you awaken to

---

1. a wooden ball, similar to a bowling ball, used in the Italian game called boccie

find yourself floating, weightless, in a sealed, windowless elevator car. A diabolical set of instructions, printed on the wall, informs you that there are two identical such elevator cars—one adrift in deep space, where it is subject to no significant gravitational influence, and the other trapped in the sun's gravitational field, plunging rapidly toward its doom. You will be rescued only if you can *prove* (not guess) in which car you are riding—the one floating in zero gravity, or the one falling in a strong gravitational field. What Einstein realized that day in the patent office was that you *cannot* tell the difference, neither through your senses nor by conducting experiments. The fact that you are weightless does not mean that you are free from gravitation; you might be in free fall. (The "weightlessness" experienced by astronauts in orbit is precisely of this sort: Though trapped by the earth's gravitational field they feel no weight—i.e., no effect of gravitation—because they and their spaceship are constantly falling.) The gravitational field, therefore, has only a *relative* existence. One is reminded of the joke about the man who falls from the roof of a tall building and, seeing a friend looking aghast out a window on the way down, calls out encouragingly, "I'm okay so far!" His point was Einstein's—that the gravitational field does not exist for him, so long as he remains in his inertial framework. (The sidewalk, alas, is in an inertial framework of its own.)

The same ambiguity applies in the opposite situation: Suppose that when you awaken you find yourself standing in the elevator car, at your normal weight. This time the instructions say that you are either (1) aboard an elevator stopped on the ground floor of an office building on Earth, or (2) adrift in zero-gravity space, in an elevator attached by a cable to a spaceship that is pulling it away at a steady acceleration, pressing you to the floor with a force equal to that of Earth's gravitation—at one "G," as the jet pilots say. Here again, you cannot prove which is the case.

CONSIDERING GRAVITATION AS A KIND OF ACCELERATION

Einstein reasoned that if the effects of gravitation are mimicked by acceleration, gravitation itself might be regarded as a kind of acceleration. But acceleration through what reference frame? It could not be ordinary three-dimensional space; the passengers in the elevator in the New York skyscraper, after all, are not flying through space relative to the earth.

The search for an answer required Einstein to consider the concept of a four-dimensional space-time continuum. Within its framework, gravitation *is* acceleration, the acceleration of objects as they glide along "world lines"—paths of least action traced over the slopes of a three-dimensional space that is curved in the fourth dimension.

A forerunner here was Hermann Minkowski, who had been Einstein's mathematics professor at the Polytechnic Institute. Minkowski remembered Einstein as a "lazy dog" who seldom came to class, but he was quick to appreciate the importance of Einstein's work, though initially he viewed it as but an improvement on [Dutch physicist Hendrick Antoon] Lorentz. In 1908 Minkowski published a paper on Lorentz's theory that cleared away much of the mathematical deadwood that had cluttered Einstein's original formulation of special relativity. It demonstrated that time could be treated as a dimension in a four-dimensional universe. "Henceforth space by itself, and time by itself, are doomed to fade away into mere shadows, and only a kind of union of the two will preserve an independent reality," Minkowski predicted. His words proved prophetic, and the special theory of relativity has been viewed in terms of a "space-time continuum" ever since. Einstein initially dismissed Minkowski's formulation as excessively pedantic, joking that he scarcely recognized his own theory once the mathematicians got hold of it. But he came to realize that if he were to explore the connection between weight and inertia, he would do well to travel farther up the trail Minkowski had blazed.

Minkowski's s space-time continuum, though suitable for special relativity, would not support what was to become general relativity. Its space was "flat"—i.e., euclidean. If gravitation were to be interpreted as a form of acceleration, that acceleration would have to occur along the undulations of curved space. So it was that Einstein was led, however reluctantly, into the forbidding territory of the noneuclidean geometries.

THE NEED FOR NONEUCLIDEAN GEOMETRIES

Euclidean geometry, as every high school math student is taught, has different characteristics depending upon whether it is worked in two dimensions ("plane" geometry) or three ("solid" geometry). On a plane, the sum of the angles of a triangle is 180 degrees, but if we add a third dimension we can envision surfaces such as that of a sphere, on which the angles of a triangle add up to *more* than 180 degrees, or a saddle-shaped hyperbola, on which the angles add up to *less* than 180 degrees. The shortest distance between two points on a plane is a straight line, but on a sphere or a hyperbola the shortest distances are *curved* lines. In the noneuclidean geometries a fourth dimension is added, and the rules are changed in a similarly consistent manner to allow for the possible curvature of three-dimensional space within a four-dimensional theater. . . .

By the time Einstein came on the scene, the rules of four-dimensional geometry had been worked out—those of spherical four-space by [mathematician] Georg Friedrich Riemann and those of the four-dimensional hyperbolas by [mathematicians] Nikolai Ivanovich Lobachevski and János Bolyai. The whole subject, however, was still regarded as at best difficult and arcane, and at worst almost disreputable. The legendary mathematician Karl Friedrich Gauss had withheld his papers on noneuclidean geometry from publication, fearing ridicule by his colleagues, and Bolyai conducted his research in the field against the advice of his father, who warned him, "For God's sake, please give it up. Fear it no less than the sensual passions because it, too, may take up all your time and deprive you of your health, peace of mind and happiness in life."

EINSTEIN'S STRUGGLE TO GET THE EQUATIONS RIGHT

Einstein rushed in where Bolyai's father feared to tread. With the aid of his old classmate Marcel Grossman—"Help me, Marcel, or I'll go crazy!" he wrote—Einstein struggled through the complexities of curved space, seeking to assign the fourth dimension to time and make the whole, infernally complicated affair come out right. He had by now begun to win professional recognition, had quit the patent office to accept a series of teaching positions that culminated in a full professorship in pure research at the University of Berlin, and was doing important work in quantum mechanics and a half-dozen other fields. But he kept returning to the riddle of gravitation, trying to find patterns of beauty and simplicity among thick stacks of papers black with equations. Like a lost explorer discarding his belongings on a trek across the desert, he found it necessary to part company with some of the most cherished of his possessions—among them one of the central precepts of the special theory itself, which to his joy was ultimately to return as a local case within the broader scheme of the general theory. "In all my life I have never before labored so hard," he wrote to a friend. ". . . Compared with this problem, the original theory of relativity is child's play." Nowhere in human history is there to be found a more sustained and heroic labor of the intellect than in Einstein's trek toward general relativity, nor one that has produced a greater reward.

He completed the theory in November 1915 and published it the following spring. Though its equations are complex, its central conception is startlingly simple. The force of gravitation disappears, and is replaced by the geometry of space itself: Matter curves space, and what we call gravitation is but the acceleration of objects as they slide down the toboggan runs described by their trajectories in time through the undulations of space. The planets skid along the inner walls of a depression in space created by the fat, massive sun; clusters of galaxies rest in spatial hollows like nuggets in a prospector's bowl.

THE QUESTION OF A FINITE OR INFINITE UNIVERSE

In marrying gravitational physics to the geometry of curved space, general relativity emancipated cosmology from the ancient dilemma of whether the universe is infinite and unbounded or finite and bounded. An infinite universe would be not just large but *infinite*, and this posed problems. The gravitational force generated by an infinite number of stars would itself be infinite, and would, therefore, overwhelm the local action of gravity; this prospect so troubled Newton that he resorted to invoking God's infinite grace to resolve it. Moreover, the light from an infinite number of stars might be expected to turn the night sky into a blazing sheet of light; yet the night sky is dark. The alternative, however—a finite euclidean universe with an edge to it—was equally unattractive: As Liu Chi posed the question, in China in the fourteenth century, "If heaven has a boundary, what things could be outside it?" The difficulty of imagining an end to space had been enunciated as early as the fifth century B.C., by Plato's colleague Archytas the Pythagorean; Lucretius summed it up this way:

Let us assume for the moment that the universe is limited. If a man advances so that he is at the very edge of the extreme boundary and hurls a swift spear, do you prefer that this spear, hurled with great force, go where it was sent and fly far, or do you think that something can stop it and stand in its way?

General relativity resolved the matter by establishing that the universe could be both finite—i.e., could contain a finite number of stars in a finite volume of space—and unbounded. The key to this realization lay in Einstein's demonstration that, since matter warps space, the sum total of the mass in all the galaxies might be sufficient to wrap space around themselves. The result would be a closed, four-dimensionally spherical cosmos, in which any observer, anywhere in the universe, would see galaxies stretching deep into space in every direction, and would conclude, correctly, that there is no end to space. Yet the amount of space in a closed universe would nonetheless be finite: An adventurer with time to spare could eventually visit every galaxy, yet would never reach an edge of space. Just as the surface of the earth is finite but unbounded in two dimensions (we can wander wherever we like, and will not fall off the edge of the earth) so a closed four-dimensional universe is finite but unbounded to us who observe it in three dimensions.

The question of whether the universe is hyperbolic and open or spherical and closed remains unanswered, as we shall see. But, thanks to Einstein, the problem is no longer clouded by paradox. By introducing the scientific prospect of a finite, unbounded cosmos, Einstein's general theory initiated a meaningful dialogue between the human mind and the conundrums of cosmological space.

The theory was beautiful, but was it true? Einstein, having been to the mountaintop, felt supremely confident on this score. General relativity explained a precession in the orbit of the planet Mercury that had been left unaccounted for in Newtonian mechanics, and he did not doubt it would survive further tests as well. As he wrote his friend [Michele Angelo] Besso, "I am fully satisfied, and I do not doubt any more the correctness of the whole system. . . . The sense of the thing is too evident."

EINSTEIN'S THEORY STANDS THE TESTS

The wider scientific community, however, awaited the verdict of experiment. There would be a total solar eclipse on

May 29, 1919, at which time the sun would stand against the bright stars of the Hyades cluster. The English astronomer Arthur Stanley Eddington led an expedition to a cocoa plantation on Principe Island off west Equatorial Africa to observe the eclipse and see whether the predicted curvature of space in the region of the sun would distort the apparent positions of the stars in the briefly darkened sky. It was a scene of high drama—English scientists testing the theory of a German physicist immediately after the end of the Great War. As the time of the eclipse approached, rain clouds covered the sky. But then, moments after the moon's shadow came speeding across the landscape and totality began, a hole opened up in the clouds around the sun, and the camera shutters were triggered. The results of Eddington's expedition, and of a second eclipse observation conducted at Sobral, Brazil on the same day, were presented by the Astronomer Royal at a meeting of the Royal Society in London on November 6, 1919, with Newton's portrait looking on. They were positive: The light rays coming from the stars of the Hyades were found to be offset to just the degree predicted in the theory.

When Einstein received a telegram from Lorentz announcing the outcome of the Eddington expedition, he showed it to a student, Ilse Rosenthal-Schneider, who asked, "What would you have said if there had been no confirmation?"

"I would have had to pity our dear Lord," Einstein replied. "The theory is correct."

Subsequent experiments have further vindicated Einstein's confidence. The curvature of space in the vicinity of the sun was established with much greater accuracy, by bouncing radar waves off Mercury and Venus when they lie near the sun in the sky, and the extent of curvature matched that predicted by the general theory of relativity. A light beam directed up a tower in the Jefferson Physical Laboratory at Harvard University was found to be shifted toward the red by the earth's gravitation to just the anticipated degree. Maelstroms of energy detected at the centers of violent galaxies indicate that they harbor black holes, collapsed objects wrapped in infinitely curved space that shuts them off from the rest of the universe; the existence of black holes was another prediction of the general theory. And the theory has been tested in many other ways as well—in examinations of entombed dead stars, the whirling of active stars around one another, the wanderings of interplanetary spacecraft well past Jupiter, and the slowing of light as it climbs up out of the sun's space well—and all these trials it has survived.

Too modest to be immodest, Einstein had written when publishing his completed account of general relativity that "hardly anyone who has truly understood this theory will be able to resist being captivated by its magic." But, even if only those mathematicians and physicists who have mastered general relativity are in a position properly to understand it, still we can all appreciate it to some degree, if, while keeping in mind its basic concepts, we contemplate the universe of effortlessly wheeling galaxies deployed across the blossom petals of gently curving space. Einstein's epitaph could be English architect Christopher Wren's: If you seek his monument, look around.

Einstein Predicts Gravity Waves

Marcia Bartusiak

Marcia Bartusiak explains that the theory of general relativity, besides predicting curved space, also predicts gravity waves, which are ripples of gravitation set off by moving masses. Because gravity waves disperse and grow weak, Einstein doubted they could ever be directly detected. Bartusiak reports that in 1974 astronomers found indirect evidence of these waves and have devised tests to find direct detection of them. Marcia Bartusiak, who is a reporter and has been news anchor for WVEC-TV in Norfolk, Virginia, has written for *Science News* and *Discover* magazine. She is the author of *Thursday's Universe*.

Gravity waves are Einstein's unfinished symphony, one of the few predictions of his theory of general relativity yet to be proved. With general relativity, this century's most illustrious physicist introduced us to a new, geometric vision of gravity. Space, Einstein taught, may be thought of not as an enormous empty expanse, but as a sort of boundless rubber sheet. Such a sheet can be manipulated in a lot of ways: it can be stretched or squeezed; it can be straightened or bent; it can even be indented in spots.

Massive stars like our sun sit in this flexible mat, creating deep depressions. Planets then circle the sun, not because they are held by invisible tendrils of force, as Newton had us think, but because they are simply caught in the natural hollow carved out by the star. As long as a heavenly body continues to exist, the indentations it creates in the mat will be part of the permanent landscape of the cosmos. What we think of as gravity—the tendency of two objects to be drawn toward each other—is a result of these indentations.

A JIGGLED MASS SENDS RIPPLES

With this concept in mind, Einstein realized that space can also be disturbed. Jiggle a mass to and fro and it should send out ripples of gravitational energy, akin to the way a ball bounced on a trampoline sends vibrations across the canvas. These gravity waves would radiate outward like light waves, striking planets, stars, and other cosmic objects. But while electromagnetic waves move through space, gravity waves would be undulations in space itself. They would expand and contract the heavenly bodies they encountered and all the space around them.

Anything in the universe that has mass is capable of sending out gravity waves—in most cases all it has to do is move. Like light and sound waves, gravity waves are expected to come in a variety of strengths and frequencies, depending on the mass of the moving body and the nature of its movement. A mammoth body like a star has a powerful gravitational pull, but since it remains essentially stationary, it emits few waves. Earth, on the other hand, continually emits weak gravitational energy as it orbits the sun; the moon sends out weaker waves still as it moves around Earth. Even hopscotch players emit a gravity wave or two as they jump up and down. Waves appreciable enough to be detected, however, will emanate from the most violent events the universe has to offer: stars crashing into one another, the explosion of supernovas, the formation of black holes.

Because gravitational energy moving through space disperses and grows weaker in the same way starlight does, Einstein himself doubted that gravity waves would ever be observed. By the time gravity waves from distant stars strike Earth, they are little more than a flutter. Were a gravity wave from a supernova in the center of the Milky Way to hit this page, it would be so weak that it would change the sheet's dimensions by a mere hundred-thousandth of a trillionth of a centimeter—a measure 10,000 times smaller than the size of an atomic nucleus.

PREDICTIONS THAT HAVE BEEN VERIFIED

Nevertheless, few people seriously doubt that gravity waves exist. Einstein had established three tests for his theory of general relativity. The first was that it account for a discrepancy in Mercury's orbit. Astronomers had long observed that Mercury's elliptical orbit is not entirely stable; rather the ends of the ellipse advance slightly each time the planet passes around the sun. Einstein showed that this could be explained by the planet subtly shifting its trajectory as it moves through the giant gravity well stamped out by the sun, and his calculations accurately predicted the elliptical advance.

Einstein also said that starlight passing by the sun should be seen to bend as it follows the curve of the same gravity pit, twice the bending predicted by Newton's theory. Additionally, Einstein announced that light beams flashed upward from Earth should shift toward the red end of the visible spectrum

---

DETECTION OF GRAVITY WAVES MAKES PROGRESS

In The Whole Shebang, *Timothy Ferris updates progress on research efforts designed to detect gravitational waves. He quotes Kip Thorne, who predicts that new devices will soon provide maps of gravitational waves emitting from black holes.*

Relativity theory predicts that colliding black holes would emit gigantic bursts of gravitational waves—ripples in the fabric of spacetime that propagate at the velocity of light. The existence of gravitational waves has already been demonstrated: Joseph Taylor and Russell Hulse of Princeton University won a 1993 Nobel Prize for studies of binary neutron stars showing that the stars are approaching each other at just the rate that relativity predicts as a consequence of energy being carried away from the system by gravitational waves. Work is under way on a pair of gravitational-wave detectors to be built by the LIGO (Laser Interferometer Gravitational-Wave Observatory) project in the United States, and a third detector, VIRGO (named after the Virgo Cluster of galaxies), is to be constructed near Pisa, Galileo's hometown. These observatories will use laser beams to detect slight changes in the geometry of local space as it expands and contracts when gravitational waves go through. Kip Thorne predicts that "gravitational-wave detectors will soon bring us observational maps of black holes, and the symphonic sounds of black holes colliding—symphonies filled with rich, new information about how warped spacetime behaves when wildly vibrating. Supercomputer simulations will attempt to replicate the symphonies and tell us what they mean, and black holes thereby will become objects of detailed experimental scrutiny."

Timothy Ferris, *The Whole Shebang: A State-of-the-Universe(s) Report.* New York: Simon & Schuster, 1997.

88   *Albert Einstein*

as the same gravitational effects stretched the light waves on their flight away from the planet. Both these predictions have been tested and verified by a host of researchers.

With all this evidence amassed in favor of Einstein's view of gravity, physicists are assured that gravity waves, a natural consequence of the theory, are whisking through the universe. Moreover, indirect evidence of their existence has been uncovered.

ATTEMPTS TO DETECT GRAVITY WAVES

In 1974 astronomers found two neutron stars in our own galaxy rapidly orbiting each other, and they noticed that the two stars are drawing closer and closer together. The rate of their orbital decay—about one yard per year—is just the change expected if this binary pair is losing its energy in the form of gravity waves radiated into space. "This is powerful evidence that gravity waves are real," says MIT physicist Ranier Weiss. But final confirmation awaits direct detection of the waves themselves.

The honor of being the first researcher to try to snag a gravity wave goes to physicist Joseph Weber of the University of Maryland. In the 1960s Weber came up with a clever technological trick for trapping a gravity wave. He surmised that a burst of gravitational energy moving through a solid cylinder would squeeze it, ever so slightly, like an accordion. Long after the wave passed through, the bar would continue to "ring." The phenomenon is similar to the vibrations that can be produced in a tuning fork when it is struck by sound waves. In both cases the dimensions and materials of the bar or the fork determine which frequency of wave will trigger the ringing.

Weber reasoned that he could position electronic devices on either the sides or ends of the cylinder and convert the extremely tiny gravity wave induced movements into electric signals that would then be recorded and scrutinized. And in 1969 he galvanized the physics community with the announcement that he had used such a system to detect pulses emanating from the center of the galaxy. The response was not unlike this year's rush to test the claimed discovery of cold fusion.[1] Many researchers built hardware of their own and attempted to detect the waves themselves.

1. a false claim regarding a nuclear reaction

And although most declared they saw nothing, a fledgling branch of astronomy was born.

In the two decades since, bars of varying designs and materials have been constructed in labs around the globe. The best are cooled with streams of liquid helium to temperatures near absolute zero, in order to cut down on the thermal noises generated when atoms in the bar jostle about. At Stanford, a five-ton aluminum bar, ten feet long and three feet wide, can detect a quiver as tiny as 10^{-16} inch.

But bars have a number of shortcomings. As their sensitivities are increased, electronic noises in the detection equipment may ultimately overwhelm any gravity wave signal. At the same time, the supercooling can be tricky; if something goes wrong, it can take several months to warm up the detector, fix it, and cool it back down again. And since manufacturing and logistical limitations prevent bars from being made much larger than the one at Stanford, they can't pick up all possible gravity wave frequencies.

For these reasons a number of researchers consider an instrument known as a laser interferometer much more attractive in their quest to catch a wave. "Bars certainly have a role, and they may yet see the first sources," says Caltech physicist Michael Zucker, who has worked on bar systems himself. "But I believe laser interferometers have the flexibility to do the long-term astronomy."

Einstein Rejects Quantum Theory

Jeremy Bernstein

Jeremy Bernstein explains the point at which Einstein rejected quantum theory, the theory that explains the behavior of radiant energy. As physicists were discovering that energy functions both as waves and as particles, Einstein was actively involved. Then physicists found that because of the dual nature of particles, their behavior could only be predicted according to laws of probability. According to Bernstein, Einstein rejected this finding as no better than dice throwing. It contradicted his belief that nature has a determined order. Jeremy Bernstein taught physics at New York University and Harvard University and was invited to do research at the Institute for Advanced Study at Princeton. He is the author of *A Comprehensible World: On Modern Science and its Origin, Elementary Particles and Their Currents,* and *The Elusive Neutrino.*

Until the mid-1920s Einstein made fundamental positive contributions to the quantum theory[1], although, after 1925, when the theory seemed to have made a decisive step forward at the hands of [physicists Werner] Heisenberg, [Wolfgang] Pauli, [Max] Born, [Niels] Bohr, [Paul] Dirac, [Erwin] Schrödinger, and others, he turned against it. Perhaps some future generation of physicists will, somehow, discover that Einstein's critical intuitions were really right, though now this does not seem likely. In fact, because of his opposition to the later developments in the quantum theory, many *physicists* have not been aware of the full scope of Einstein's contributions to the quantum physics of the 1920s. It is only re-

1. The theory that radiant energy—light, for example—is transmitted in discrete units, or particles.

cently that historians of modern science have begun to untangle the complicated web of influences that led to the invention of the quantum theory and the discovery of the wave nature of matter—only to find, once again, Einstein as a pivotal figure.

EARLY METHODS OF DOING QUANTUM STATISTICS

Einstein's great work of the 1920s had to do with the quantum statistical mechanics of gases—what we now call the Bose-Einstein gas. S.N. Bose, an Indian physicist working in Dacca, had sent Einstein a short manuscript in English in 1924, and in July of that year, the *Zeitschrift für Physik* received a rather unusual communication: a paper written by Bose, entitled "Planck's Law and the Hypothesis of Light Quanta," but submitted by Einstein. After reading the English manuscript Einstein had been so impressed by it that he had translated it himself into German and had sent it, on Bose's behalf, to the journal.

Bose had discovered a new method of doing quantum statistics and had applied it to give a new derivation of Planck's radiation formula[2]. Einstein realized that the same methods could be applied to ordinary gases but that if one did so it would necessarily imply that the "particle" composing such gases would behave statistically like light quanta and therefore should, or *could*—since there was no experimental evidence at that time—also show wave characteristics. It was while he was carrying out these calculations that he received a copy of [physicist Louis] de Broglie's thesis in which de Broglie—for other reasons—had made the same conjecture and, in Einstein's words, had "lifted a corner of the great veil." By 1925, Einstein had sufficient confidence in the whole scheme so that he could write, "A beam of gas molecules which passes through an aperture must, then, undergo a diffraction analogous to that of a light ray." That this in fact happens was confirmed by [physicist] C.J. Davisson and L.H. Germer and, independently, by G.P. Thomson in their celebrated experiments of 1927. (These experiments actually used electrons, but the principle is the same.) This means that not only is light schizophrenic—exhibiting both wave and particle aspects—but "particles" such as the electron are

---

2. German physicist Max Planck was first to discover that energy is not continuous, that it has discrete parts. He discovered a formula relating the energy of a photon to the frequency of that photon.

92   *Albert Einstein*

equally schizophrenic. Under suitable circumstances electrons act like "waves," i.e., beams of electrons can interfere
with each other like interfering beams of light waves.

In 1925 Erwin Schrödinger and Heisenberg made the
great theoretical breakthroughs that led to modern quantum
mechanics. At first it looked as if each of them had invented
a different theory, so that there were two separate quantum
theories. But by 1926 Schrödinger proved that the two theories were mathematically equivalent. He discovered the
equation that described the behavior of the de Broglie waves
or, as he insisted on calling them, "the de Broglie-Einstein"
waves. As he wrote, "My theory was stimulated by de
Broglie's thesis and by short but infinitely far-seeing remarks by Einstein." Einstein greeted Schrödinger's first paper with enthusiasm, and he wrote to Schrödinger, "The
idea of your article shows real genius."

EINSTEIN REJECTS THE FINDING THAT BEHAVIOR OF
PARTICLES IS *PROBABLE*, NOT DETERMINED

Both Einstein and Schrödinger rejected the next step, which
was taken by Born and his colleague Pascual Jordan. This
had to do with the question of what the waves were supposed to represent. The first interpretation, going back to de
Broglie, was that particles such as the electron were classical particles—small billiard balls—but that the waves determined the trajectories of these particles when, for example,
they circulated around an atomic nucleus. This was a picture that was based as closely as possible on classical
physics. But Born and Jordan argued that it was inconsistent
and that the only possible interpretation of the waves was
that from them—from their mathematical form as given by
the Schrödinger equation—one could calculate the *probable*
behavior of the particles and *nothing else.*

One may illustrate this graphically with the light quanta.
As we have seen, if a light ray is sent through a small aperture, because of the interference effects, a diffraction pattern
will be formed on a screen at the other side of the aperture.
Now the same experiment can be performed by sending
light quanta, one at a time, through the aperture. Each light
quantum will pass through and hit some point on the
screen. According to the Born-Jordan interpretation one
cannot predict with certainty what an individual light quantum will do when it arrives at the aperture. One can only

state what it is *most likely* to do—something that is determined by the Schrödinger wave function; i.e., the solution to the Schrödinger wave equation.

In fact, according to the theory, the light quantum is most likely to hit that point on the screen where, according to the wave picture, the diffraction pattern is brightest. This resolves the wave-particle schizophrenia, but at the cost of giving up a deterministic description of physical events. Strict determinism in the sense that physicists had become accustomed to from Newton to Einstein had to be abandoned, and this Einstein, and Schrödinger as well, would not accept. As Einstein said again and again, "God does not play dice with the world."

THE CONCLUSION THAT THE UNCERTAIN POSITION OF A PARTICLE IS A FACT OF NATURE

The next steps were taken by Heisenberg and Bohr at Bohr's institute in Copenhagen, where Heisenberg was a frequent visitor. The main consequence of this work was the idea that the particle-wave duality was not an incidental feature of atomic physics but was, rather, a basic fact about nature that could be traced back to a careful analysis of the meaning of "measurement" on the atomic scale, which Heisenberg expressed in terms of his "uncertainty principle." The most famous elementary example is the "Heisenberg microscope." This is an imaginary device capable of generating light quanta of such short wave length that, in principle, one could use it to try to measure the positions of electrons in atoms. Heisenberg argues that such quanta would have to be so energetic that after each measurement the electron would be knocked out of the atom—hence that the idea of an electron "orbit" in an atom was meaningless since it was unmeasurable. One could predict where the electron could be found in the atom with the greatest probability, using the Schrödinger wave function, but nothing more. Bohr saw in this something even deeper—a whole new philosophical outlook which he called "complementarity," and which he felt illuminated the limitations on the use of concepts not only in physics but throughout science and philosophy. Just as in physics where there are pairs of complementary variables such as position and momentum of such a character that the more precisely one is determined then, necessarily, the more imprecise must be the determination of the other, Bohr saw in such ancient philosophical questions as the separation of subject from object, or the role of love versus justice, the interplay of mutually restrictive complementary concepts.

EINSTEIN STICKS TO HIS POSITION THAT CERTAINTY EXISTS AND CAN BE DISCOVERED

From the beginning Einstein rejected the uncertainty principle. As he wrote to Schrödinger in 1928, "The Heisenberg-Bohr tranquilizing philosophy—or religion?—is so delicately contrived that, for the time being, it provides a gentle pillow for the true believer from which he cannot very easily be aroused. So let him lie there." As one might imagine, Einstein was not content to let "the true believers"—who, after a while, included most physicists—lie on their pillows. He began almost at once to formulate apparent paradoxes in the theory which Bohr responded to, one after the other, even after Einstein's death. As people who knew Bohr often pointed out, it was as if each day he began from the beginning reviewing all of his arguments in real or imaginary dialogues with Einstein to make sure he had left nothing out. In 1948 Bohr wrote a masterly summary of his discussions with Einstein over the years which he concluded by stating, "Whether our actual meetings have been of short or long duration, they have always left a deep and lasting impression on my mind, and when writing this report I have, so-to-say, been arguing with Einstein all the time even when entering on topics apparently far removed from the special problems under debate at our meetings." Bohr recounted one of their most celebrated discussions, which took place at the Solvay Conference in Brussels in 1930. For this occasion Einstein had invented a remarkable imaginary device involving clocks and scales—perhaps drawing on his experience examining patents in Bern—which appeared to violate the uncertainty principle. After a sleepless night Bohr discovered that in his reasoning Einstein had forgotten to take into account the effect of *his own discovery* that clocks run at a slower rate in a gravitational field, and that, indeed, the uncertainty principle was secure.

All of the principles in this debate—which lasted nearly three decades—remained unbudgeable to the end. ([Paul] Ehrenfest, who knew both men well and witnessed many of their discussions, was tormented by his own conflicting feelings as to who was right, and this, it is generally agreed, was one of the factors that led to his suicide in 1933.) Max Born summarized the attitude of many physicists when he wrote in 1948 of Einstein, "He has seen more clearly than anyone before him the statistical background of the laws of physics, and he was a pioneer in the struggle of conquering the wilderness of quantum phenomena. Yet later, when out of his own work a synthesis of statistical and quantum principles emerged which seemed acceptable to almost all physicists he kept himself aloof and sceptical. Many of us regard this as a tragedy—for him, as he gropes his way in loneliness, and for us, who miss our leader and standard-bearer." Sometime before writing this Born had received a letter from Einstein in which he wrote, "In our scientific expectation we have grown antipodes. You believe in a dice-playing God and I in perfect laws in the world of things existing as real objects, which I try to grasp in a wildly speculative way."

The Search for a Unified Field Theory

Loyd S. Swenson Jr.

Loyd S. Swenson Jr. argues that Einstein's contributions to science were primarily completed when he was awarded the Nobel Prize in 1922. Einstein, however, worked diligently for thirty more years hoping to find a theory that synthesized gravitation and electromagnetism—a unified field theory. Swenson explains that in the 1920s and 1930s many of the world's leading physicists turned their attention to particle physics and the development of quantum mechanics. Consequently, Einstein, who rejected quantum mechanics, became more and more isolated in his search; he died without achieving his goal. Loyd S. Swenson Jr. has taught history at Harvard and at the University of Houston. He is the author of *The Ethereal Aether* and *Chariots for Apollo: A History of Manned Lunar Spacecraft.*

After Einstein's recognition by his peers about 1910, by the public about 1920, and with *the* [Nobel] prize, acknowledged on 11 July 1923 by his lecture delivered in Göteborg, Sweden, Einstein's greatest achievement was essentially finished. His character and reputation were matched and his major syntheses were, if not fully accepted, being explored for their implications.

But Einstein himself did not recognize this historical judgment. Being only forty-eight years old and in fairly good health, he set forth on the quest that would occupy the next thirty-two years of his life. He considered this search for *the* unified field theory truly a piece of *re*-search, trying to synthesize mathematically the logical foundations for gravitation and electromagnetism. Within the decade he achieved and published *a* unified field theory, but already it had been

Excerpted from *Genesis of Relativity,* by Loyd S. Swenson Jr. (New York: Burt Franklin, 1979). Reprinted by permission of the author.

made obsolete by other advances in physics. And within another decade he would have to account for the strong (and later the weak) "forces" of nucleonic particle interactions. His commitment to the field concept, to continuity, rationality, and causality in nature, was never a blind commitment. But it did become, after the quantum mechanical revolution of the mid-1920s and especially after the fifth Solvay conference, in 1927, a minority position that grew ever less popular. Only after his death was there sizable evidence of a resurgence toward the unification of relativistic and quantum field theories.

NEW SCIENTIFIC TRENDS DURING THE 1920S

To see something of the way in which Einstein moved toward generalizing his general theory, we shall look briefly at a few of the trends and events in observational astrophysics and quantum mechanics that changed the tenor of the times during the 1920s.

The first independent check of the results of the Eddington eclipse expedition to test Einstein's predictions of the bending of starlight was carried out in 1922 by American astronomers R.J. Trumpler and W.W. Campbell, director of the Lick Observatory on Mount Hamilton near San Francisco. Trumpler went to Tahiti in May to prepare instruments and check patterns for comparisons later. On 21 September 1922, at Wallal in Western Australia, W.W. Campbell and his aides succeeded in making good photographs of about seventy-five stars during a total solar eclipse. After data reduction and correlation, they announced their results in April 1923 as being in excellent agreement with Einstein's predictions. Given Campbell's position as an authority on stellar motions and as a former skeptic regarding relativity, his report was especially significant. And it spurred other Californians farther south on to a variety of similar activities. . . .

Meanwhile, throughout the 1920s, Einstein had continued to struggle with his quest for a unitary field theory. After the rather shocking reports in 1923 from [physicist] Arthur H. Compton at St. Louis that he had been able to produce experimental proof that X rays can be *totally* reflected from glass or silver mirrors at small angles of incidence *and* that X rays experience a change in wave length, a "softening," in scattering experiments, physicists had to cope with this strong direct evidence that X rays show *both* a wave and a particle nature. Thus the dilemma of wave-particle duality, reinforced thereafter by similar news from elsewhere, led physicists much more deeply into the quantum interpretations of [physicist Max] Planck and Einstein regarding radiant energy transfer. In Paris, the younger brother of Maurice de Broglie, Prince Louis de Broglie, was finishing his doctoral thesis and publishing during 1923–24 a series of papers showing how matter (in the form of electrons and protons) and radiation (in the form of quanta or "atoms of light") might be reconciled. . . .

After their Nobel prizes had been awarded[1], Einstein and [Danish physicist Niels] Bohr began to notice certain subtle differences in their taste and style of doing physics. This divergence ripened through the crisis that was approaching. The best of [physicist] Max Born's students at Göttingen— Wolfgang Pauli and Werner Heisenberg—were visiting Bohr's institute in Copenhagen more than Einstein's institute in Berlin. It seemed as if the problem of atomic structure was more compelling, if not more tractable, than that of the unified field. Theoretical spectroscopy based on laboratory results seemed more promising than that based on observatory data. And yet Einstein retained a foot in both camps, as was recognized by physicists like Alfred Landé and Erwin Schrödinger.

In June and July of 1925, the first fruits from the divergent but prepared minds of Heisenberg and Schrödinger began to appear. These works were destined within a year or two to transform the old quantum theory into the new quantum mechanics. . . .

Despite the superficial similarities and profound differences between Heisenberg's and Schrödinger's systems for understanding microphysics, yet another system came forth during 1926 to complement matrix and wave mechanics and to translate the whole of classical dynamics into quantum theory. This brilliant achievement of [physicist] Paul A.M. Dirac of Cambridge University brought a third scheme of explanation into play. And thus the revolution characterized by three equally powerful mathematical approaches to matter and radiation, known collectively as quantum mechanics, proved irresistible.

---

1. Einstein received the 1921 Nobel Prize and Bohr received the 1922 Prize, but both were awarded in 1922 since none was awarded in 1921.

EINSTEIN'S GROWING DISAGREEMENT WITH BOHR

In 1927, theory, it seemed, had finally caught up with experimentation. And yet at the fifth Solvay conference [of physicists] in Brussels, that year, devoted to the theme "Electrons and Photons," the senior theoretical physicists found themselves profoundly polarized by conflicting philosophies. Bohr came to explain his schools' working consensus that operational meanings alone should be trusted, that probabilities within the various forms of quantum statistics should replace the search for causal laws, and that all observers should recognize henceforth that the act of observation may change or otherwise affect what is observed. . . .

In September 1927 at Lake Como in Italy, Bohr had launched his principle of complementarity to another congress of physicists: "Evidence obtained under different experimental conditions cannot be comprehended within a single picture, but must be regarded as *complementary* in the sense that only the totality of the phenomena exhausts the possible information about the objects."

In Brussels, Einstein arose in response to this challenge, arguing forcefully against such trust placed in discontinuities, probabilities, indeterminacy, and complementarity. All his instincts by now inveighed against accepting the Dane's doctrines. To Einstein it seemed puerile to think that physics had reached a state of perfection or completeness. To Bohr it seemed equally futile or childish to believe that men will ever become divine enough to know everything in detail about either universal or individual events. Bohr and his allies felt that quantum-mechanical descriptions would eventually and essentially exhaust the possibilities of accounting for observable phenomena. Einstein vehemently disagreed, lamenting the loss to science of causality, continuity, and determinism.

Three years later, at the sixth Solvay conference, the Einstein-Bohr debate continued even more dramatically. The year before, in 1929, Einstein had with great hope published a unified field theory; it was poorly received, probably because quantum mechanics and atomic and nuclear physics promised so much more in return. Then, too, all the developments from quantum theory fed back into electromagnetism and thus modified half of what Einstein had unified. At any rate, Einstein confronted Bohr in 1930 with a new thought-experiment that attempted to prove the principle of complementarity was untenable. To Einstein, Bohr had made the mistake of permitting theoretical description to be too directly dependent on mere observations or experiments. But Bohr defended himself heartily, and after he showed Einstein had forgotten certain implications of his own general theory of relativity, Einstein again had to retreat. Each felt that the other was verging on a betrayal of the spirit of physics.

EINSTEIN'S FAITH IN NATURE'S ORDER

In Albert Einstein: A Biography, *Albrecht Fölsing maintains that Einstein searched for a unified field theory with the fervor of deep religious faith. Because Einstein believed that nature has an orderly structure, he remained determined in his quest, beginning anew after each failed theory.*

In his later years Einstein saw beauty in the laws of nature. He profoundly believed, with religious fervor, that simple laws existed, and that these could be discovered. Except for a brief phase during his adolescence, he never had any use for the personified God of the Judeo-Christian tradition. But even in his younger years, he saw God as the guarantor of the laws of nature. Initially this sounded like a playful formulation, but as he grew older the metaphor became a kind of heuristic principle: Einstein would attempt to slip into the role of the creator of the world and its laws. He surprised Banesh Hoffmann with his criterion: "When I am judging a theory, I ask myself whether, if I were God, I would have arranged the world in such a way."

This belief in a lawful structure of the world gave him the strength and perseverance he needed throughout the decades when he was searching for a unified theory. He was capable of pursuing a theoretical concept, with great enthusiasm for months or even years at a stretch; but when grievous flaws emerged—which invariably happened in the end—he would drop it instantly at the moment of truth, without sentimentality or disappointment over the time and effort wasted. The following morning, or a few days later at the most, he would have taken up a new idea and would pursue that with the same enthusiasm. . . .

He never wavered in his conviction that although the statistical laws of quantum mechanics were useful tools, they were not the foundations of physics.

Albrecht Fölsing, *Albert Einstein: A Biography.* Trans. by Ewald Osers. New York: Viking, 1997.

EINSTEIN'S LONE SEARCH FOR A UNIFIED FIELD THEORY

By 1930, the leaders of the profession could see an obvious epistemological split between the rationalism of Einstein and the relativism of Bohr. Ironically, as the years passed, Einstein became less a leader of revolutionary relativism, a critic of accepted concepts, and a creator of startling new syntheses, and more a conservative spokesman for what the younger generation thought of as "classical" physics. He was still deeply immersed in his quest for a unified field theory, but he recognized his growing loneliness in that search. With wry humor he tried to keep up with the avalanching advances in physical discovery while maintaining as a personal program the research for a set of continuous functions in the four-dimensional space-time continuum. (He could afford this pursuit of a possible chimera; younger men could not.) The basic obstacle to achieving a larger field theory for the synthesis of gravitation and electromagnetism was the perpetual appearance of "singularities," that is, places or parts of space-time where the field equations are not valid. In his efforts to avoid such singularities, Einstein was led farther from science and deeper into philosophy.

CHAPTER 3

THE PUBLIC EINSTEIN—HIS FAME AND CAUSES

ALBERT EINSTEIN

Fame Transformed into Legend

Anton Reiser

Writing in the late 1920s, Anton Reiser (pseudonym
for Rudolf Kayser) describes how Einstein, first
merely famous, became a legend. Reiser identifies
factors that caused Einstein's reputation to mush-
room out of proportion: the misunderstanding by the
public of "relativity," the appearance of Einstein's
picture with his crown of hair and kindly face, the
hopes of writers and seekers who believed he could
help them. Reiser credits Einstein for his patience
and understanding with the disruptions, and for his
courage to promote peace after World War I by lecturing in nations that had been Germany's enemies
during the war. Anton Reiser was a journalist who,
because he was married to Einstein's stepdaughter,
knew the physicist well. Reiser is the editor of *Mein
Weltbild*, a collection of Einstein's writings.

Einstein's life work could not be misunderstood more thor-
oughly. How could this misunderstanding arise? The word
relativity was responsible in the first place. The word was
confused in lay circles and, to-day, is still confused with the
word *relativism*. Einstein's work and personality, however,
are far removed from the ambiguity of the concept of relativism, both in the theory of knowledge and in ethics. The
theory of relativity in nowise teaches the idea that our impressions are relative, that they do not grasp objects themselves, but only their interrelations and conditions. On the
contrary, the theory of relativity has succeeded in determining the physical phenomena with greater exactness and sim-
plified the whole physical system by means of the combination of space and time into a continuity and by means of the
new explanation of gravitation. Ethical relativism, however,

Excerpted from *Albert Einstein: A Biographical Portrait*, by Anton Reiser (New York:
Albert and Charles Boni, 1930).

which denies all the generally obligatory moral norms, totally contradicts the high social idea which Einstein stands
for and always follows. Nevertheless, these misunderstandings have not entirely disappeared. Even to-day, they completely misrepresent his achievement and personality. These
misunderstandings read intentions into a theoretical work
which arise only in the attitude of the times.

EINSTEIN'S FAME BECOMES LEGENDARY

And yet Einstein's great fame is a fact which is not only justified by his incomparable achievement, but a fact which has
become more and more a part of the consciousness of our
times. This fact provokes thought and presents us with the
problem of solving a mystery which cannot consist of misunderstandings only. The legend of a man, the immense
popularity of a name in all parts of the world—these facts as
they reappear in history from epoch to epoch, find explanation only in the one miracle of history and life, namely the
magic of a great personality. Every fame that lasts more than
a day, every real human legend has this magic for its cause.
Even though the work of a personality is open to a very small
circle, and even though the profit and the enjoyment derived
from this work may for all future times be open only to a
small part of humanity, the great significance of this work
impresses the simple human mind all the more, inasmuch
as it senses the magic and the magnitude of a creator even
in the most ordinary things.

At the beginning of the Einstein legend, there were dis-
sensions and misunderstandings; there was unbounded excitement in the various camps of the scientists; and, at the
same time, there was a premonition of greatness which does
not deceive. There was the premonition that Einstein's
achievement, quietly attained and not intended for the great
public, had suddenly made a scientist the center of all discussions of the world, and this at a moment when Germany
was in a more pitiable and helpless position than ever before. In April of the year 1922, there appeared in the Parisian
paper *Œuvre* a cartoon that amusingly yet seriously illustrated this situation. In the cartoon, the French government
is asked: "But you do admit that Einstein has revolutionized
science?!" The answer is "As long as Germany doesn't pay—
never!" This cartoon is significant of the political moment
during which Einstein's great fame began. Back in the year

1919, there appeared, on the title page of the *Berliner Illustrierte Zeitung*, the portrait of Albert Einstein. Hundreds of thousands of people saw this face for the first time; heard for the first time the name of this Berlin professor of physics; learned for the first time, through the printed article, about the problems of the theory of relativity. In all probability, his face made as deep an impression on the readers as the popular and abbreviated summary of his great discoveries. From then on, it became the property of the great number of people who derive from these features a living impression at once undeceiving and unforgettable.

A calm and serious face. Beneath the strongly arched forehead, there are dreamy and kindly eyes. And above the forehead, the long gray hair—this face speaks a clear language. Every one understands this language and receives the impression of creative greatness, of achievement and vision, of loneliness and kindliness, of intellectual mastery and social service. The more successful Einstein's theory became, the more silent his opponents, the greater the admiring appreciation from scientists of all countries, the deeper became the impression of his personality and the impression of this, now so often published, portrait. This legend of a great personality creates an impression all the more powerful in a democratic age characterized by the mass of mechanized life.

LETTERS AND REQUESTS FROM ALL PARTS OF THE WORLD

The cardinal points of the Einstein legend are his scientific work and his humanity. The world needs both at all times. The hopes and wishes of innumerable people cling to both. When one sees how these hopes and wishes find their way day after day into the quiet study of the scholar, when one sees the tireless zeal with which this man devotes himself to all the petitions and requests which are placed before him, one sometimes receives the impression of a man who has set himself to gather the tears of the world in his hands. People turn to him as to a miraculous Rabbi who can always heal and help. People write to him from the four corners of the world. They submit to him their most intimate worries; they tell him things that are totally foreign to him and which often make him smile, and this all happens in the firm belief that "this man can help us, this man will help us."

Poor people beg for money, for clothing, and jobs. A young man has taken the notion to become an explorer; won't Einstein help him to get to India or Africa? A woman telegraphs would the professor please obtain a visé. Actors ask for engagements; young people in small towns who have hardly attended high school would like to come to Berlin and become his disciples. Einstein reads all these requests with kindliness and understanding and also with a sense of humor. These are obligations of fame which one must bear with a smile, but this fame has other consequences frequently responsible for bitterness. There are letters and magazine articles filled with hatred, malice, envy and vulgarity. And since Einstein is a Jew and an opponent of all nationalistic pride, all the garbage of political strife is also cast at him. In addition, there come the fools and the prophets, who sprout like mushrooms, especially in the years of insecurity and anarchy. This one writes that he has finally discovered the essence of sleep. That one writes that he has found the only correct way to lower the price of coal. Another one has invented new senses, since the old five senses are no longer sufficient for man's use. Technicians report on their new inventions. They send blue prints of new contraptions and flying machines. Still another is engaged in overthrowing the traditional astronomy and building up a new one. Still another believes that he has found new mathematical formulæ—and all these piles of patient paper that fools and wise men, good and bad men, have written upon pass through Einstein's hands, and not one but is read. The human world, in view of these daily letters, must seem queer to him: a mixture of need, despair, foolishness, humanity and misanthropy. Touching tokens of admiration are among them. For instance, poor people, who have heard that Einstein helps the oppressed, congratulate him on his birthday; or somebody writes that he has named his son Albert in Einstein's honor; or a cigar manufacturer informs him that he has given the name "Relativity" to his new brand. How human all this is, both the good and the bad. And Einstein has such a deep understanding of all things human.

But he does not desire this noisy fame. He does not want to stand exposed to the gaze of the people. He suffers when popularity oppresses and injures him too much. Then it often happens that he complains, "What do these people want of me? Why am I not permitted to live like anybody else? What barbarous nonsense all this is." And when the more intrusive tools of this popularity, interviewers, photographers and autograph hunters, take after him too hard, it happens that his kindliness is transformed into anger and that he forbids these too obtrusive importunities.

SPREADING PEACE AFTER WORLD WAR I

Albert Einstein is the first German whose name attained national significance after the World War. He is also the first intellectual personality who found his way beyond the German boundaries and into formerly hostile capitals, to be honored and welcomed. When, in the year 1921, he accepted an invitation to deliver lectures in Paris, he was attacked most violently on nationalistic grounds. He received letters from unknown persons who wrote him that for the honor of Germany he should not enter a country whose troops were occupying German soil. These persons overlooked the fact that nothing could be more advantageous for Germany than this peaceful conquest by means of creative achievement. No better start could be conceived for a new European community than the eternal internationalism of science. As a matter of fact, at that time there was still present on both sides of German boundaries a cool reserve towards all attempts to reconstruct European society. Thus Einstein's visit to Paris bore fruit by inducing France to think again of its great European mission of culture and to enter upon a closer intellectual affiliation with its German neighbors. Since then this affiliation has been greatly strengthened. At first, of course, a certain portion of the Parisian press found it necessary to excuse Einstein's visit with the explanation that he was not a German but a Swiss. That was intended as a kind of sedative for nationalistically heated minds at a time when it was still dangerous to talk German on the streets of Paris. However, the effects of his personality and of his teaching, which found strong approval, especially in French scientific circles, so that Einstein, even to-day, stands in close touch with French fellow scientists, were so great that the political question of nationality subsided of its own accord.

There was a repetition of this event soon after in London. In the first years after the war, the tension between Germany and England was not as great as that between Germany and France, but nevertheless, the English were cool and reserved towards everything German. In spite of that, London prepared a very warm reception for the German scholar. [Government minister] Lord Haldane introduced Einstein's lectures in Kings College with a speech in which he unreservedly gave Einstein the prominent position which is due him. "You see here before you," he turned toward the audience, "the Newton of the twentieth century, a man who has called forth a greater revolution of thought than even Copernicus, Galileo, or Newton himself." The reception bestowed upon Einstein's lecture was vividly described by the London periodical *The Nation*:

EINSTEIN'S HEAD

In his biographical essay, "Einstein," C.P. Snow describes his first impression of Einstein's lined face and white hair when the two men first met.

At close quarters Einstein's head was as I had imagined it: magnificent, with a humanising touch of the comic. Great furrowed forehead: aureole of white hair: enormous bulging chocolate-brown eyes. I can't guess what I should have expected from such a face if I hadn't known. A shrewd Swiss once said it had the brightness of a good artisan's countenance, that he looked like a reliable old-fashioned watchmaker in a small town who perhaps collected butterflies on a Sunday.

C.P. Snow, "Einstein." In *Einstein: The First Hundred Years*. Ed. by Maurice Goldsmith, Alan Mackay, and James Woudhuysen. New York: Pergamon, 1980.

"There was at first no applause. Something like a light tremor was felt in the air. Is not Einstein really a German? But Lord Haldane, smiling, clever and merciless, passed over this point. A fact like this must be suppressed. The dose, however, is not diminished no matter how distasteful the truth is: the greatest investigator whom the last centuries have produced is a German Jew. They gazed at Einstein. He was calm, dreamy and looked at nothing.

"The great reception bestowed upon Einstein's lecture, in proportion to his importance and his presentation, certainly represents a turning-point in the emotions of the post-war period in this country. Science and the arts have no boundaries. This is a fact, but this fact, like many others, was denied in the general conflagration of the war. The appreciation of obvious genius is a symptom of returning health, and we may now justifiably hope for the gradual restoration of the sane conditions of pre-war times, if an Austrian artist like [violinist and composer] Fritz Kreisler and a German scholar like Albert Einstein are heard with avidity and welcomed enthusiastically in the capital of a formerly hostile country. The position of scholars, English as well as German, was not irreproachable during the war, but this welcome shows that genius is no longer denied admiration, for the admiration of genius is rooted as deeply in human nature as the desire to injure the enemy. Our outlook on life, our ability to distinguish the noble from the bad, has been crippled and shamed long enough by the passions of war. It seems sanity, understanding, and harmony are being restored by men of creative genius."

The last words of this report completely express Einstein's own opinion. How can anybody live the life of an intellectual human being when one reaches, after a trip of a few hours on the train, a boundary beyond which one is considered an enemy, a member of an inferior nation, a person potentially harmful? How is it possible to preserve the century-old tradition of European science as an essential inner experience when it is possible that the brutal violence of war may suddenly destroy this noble tradition and annihilate everything that sums up the real meaning of life to a man of intellect? How can it be possible to have one's own work known only in one's own native land when the premises of this work were created in such a great diversity of countries? Einstein's visits and lectures in the European capitals proved the existence of a scientific community superior to nationalism. This proof was completely successful. The miracle happened; since these visits, the scientific circles of all European countries are again in close touch with each other; the former exchange of ideas and the former fellowship of labor among scholars has been resumed and is starting productive work.

OUTSPOKEN GERMAN OPPONENTS

In Germany itself, the opponents of Einstein had not as yet been silenced. To a large extent, they were led by political, anti-Semitic motives. There could be recognized also amidst this opposition the old, hoary, pedantic scholasticism which can endure no scientific revolution and refuses every new thought which might cause the traditional system of science to totter. Of course, in time, resistance diminished. Many a Saul became a Paul. Many a skeptic or opponent of the theory of relativity gave up his resistance and became a disciple of the new doctrine. But the smaller the opposition to Einstein became, the more bitterly it fought. Thus the most fanatical opponent of the theory of relativity among the German professors of physics refused, at a scientific convention, to shake hands with Albert Einstein. When, in the year 1922, the Society of German Scientists and Physicians, assembled at Leipzig for their Centennial, announced lectures on the theory of relativity, a group of physicists, mathematicians, and philosophers expressed in the press their regret as to "the misleading of public opinion, to which the theory of relativity is offered as a solution of the riddle of the universe, and which is kept in ignorance of the fact that many highly-respected scholars in the three above-mentioned subjects not only consider the theory of relativity a hypothesis without proof, but even deny it as a fundamentally erroneous and logically untenable fiction." The manifesto concluded with this shameful sentence: "The undersigned consider it irreconcilable with the seriousness and the dignity of German science that a theory extremely open to attack is prematurely and vulgarly broadcast to the lay world and that the Society of German Scientists and Physicians is used to support such endeavors."

A really shameful document which has deservedly disappeared into complete oblivion! How many of the signers would now be overcome with shame if they again saw this manifesto! Einstein himself bears such hostility with a sense of humor. He can not be angry with anybody. He has a sympathetic understanding for everything and a hearty laugh. He finds a too-obtrusive friendship much more unbearable than hostility. He dislikes the noisy and distasteful worship which endeavors to turn the personality of the scientist and his discoveries into a sensation. Nothing is more distasteful to him than the fact that the public busies itself with his private life. Members of his family must carefully keep from him all newspapers which contain articles about him or pictures of him. If, accidentally, such a sheet does fall into his hands, he throws it away infuriated, or looks at his picture with a laugh, and says: "Bah! What a nasty, fat fellow."

Although lecture tours repeatedly expose him to the disadvantages of fame, to the annoyances and intrusions of publicity, and to the painful experience of the sensational, Einstein has often been lured by far-away places. Travel increases inner freedom. It makes one conscious of the diversity of man, peoples and landscapes. It brings about an emotional experience which bears fruit forever.

Einstein Lends Support to Causes

Philipp Frank

According to Philipp Frank, Einstein felt that his fame, fostered by the confirmation of his general relativity theory, carried with it public responsibility. Without joining any political organizations, Einstein supported a number of causes and organizations, such as pacifists who chose to be conscientious objectors, the Zionist movement, the Hebrew University, and the League of Nations. Philipp Frank, a German physicist, is the author of *Foundations of Physics, The Validation of Scientific Theories,* and *Modern Science and its Philosophy.*

With the intense public interest aroused by the confirmation of his theory, Einstein ceased to be a man in whom only scientists were interested. Like a famous statesman, a victorious general, or a popular actor, he became a public figure. Einstein realized that the great fame that he had acquired placed a great responsibility upon him. He considered that it would be egoistic and conceited if he simply accepted the fact of his recognition and continued to work on his researches. He saw that the world was full of suffering, and he thought he knew some causes. He also saw that there were many people who pointed out these causes, but were not heeded because they were not prominent figures. Einstein realized that he himself was now a person [to] whom the world listened, and consequently he felt it his duty to call attention to those sore spots and so help eradicate them. He did not think of working out a definite program, however, he did not feel within himself the calling to become a political, social, or religious reformer. He knew no more about such things than any other educated person. The advantage he possessed was that he could command public attention, and

From *Einstein: His Life and Times,* by Philipp Frank, translated by George Rosen. Copyright 1947, 1953 by Alfred A. Knopf, Inc. Used by permission of Alfred A. Knopf, a division of Random House, Inc.

he was a man who was not afraid, if necessary, to stake his great reputation.

EINSTEIN'S POSITION TOWARD PUBLIC INVOLVEMENT

It was always clear to him that anyone venturing to express his opinion about political or social questions must emerge from the cloistered halls of science into the turmoil of the market place, and he must expect to be opposed with all the weapons common to the market place. Einstein accepted this situation as self-evident and included in the bargain. He also realized that many of his political opponents would also become his scientific opponents.

In the years immediately following the World War it was only natural that the main problem of all political reformers was the prevention of another such catastrophe. The obvious means to this goal were the cultivation of international conciliation, struggle against economic need, for disarmament, and the emphatic rejection of all attempts to cultivate the militaristic spirit. The surest and indeed an infallible method of obtaining the desired end seemed to be the refusal of military service by the individual, the organization of "conscientious objectors" on a large scale. All these ideas appeared as obvious to Einstein as they did to so many others. Only he had more courage and more opportunity than others to advocate them. Einstein did not have the self-complacency with which scholars, especially in Germany, liked to retire into the ivory tower of science. But the means toward the goal appeared to him at that time, as to many thousands, much simpler and more certain than was later found to be the case.

Einstein's political position, like that of all the intellectuals in the world, changed during the twenty years of armistice between the two World Wars, but he was never a member of any political party. Parties made use of his authority where they could do so, but he was never active in any group. This was due fundamentally to the fact that Einstein was never really interested in politics.

Only to very superficial judges does Einstein appear to be a genius so buried in his researches that he finds all his happiness in them without being influenced by the outside world. There are many more unresolved contradictions in Einstein's character than one would believe at first glance, and these, as I have mentioned already, are due to the contrast between his intense social consciousness on the one hand and the aversion to entering into too intimate relations with his fellow men on the other. . . .

Einstein realized very well that everything has several aspects and that by supporting a good cause one must often help one that is less worthy. Many people who are essentially hypocrites seize upon such situations and refuse to participate in any good cause because of "moral scruples." Such behavior was not Einstein's way of acting. If the basic cause was good he was occasionally ready to take into the bargain a less worthy, secondary tendency. He was much too realistic and critical a thinker to believe that any movement conducted by human beings to attain human aims could be perfect.

EINSTEIN AIDS THE ZIONIST MOVEMENT

He helped the Zionist movement, for instance, because he believed that it was of value in creating a feeling of self-respect among the Jews as a group and in providing a refuge for homeless Jews. He was well aware, however, that at the same time he was helping occasionally the development of nationalism and religious orthodoxy, both of which he disliked. He saw that at present no other instrument than a kind of nationalism was available to produce a feeling of self-respect in the rank and file of the Jewish community. . . .

During the World War, when the British government declared its willingness to support the development of a national home for the Jews in Palestine, the Zionist movement experienced a powerful revival in all countries. Its goal was to establish a Jewish state in the ancient historical homeland of the Jews in order to give the Jews of the entire world a national and cultural center. In the British promise they saw the first step toward this goal. It was hoped that the cooperation of all the Jews in the world would enable them to throw off the humiliating feeling that they alone among all people had no national home and were everywhere tolerated only as guests.

From the beginning Einstein had various doubts about the Zionist aims. He was not sympathetic to the strong nationalistic emphasis, and he saw no advantage in substituting a Jewish for German nationalism. He also realized the difficulties inherent in the Palestine plan. He thought the country was too small to receive all the Jewish immigrants who might want to settle in a national home, and he foresaw the clash between Jewish and Arab nationalism. Zionists often have tried to minimize the magnitude of these problems, but Einstein considered this due to wishful thinking.

But in spite of all these doubts and scruples, Einstein saw many reasons in favor of Zionism. He saw in it the only active movement among the Jews that appeared capable of arousing in them the sense of dignity, the absence of which he deplored so much. He did not much care to have this ed-

PROGRESS OF THE ZIONIST MOVEMENT

Speaking in America in 1931, ten years after he began supporting the Zionist movement, Einstein reviews progress and reminds his listeners that establishing good relations with Arab Palestinians is as important as establishing a Jewish state. His talk is recorded in Ideas and Opinions by Albert Einstein, *based on Mein Weltbild, edited by Carl Seelig.*

Ten years ago, when I first had the pleasure of addressing you in behalf of the Zionist cause, almost all our hopes were still fixed on the future. Today we can look back on these ten years with joy; for in that time the united energies of the Jewish people have accomplished a piece of splendidly successful, constructive work in Palestine, which certainly exceeds anything that we dared then to hope for.

We have also successfully stood the severe test to which the events of the last few years have subjected us. Ceaseless work, supported by a noble purpose, is leading slowly but surely to success. The latest pronouncements of the British government indicate a return to a juster judgment of our case; this we recognize with gratitude.

But we must never forget what this crisis has taught us—namely, that the establishment of satisfactory relations between the Jews and the Arabs is not England's affair but ours. We—that is to say, the Arabs and ourselves—have got to agree on the main outlines of an advantageous partnership which shall satisfy the needs of both nations. A just solution of this problem and one worthy of both nations is an end no less important and no less worthy of our efforts than the promotion of the work of construction itself. Remember that Switzerland represents a higher stage of political development than any national state, precisely because of the greater political problems which had to be solved before a stable community could be built up out of groups of different nationality.

Albert Einstein, *Ideas and Opinions.* Trans and rev. by Sonja Bargmann. Based on *Mein Weltbild,* ed. Carl Seelig. New York: Wings Books, 1954.

ucational process put into effect by an emphasis on nationalism, yet he felt that the Jewish psyche, and in particular that of the German Jews, was in such a pathological state that he recommended every educational means that tended to alleviate and remedy this situation.

He therefore decided in 1921 to appear publicly as a supporter of Zionism. He was well aware that this action would produce an astounding impression within German Jewry, since almost all the Jews in Germany who were active in public life as scholars and writers considered the Zionist movement as a mortal enemy of the development that they sought—the gradual complete assimilation of the Jews among their fellow citizens. When a man like Einstein, certainly the greatest of the Jewish scientists in Germany and a man of world reputation, stepped forth in this manner and thwarted their efforts, it was obvious that by many German Jews his action would be regarded as a "stab in the back." But Einstein was not the man to be afraid of any such reaction. He even felt that this antagonism was already the beginning of the educational process at which he was aiming. Also, since Einstein had taken upon himself to say so much that other people did not dare express, self-expression became easier and inhibitions were abated.

Thenceforth Einstein has been regarded by many people as a "black sheep" among the German scholars of Jewish origin. Attempts were made to explain his conduct on the basis of all sorts of causes, such as his misunderstanding of the German character, his wife, the propaganda of skillful journalists, or even his being, allegedly, a "Russian draft-dodger." They did not realize that Einstein was utilizing the credit he had obtained through his scientific achievements to educate the Jewish community.

EINSTEIN SUPPORTS THE HEBREW UNIVERSITY

Einstein's participation in the work of the Zionists, however, was due not only to the primary aim of this movement, but as well to a secondary plan that struck a responsive chord in his innermost being. This was the plan to establish a Jewish university in Jerusalem.

It had always been very painful for Einstein to see many Jewish youths who wished to acquire a higher education prevented from doing so on account of the discrimination against them. Most universities in eastern Europe were averse to admitting a large number of Jewish students. In central Europe, again, this attitude prevailed against the admission of Jewish students barred from the eastern universities. To Einstein it appeared as a special form of brutality—indeed, a paradoxical brutality—that just these people who had always had a special respect and love for intellectual pursuits should be thwarted in their ambitions. Although the Jewish students were often among the most interested and industrious, every admission of an Eastern Jew to a Germanic university was regarded as a special act of tolerance. Thus even the few fortunate ones who were admitted were not fully regarded by the others as fellow students and friends, and they never felt really at ease. The same prejudice was also felt by quite a few Jewish teachers. For this reason Einstein felt that it was necessary to found a university that would belong to the Jews and where students and professors would be free of the tension that arises through constant contact with an unfriendly environment.

It was through this plan for a university that Einstein came into contact with Chaim Weizmann, the recognized leader of the Zionist movement. Like Einstein, Weizmann was a scientist, but he was more interested in the application of science to technical problems. He was a professor of chemistry at the University of Manchester in England, and his work in the war research had been of great service to the British government during the World War. As a result he had become associated with influential English circles and had thus been able to propagate the Zionist plan. Einstein certainly intended to collaborate with the party led by Weizmann for a definite purpose, and the plan for the establishment of a university in Jerusalem rendered this collaboration easier. Weizmann himself characterized the aims of the university in a far-sighted way that Einstein must also have found sympathetic. He said: "The Hebrew University should further self-expression and shall play a part as interpreter between the Eastern and Western world."

EINSTEIN'S PACIFISM AND THE LEAGUE OF NATIONS

From his childhood Einstein had been terribly depressed at the sight of people being trained to become automatons, whether they were soldiers marching through the streets or students learning Latin at the gymnasium. Aversion to mechanical drill was combined in him with an extreme abhorrence of all violence, and he saw in war the culmination of all that was hateful—mechanized brutality.

Einstein placed this aversion above and apart from any political conviction. On one occasion, speaking to a group of Americans who visited him in Berlin in 1920, he said:

> "My pacifism is an instinctive feeling, a feeling that possesses me because the murder of men is disgusting. My attitude is not derived from any intellectual theory but is based on my deepest antipathy to every kind of cruelty and hatred. I might go on to rationalize this reaction, but that would really be a *posteriori* [from effects to causes] thinking."

Because Einstein's attitude to war was based on general human grounds rather than on political ones, it was very difficult for him to work together with institutions that also considered themselves to be working for world peace. In 1922 Einstein was appointed to the "Commission pour la Coopération Intellectuelle" of the League of Nations. The purpose of this body was to make intellectuals acquainted with the aims of the League and to induce them to use their knowledge and talents for the achievement of these aims. The commission never got beyond certain vague beginnings. At first, however, Einstein believed that he ought not to refuse to co-operate, and in his letter of acceptance he wrote as follows: "Even though I must admit that I am not at all clear as to the character of the work to be done by the commission, I consider it my duty to obey its summons since nobody in these times should refuse assistance to efforts toward the realization of international co-operation."

But after one year Einstein recognized that the League did not prevent the use of force by great powers and sought only for means to induce weak nations to submit without resistance to the demands of the strong ones.

Consequently he resigned from the commission, giving the following reason for his action: "I have become convinced that the League possesses neither the strength nor the good will necessary to accomplish its task. As a convinced pacifist it does not seem well to me to have any relation whatever with the League.

In a letter to a pacifistic magazine he presented an even sharper formulation of this step:

> I did so because the activities of the League of Nations had convinced me that there appeared to be no action, no matter how brutal, committed by the present power groups against which the League could take a stand. I withdrew because the

League of Nations, as it functions at present, not only does not embody the ideal of an international organization, but actually discredits such an ideal."

The correctness of his judgment was shown already in the fall of that year (1923) when in the conflict between Greece and Italy the League endeavored only to make Greece, the weaker party, yield. It did not wish to hurt the feelings of Italy, which was then celebrating the honeymoon of Fascism.

Soon, however, Einstein realized that the matter had another aspect. He noticed that his resignation from the commission was greeted with glee by the German nationalist groups. Thereupon, as on so many other occasions, he reflected that even though one sees many mistakes in a movement, yet it is not right to refuse to support it if its essential principle is a good one. In 1924 he therefore rejoined the commission. On the occasion of the tenth anniversary of the League (1930) he expressed the essence of his opinion as follows: "I am rarely enthusiastic about what the League has done or has not done, but I am always thankful that it exists." He always emphasized, however, that without the collaboration of the United States the League would never become a factor for international justice.

Einstein's Widespread Influence

Gerald Holton

Gerald Holton analyzes Einstein's influence beyond physics, an influence that began with immediate, worldwide fame following the 1919 verification of the theory of general relativity. Holton argues that the application of Einstein's theories led to devices that people encounter in their daily lives, from television cameras to calculators. Moreover, his influence extended to philosophers, art critics, and writers, who, enamored of the significance of general relativity, adapted—and often misapplied—Einstein's ideas to their own work. Finally, Holton credits Einstein with lending his celebrity status to causes of peace and Zionism. Gerald Holton, who teaches physics at Harvard University, is the author of *The Scientific Imagination* and *Thematic Origins of Scientific Thought, Kepler to Einstein.*

In addition to his role as builder of a new view of the physical universe, and as contributor to many branches of physical science, Einstein came to influence twentieth-century culture in ways no other scientist did. His ideas, or views attributed to him, reverberate to this day in fields as distant from his own direct scientific contributions as psychology, linguistics, the analysis of modern art, and the study of the impact of science and technology on ethics. . . .

EINSTEIN'S IDEAS PERMEATE DAILY LIFE

Apart from changing science itself, Einstein has reached into the daily life of virtually every person on the globe in direct or indirect ways through the incorporation of his ideas on physics into a vast range of technical devices and processes. I need cite only some of the most obvious ones. Every photo-

Excerpted from "Einstein and the Shaping of Our Imagination," in *The Advancement of Science, and Its Burdens: The Jefferson Lecture and Other Essays*, rev. ed., by Gerald Holton (Cambridge, MA: Harvard University Press, 1998). Copyright © Gerald Holton, 1986, 1998. Reprinted with permission.

electric cell can be considered one of his intellectual grand-children. Hence, we are in his debt whenever photo emission or absorption is used, in the home or on the job, to capture an image by means of a television camera, or to project the optical soundtrack of a motion picture, or to set the page of a book or newspaper by photocomposition, or to make a telephone call over a modern fiber cable, or (eventually) to replace the oil-fired heater by an array of photovoltaic cells[1]. In each case, if a law required a label on the appliance giving its intellectual content or pedigree, such a display would list prominently: "Einstein, *Annalen der Physik*, 17 (1905), pp. 132–148; 20 (1906), pp. 199–206," and so forth.

One would find an entry of this sort also on the laser, whose beam was probably used to lay out the highway on which one travels to the office or to site the office building itself. Or again, the same kind of answer comes if one lists key ideas that helped to make possible modern electric machinery, such as power generators, or precision clocks that allow the course of planes and ships to be charted. Einstein appears also, if one looks for the ancestry of the ideas in quantum and statistical physics by which solid-state devices operate, from calculators and computers to the transistor radio and the ignition system—and perhaps even when one takes one's vitamin pill or other pharmaceutical drug, for it is likely that its commercial production involved diffusion processes, first explained in Einstein's papers on Brownian movement[2] and statistical mechanics.

As [physicist] Edward M. Purcell remarked in his lecture at the Einstein Centennial Symposium at Princeton in 1979, since the magnetism set up by electric currents is a strictly relativistic effect, derivable from Coulomb's law of electrostatics and the kinematics of relativity, and nothing more, it requires no elaboration to discuss "special relativity in engineering": "This is the way the world *is*. And it does not really take gigavolts or nanoseconds to demonstrate it; stepping on the starter will do it!" It is not too much to say that even in our most common experiences, that unworldly theoretician's publications help to explain what happens to us all day—from the moment we open our eyes on the light of the morning, since the act of seeing is initiated by a photochemical reaction.

---

1. cells capable of producing voltage when exposed to radiant energy, especially light
2. papers that proved the existence of atoms

The proverbial man in the street is quite blissfully ignorant of all that, and has preferred to remain so, even while expecting fully that, mysteriously yet automatically, a stream of practical, benign "spin-offs" continues from the pursuit of pure science. But the philosopher, the writer, the artist, and many others outside the scientific laboratories could not help but be caught up to some extent by the wave that spread beyond science and technology, at first slowly, then with astonishing intensity. As the best scientists were coming to understand what Einstein had done, the trumpets began to sound. When in London on November 6, 1919 the result of the British eclipse expedition was revealed to bear out one of the predictions of general relativity theory, the discussion of implications rose to fever pitch among scholars and laymen, beginning with declarations such as that in *The Times* of London (November 8, 1919): the theory had served "to overthrow the certainty of ages, and to require a new philosophy, a philosophy that will sweep away nearly all that has hitherto been accepted as the axiomatic basis of physical thought." It became evident that, as Newton had "demanded the muse" after the *Principia*, now it would be Einstein's turn. . . .

RELATIVITY APPLIED AND MISAPPLIED TO OTHER DISCIPLINES

Philosophy was no doubt destined to be the most obvious and often the earliest and most appropriate field, outside science itself, that the radiation from Einstein's work would reach. But soon there were others, even though the connections made or asserted were not always valid. From Einstein's wide-ranging output, relativity was invoked most frequently. Cultural anthropology, in [French social anthropologist] Claude Lévi-Strauss's phrase, had evolved the doctrine of cultural relativism "out of a deep feeling of respect toward other cultures than our own"; but this doctrine often invited confusion with physical relativity. Much that has been written on "ethical relativity" and on "relativism" is based on a seductive play with words. And painters and art critics have helped to keep alive the rumor of a supposed genetic connection of visual arts with Einstein's 1905 publication.

Here again, Einstein protested when he could and, as so often, without effect. One art historian submitted to him a draft of an essay entitled "Cubism and the theory of relativity," which argued for such a connection—for example, that in both fields "attention was paid to relationships, and allowance was made for the simultaneity of several views." Politely but firmly, Einstein tried to put him straight, and he explained the difference between physical relativity and vulgar relativism so succinctly as to invite an extensive quotation:

> The essence of the theory of relativity has been incorrectly understood in it [your paper], granted that this error is suggested by the attempts at popularization of the theory. For the description of a given state of facts one uses almost always only one system of coordinates. The theory says only that the general laws are such that their form does not depend on the choice of the system of coordinates. This logical demand, however, has nothing to do with how the single, specific case is represented. A multiplicity of systems of coordinates is not needed for its representation. It is completely sufficient to describe the whole mathematically in relation to one system of coordinates.

> This is quite different in the case of Picasso's painting, as I do not have to elaborate any further. Whether, in this case, the representation is felt as artistic unity depends, of course, upon the artistic antecedents of the viewer. This new artistic "language" has nothing in common with the Theory of Relativity.

. . . It was therefore doubly wrong to invoke Einstein as authority in support of the widespread misunderstanding that physical relativity meant that all frameworks, points of view, narrators, fragments of plot, or thematic elements are created equal, that each of the polyphonic reports and contrasting perceptions is as valid or expedient as any other, and that all of these, when piled together or juxtaposed, *Rashomon*[3]-like, somehow constitute the real truth. If anything, twentieth-century relativistic physics has taught the contrary: that under certain conditions we can extract from different reports, or even from the report originating in one frame properly identified, all the laws of physics, each applicable in any framework, each having therefore an invariant meaning, one that does not depend on the accident of which frame one inhabits. It is for this reason that, by comparison with classical physics, modern relativity is simple, universal, and, one may even say, "absolute." The cliché became, erroneously, that "everything is relative," whereas the whole point is that out of the vast flux one can distill the very opposite: "some things are invariant." . . .

In April 1921, at the height of what Einstein on his first journey to the United States all too easily diagnosed as a

---

3. a word used in titles of Japanese poetry collections literally translated as, "in the bush"

pathological mass reaction, William Carlos Williams published a poem entitled "St. Francis Einstein of the Daffodils," containing such lines as "April Einstein / . . . has come among the daffodill shouting / that flowers and men / were created / relatively equal. . . ." Declaring simply that "relativity applies to everything" and that "Relativity gives us the clue. So, again, mathematics comes to the rescue of the arts," Williams felt encouraged to adopt a new variable measure for his poems—calling it "a *relatively* stable foot, not a rigid one"—that proved of considerable influence on other poets.

Williams was of course not alone. [American poets] Robert Frost, Archibald MacLeish, E.E. Cummings, Ezra Pound, T.S. Eliot, and some of their disciples (and outside the English-speaking world, others such as [German writers] Thomas Mann and Hermann Broch) referred directly to Einstein or to his work. Some were repelled by the vision thought to be opened by the new science, but there were at least as many who seemed to be in sympathy with [French writer] Jean-Paul Sartre's remark that "the theory of relativity applies in full to the universe of fiction." . . .

A FEW WRITERS SUCCEED WITH SPACE-TIME METAPHOR

If I have spelled out some of the misunderstandings by which Einstein's work, for better or worse, has been thought to have found its way into contemporary culture, the examples of incorrect interpretation prepare us to appreciate that much more the correct ones. I should confess that my own favorite example of the successful transmutation of scientifically based conceptions in the writer's imagination is a novel, and a controversial one. William Faulkner's *The sound and the fury* is more like an earthquake than a book. Immediately on publication in 1929 it caused universal scandal; for example, not until Judge Curtis Bok's decision in 1949 was this, among Faulkner's other novels, allowed to be sold in Philadelphia. On the surface it seems unlikely that this book—even a friendly reviewer characterized it as "designedly a silo of compressed sin"—has any resonance with the ideas of modern physics, by intent or otherwise. At the time he poured himself into the book, Faulkner was still almost unknown, largely self-taught, eking out a meager living as a carpenter, hunter, and coal carrier on the night shift of a power station, his desk the upturned wheelbarrow on which he would write while kneeling on the floor. Yet, even there, he was not isolated if he read even a small part of the flood of articles in newspapers, periodicals, and popular books in the 1920s dealing with the heady concepts of relativity theory—such as the time dilation experienced by a clock traveling through space, the necessity to recognize the meaninglessness of absolute time and space—and the recent quantum physics, with its denial of the comforts of classical causality. Particularly in America, Einstein was quoted down to the level of local evening papers and *Popular Mechanics,* resulting in wide circulation of such haunting epigrams as his remark, made in exasperation to [German physicist] Max Born (1926), that "God does not throw dice." Could any of this have reached Faulkner? . . .

If the poet neither settles for the relief of half-understood analogies nor can advance to an honest understanding of the rational structure of that modern world picture, and if he is sufficiently sensitive to this impotency, he must rage against what there is left him: time and space are then without meaning; so is the journey through them; so is grief itself, when the very gods are playing games of chance, and all the sound and the fury signify nothing. And this leads to recognizing the way out of the dilemma, at least for a few. At best, as in the case of Faulkner, this rage itself creates the energy needed for a grand fusion of the literary imagination with perhaps only dimly perceived scientific ideas. There are writers and artists of such inherent power that the ideas of science they may be using are dissolved, like all other externals, and rearranged in their own glowing alchemical cauldron.

It should not, after all, surprise us; it has always happened this way. [Italian poet] Dante and [British poet John] Milton did not use the cosmological ideas of their time as tools to demarcate the allowed outline or content of their imaginative constructs. Those college students of ours who, year after year, write us dutifully more or less the same essay, explaining the structure of the *Divine comedy or Paradise lost* by means of astronomy, geography, and the theory of optical phenomena—they may get the small points right, but they miss the big one, which is that the good poet is a poet surely because he can transcend rather than triangulate. In Faulkner, in Eliot's *The Waste land,* in Woolf's *The waves,* in Mann's *Magic mountain* it is futile to judge whether the traces of modern physics are good physics or bad, for these trace elements have been used in the making of a new alloy. It is one way of understanding

Faulkner's remark on accepting his Nobel Prize in 1950: the task was "to make out of the material of the human spirit something which was not there before." And insofar as an author *fails* to produce the feat of recrystallization, I suspect this lack would not be cured by more lessons on [Hermann] Minkowski's space-time, or [Werner] Heisenberg's indeterminacy principle, or even thermodynamics, although such lessons could occasionally have a prophylactic effect that might not be without value. . . .

EINSTEIN'S CONTRIBUTIONS TO CAUSES

It remains to deal with one more, somewhat different mechanism by which Einstein's imprint came to be felt far beyond his own field of primary attention: the power of his personal intervention on behalf of causes ranging from the establishment of a homeland for a persecuted people to his untiring efforts, over four decades, for peace and international security. In retrospect we can see that he had the skill, at strategic periods of history, to lend his ideas and prestige to the necessary work of a Chaim Weizmann or a Bertrand Russell[4]. Even the most famous of these personal interventions, the call on President Roosevelt in 1939 to initiate a study of whether the laws of nature allow anyone to produce an atomic weapon, was of that sort, although it has perhaps been misunderstood more widely than anything else Einstein did. He was, after all, correct in his perception that the Germans, who were pushing the world into a war, had all the skill and intention needed to start production of such a weapon if it was feasible. In fact, they had a head start, and but for some remarkable blunders, they might have fulfilled the justified fears, with incalculable consequences on the course of civilization. . . .

Looking back at the variety of ways in which Einstein came to impress the imagination of his time and ours, we can discern some rough categories, spread out, as it were, in a spectrum from left to right. At the center portion, corresponding to the largest intensity, one finds the widespread but unfocused and mostly uninformed fascination, manifested in a variety of ways, from enthusiastic mass gatherings to glimpse the man, to the outpouring of popularizations with good intentions, to responses that betray the vague discomfort aroused by the ideas. . . .

---

4. Einstein collaborated with Weizmann on creating a homeland for Jews and with Russell on peace and elimination of nuclear bombs.

CHAPTER 4

EINSTEIN IN AMERICA

PEOPLE WHO MADE HISTORY

ALBERT EINSTEIN

California Trips Highlight Einstein's Fame and Politics

Albrecht Fölsing

Albrecht Fölsing provides a detailed account of Einstein's 1930 trip to California via New York—throngs of reporters, hoards of activists, public ceremonies, and militant political speeches by Einstein. At California Institute of Technology in Pasadena, Einstein worked with scientists at the Wilson Observatory before returning to New York by train, stopping along the way where he was again treated to receptions worthy of a celebrity. His second trip to California was less hectic. By the time he made his third trip, conditions in Germany had worsened, and Einstein, thinking America might become his home, deflected criticism from political conservatives by softening his pacifist rhetoric. Albrecht Fölsing, a German physicist, has published widely in German scholarly journals.

The long voyage to California started in Antwerp on December 2, 1930, on board the *Belgenland*, a Belgian steamship on which Einstein was to travel several more times over the next few years. His party included his wife; his secretary, Helen Dukas, as "girl Friday"; and the "calculator," Walther Mayer, because Einstein intended to work during the voyage. In his luxury suite on the upper deck he felt "uncomfortable, like a con man and indirect exploiter"; compared with the elegantly restrained demeanor of the staff, he felt "odd with his peasant manners," and he invariably "dressed negligently, even for the sacred sacrament of dinner." During the stopover at Southampton, he had an opportunity to admire the results of British education: "In England even the reporters are re-

strained. Honor where honor is due. A single 'No' is enough."
This would be very different in the New World.

Originally, Einstein had not intended to go ashore during
the five days when the *Belgenland* was in New York harbor, in
order to avoid attention. But *The New York Times* had already
decided that it would be impossible for him to avoid the press,
unless of course he had himself locked up in the purser's safe,
"and even then there would be photos—of the safe."

A RAUCOUS STOPOVER IN NEW YORK

As the *Belgenland* approached New York, there were "countless telegrams, so that the ship's radio operators were sweat-
ing," a foretaste of what was to come. The arrival in New
York was "worse than the most fantastic expectation. Hordes
of reporters came on board at Long Island, as well as the
German Consul with his fat assistant Schwartz. Plus an
army of photographers who pounced on me like hungry
wolves. The reporters asked exquisitely stupid questions, to
which I replied with cheap jokes, which were enthusiastically received." Everything was just as on his first visit ten
years earlier, but possibly even more frenzied.

As Einstein was still not familiar with the English language, he spoke only German, even for his first greetings,
which two broadcasting companies transmitted live from
aboard. The manner in which he greeted American soil and
the American people was almost papal—if popes had then
ever gone on tour.

In all this hullabaloo Einstein's wife proved a circumspect
impresario, organizing the professor's appointments and
making sure that for every photograph and every interview
a small fee was paid—not into Einstein's pocket, but for the
poor in Berlin and for draft refusers all over the world. In
this respect he had every reason to be satisfied: "Thanks to
Elsa's shrewd management I earned $1,000 for the charity
box. By midday I was dead."

Contrary to all plans, then, there were five exciting and ex-
hausting days in New York while the *Belgenland* lay at anchor.
Einstein was handed from one event to another and met the
elite of the city as well as other celebrities passing through,
such as [composer and violinist] Fritz Kreisler and [Bengali
poet] Rabindranath Tagore—both of whom he already knew-
-and [Italian conductor] Arturo Toscanini, with whom he
now shook hands for the first time. He was even able to see

himself hewn in stone on the tympanum[1] of Riverside Church above the Hudson, which was adorned with statues of great figures in world history, Einstein being the only living person among them. Some grotesque situations inevitably arose, on the lines of "Einstein escaping from reporters"; and it was only in his stateroom at night that he found any rest—the approach to his cabin was guarded by policemen.

In a festive ceremony with speeches by the mayor and the president of Columbia University, Nicholas Murray Butler, Einstein was made an honorary citizen of New York City. He himself made a speech at a Hanukkah celebration in Madison Square Garden, where he was claimed by the Zionists as one of their own. His most controversial speech, however, was to a smaller audience at a meeting of the New History Society at the Ritz-Carlton Hotel on December 14. This was devoted to his great political passion, pacifism.

EINSTEIN ADVOCATES MILITANT PACIFISM

In his message of greeting from on board ship, Einstein had said that the Americans had the strength "to overcome the threatening specter of our era, militarism." He now defined his own position and deplored the fact that "under the present military system any person can be compelled to commit murder in the name of his country." He also knew what was to be done about it: "uncompromising opposition"—that is, refusal of military service. "If even two percent of those called up declare that they will not serve, and simultaneously demand that all international conflicts be settled in a peaceful manner, governments would be powerless." Finally, he called for the "creation of an international organization and of an international pacifist fund" to help those who found themselves in difficulties as a consequence of refusing to serve in the armed forces.

For a number of years this "two percent" speech became something of a Magna Carta of militant pacifism. It was extensively reprinted: in *The New York Times* for example, and also—excerpted—in Germany. An abridged version appeared under an outraged headline, "Einstein Begging for Military Service Objectors—Scientist's Unbelievable Publicity Methods in America"; and this was sent by the ministry to [Max] Planck as president and [Friedrich] Glum as director-

---

1. a recessed space above a door or window

general of the Kaiser Wilhelm Society, with a request for information on "what attitude Herr Prof. Einstein adopts in the Kaiser Wilhelm Society." In the United States, the speech did not meet with unanimous applause, but Einstein would have been pleased to note that many young Americans in the streets and on campuses were wearing buttons with the provocative slogan "Two Percent"—and everybody knew what that meant.

By the time the *Belgenland* left New York, on December 16, Einstein had had "to stand up to a trying amount of his fellow men's love," but he was probably highly satisfied with the way his visit had gone so far.

TO PASADENA AND ANOTHER SPECTACULAR WELCOME

The voyage south and through the Panama Canal provided Einstein with unforgettable impressions of scenery and with some amusing folklore of Central American revolutions, which took place harmlessly but probably confirmed him in his dislike of using the term "revolution" in connection with science: "In Havana they were in the process of having a revolution while we were there, and in Panama shortly after our departure. Their president, a former fellow student from the Zurich Polytechnic, was deposed on this occasion." He bore the interest of his fellow passengers with black humor. "Passengers becoming more importunate. Perpetual photographing," he noted in his diary. "The charity business with my autographs is booming. . . . They have gone crazy about me. How will it all end?" The voyage ended in San Diego on December 30, where the docking was attended by a spectacle suggesting that a reincarnated Columbus was about to step onto the shore of a new continent. There was a four-hour show of the most garish American kind, with speeches and interviews, but it evidently gave him pleasure. Back home, his friends—watching his arrival in California in newsreels—feared that he was "totally immersed in the hullabaloo and razzmatazz of the Americans." Hedwig Born [wife of Max Born, physicist and friend of Einstein], faintly irritated, wrote to him that it was "great fun to see and hear you in the newsreel. To see you (San Diego) presented with flower floats and beautiful mermaids, and suchlike! The world certainly has some amusing aspects. Even though these things look meshugge [crazy] from outside, I still have the feeling that the good Lord knows what he is doing."

In Pasadena, the Einsteins moved into a "small ginger-bread cottage" in the immediate neighborhood of the Cal-tech campus. "Here in Pasadena it is like Paradise," he de-lightedly reported back to Berlin. "Always sunshine and clear air, gardens with palms and pepper trees and friendly people who smile at one and ask for autographs."

During his first week, the famous man was immediately invited to Hollywood, where he watched a special screening of *All Quiet on the Western Front*, a film made from Erich Maria Remarque's novel; because of its realistic portrayal of men dying during World War I, the film was banned in Ger-many. Einstein declared the ban to be "a diplomatic defeat for our government." He was the guest of Charlie Chaplin, "who had set up in his home a Japanese theater, with genuine Japanese dances being performed by genuine Japanese girls. Chaplin is an enchanting person, just as in his film parts." On several occasions Einstein met the social critic Upton Sin-clair: "He is in the doghouse here because he relentlessly lights up the dark side of the American bustle." Over the next two months, though, Einstein also came to know the pleasant side of the American bustle, with brief excursions to fashion-able places like Santa Barbara and Palm Springs; and Mil-likan[2] invited him to go sailing on the Pacific.

EINSTEIN CREDITS SCIENTISTS

Science, too, had its ceremonies. On January 15, Millikan gave a festive dinner at the Athenaeum, the elegant faculty club of Caltech. Two hundred rich patrons of Caltech, in recognition of their donations, were invited to eat with the legendary Einstein, though he himself was more interested in talking to the physicists and astronomers who were pre-sent. In a brief after-dinner speech he thanked his colleagues for their work, without which his theory of relativity would "today be scarcely more than an interesting speculation": William Wallace Campbell, for his determination of the de-flection of light in the sun's gravitational field; and Charles Edward St. John, for his efforts to prove the red shift. . . .

Einstein also paid tribute to "the work of your wonderful observatory," which had been a major reason for his accep-tance of the invitation to Pasadena: it had "led to a dynamic concept of the spatial structure of the universe, for which

2. Robert Millikan was the president of California Institute of Technology in Pasadena.

[Richard Chace] Tolman's work has provided an original and exceedingly clear theoretical expression."

As a result of that wonderful observatory on Mount Wilson, the structure of the universe now looked entirely different from what had been mapped out by Einstein in his pioneering cosmological study thirteen years earlier. . . .

CROSSING AMERICA BY TRAIN

After two months Einstein had temporarily had enough of "this land of contrasts and surprises, where one in turns admires and shakes one's head. One feels that one is attached to the old Europe with its pains and hardships, and is glad to return there." The homeward journey began by rail, across the continent. On a visit to an Indian reservation near the Grand Canyon on February 28 Einstein received from the Hopi not only a rich headdress but an amusingly punning title, "the Great Relative." In Chicago, where his train stopped for two hours, he was met by several hundred supporters of peace; to their great delight, he treated them to an abridged version of his "two percent" speech.

The following morning, when the night train arrived in New York, where the steamship *Deutschland* was to sail at midnight, all hell once more broke loose, for the next sixteen hours. The German consul general recorded that "Einstein's personality, without any clearly recognizable reason, triggers outbursts of a kind of mass hysteria, not only among specially thus inclined groups of 'friends of peace' and the romantic dreamers of newly founded mystical religious communities, but also among relatively levelheaded circles, such as the American supporters of the Palestine program."

Pacifist organizations claimed their hero immediately on his arrival in New York. Einstein invited them on board the *Deutschland* to a meeting restricted to four hundred persons and called for radical action: "The struggle against militarism will have a dramatic effect because it will create a conflict that will directly challenge our opponents." These words set off such "a delirium of enthusiasm that numerous persons kissed Einstein's hands and clothing, and the poor man had eventually to be forcibly taken to his cabin in order to put an end to these demonstrations." For the afternoon Einstein moved into a hotel, where he had to deal with an unending stream of journalists, visitors, and admirers.

The evening had been reserved for Einstein's other passion—Jewish development in Palestine. With funds running low, Weizmann had implored Einstein as early as the beginning of February to make himself available for an urgently needed fund-raising drive. This was a request Einstein could not deny, and so he agreed to be the guest of honor and speaker at a great banquet given by the American Palestine Campaign at the Astor Hotel on the evening of his departure. The guests had to pay $100 each, but despite this high fee—in the midst of the Depression—the target figure of one thousand participants who wanted to see and hear Einstein was actually exceeded. He was celebrated as a "prince of the intellect," and the applause became an ovation when a telegram from President Hoover was read out. Hoover certainly had no sympathy for pacifism or socialism, but he could not avoid saluting the visitor: "My hope is that your visit to the United States has been as satisfying to you as it has been gratifying to the American people." In his address, Einstein again appealed to the Jews to cooperate with the Arabs and pleaded for an arrangement on the model of the Swiss constitution.

When Einstein returned to his ship shortly before midnight, pacifists were again lining the pier; as the ship pulled away, they chanted in unison, "No war forever."

EINSTEIN RETURNS TO UNCERTAINTY IN GERMANY

On the stormy voyage, Einstein learned enough about conditions in Germany to view his return with mixed feelings. "In Germany everything is rocking, much worse than on this ship. But one is used to it and one cuts one's clothes according to one's cloth at the time. For the moment, at least, the Republic still stands." But it was standing on very shaky feet. . . .

In this uncertain situation Einstein intended to ask Planck "to see to it that my German citizenship is rescinded. . . . Concern for the many people dependent on me, as well as a certain need for independence, compels me to take this step." This letter was never sent; it was found, in its envelope, among Einstein's papers after his death. Nevertheless, it shows that in the summer of 1931 Einstein was beginning to accustom himself to the idea that before long he would sever his ties with Germany. . . .

Einstein had returned to a threatened Germany in the knowledge that he would always have an acceptable—and superbly paid—fallback position in California. When in April

1931 he approached a senior official in the Prussian Ministry of Education with a request to establish an extraordinary professorship for his collaborator Walther Mayer, he frightened the official with the disclosure that he himself had received an offer from Pasadena, at an annual salary of $35,000. Unless a satisfactory solution was found for Mayer, who by then was forty-five, Einstein threatened, he "would otherwise have to go to Pasadena, because there the remuneration of Dr. Mayer would be no problem."

In fact, whatever had been discussed in Pasadena, there can have been no firm contract but only an oral statement of intent by Arthur Fleming, the chairman of the Caltech board, who was inclined to act on his own. Over the summer, there had been exchanges of letters and telegrams between Pasadena and Berlin, but the figure mentioned in them was $20,000 for a ten-week stay at Caltech. While Einstein was waiting for the contract to be mailed to him for his signature, Millikan, on a trip to Europe, visited him at Caputh and offered him a salary of $7,000 for his next visit, with a permanent arrangement to be settled the following year.

Einstein was irritated by this confusion in California and first went to give a lecture in Vienna, where Austrian officialdom "observed special reserve because he is a Jew and believed to be on the left politically." After thinking the Pasadena offer over for a week, he wrote a grand refusal on October 19, informing both Fleming and Millikan that over the winter he would take a rest from these tiresome negotiations and seek out the sun of southern Europe. He intended to leave Berlin in any case. He informed his friend [Michele] Besso that he would probably come to Switzerland in the winter "because things are getting uncomfortably hot for me here."

RETURNING TO CALIFORNIA WITH LESS FANFARE

Then, in a sudden change of mind, the reasons for which we do not know, Einstein after all accepted the offer from California on Millikan's terms; on November 14, he sent the signed contract back to Pasadena. A week later, he left Berlin, accompanied by his wife. He spent a few days in Belgium and Holland before embarking on the four-week voyage on December 2, this time on the American steamship *San Francisco*, which took him direct to California, sparing him the stress of a stopover in New York.

When the ship had left the coast of Europe behind, Einstein noted in his diary a decision of crucial importance for his future life: "Today I resolved in essence to give up my Berlin position. Hence a migrating bird for the rest of my life! Seagulls are still accompanying the ship, always on the wing. They are said to come with us as far as the Azores. These are my new colleagues, but, Heaven knows, more efficient than me." He remained silent about his reasons, and also about his specific intentions. Presumably he had in mind shuttling between Pasadena and Oxford. As if to confirm the seriousness of his decision, he added: "I'm also learning English, but it won't stick in my elderly braincase."

Einstein arrived in Los Angeles shortly before the end of the year. This time, unlike the previous year, his arrival was almost normal. As a small compensation for the financial confusion, Einstein was able to move into Arthur Fleming's splendid accommodation at the Athenaeum. Among the colleagues with whom he met to work was Willem de Sitter, the Leyden astronomer—an expert on relativity, and like himself a visiting scientist. Jointly they produced a paper on an aspect of the expanding universe. Einstein gave a few lectures on cosmological problems, and especially on a new variant of the unified theory, which he had worked out with Mayer. But he did not give up his pacifist sermons; and, much to the displeasure of Millikan, he also meddled in American domestic problems such as racial discrimination. . . .

When Einstein, in early March, once more boarded the *San Francisco* to return to Europe, he knew that he would return to Caltech the following year. But no permanent arrangements had yet been agreed on, and the idea of a permanent move to America did not greatly appeal to him anyway. As he explained to his friend [Paul] Ehrenfest, who had asked him to look out for a possible position for him: "I must tell you quite frankly that in the long term I would prefer to be in Holland rather than in America, and that I am convinced that you would come to regret a change. Apart from the handful of really fine scholars, it is a boring and barren society that would soon make you shiver.". . .

WORSENING GERMAN DEVELOPMENTS MAKE AMERICAN OFFERS ATTRACTIVE

As political developments in Germany went from bad to worse, Einstein must have frequently thought of his contract with

Flexner[3]. Although in the spring Hindenburg once more won the presidential election[4], more than thirteen million votes had been cast for Hitler. Nevertheless, Einstein for the time being wanted to stay in Berlin. "He has wholly adapted to Caputh," his wife reported, "and keeps telling me that no one is going to make him leave. He knows no fear." But Elsa was worried and urged him "not to sign any appeals anymore and to live solely for his problems. He answered that . . . if I were as you want to have me, then I just wouldn't be Albert Einstein.". . .

Einstein had kept quiet about his obligation to spend half the year in America; the authorities in Berlin and the Prussian Academy were taken by surprise by newspaper reports, at the end of August, that the Institute for Advanced Study in Princeton would start functioning in the fall of 1933 and that Einstein was its most prominent acquisition.

Only in September, in response to a query, did Einstein feel inclined to inform the academy of his arrangement with Flexner, although he pointed out that he had already talked to Planck about it. Nonchalantly, he left it to the Ministry of Education to decide "if under these new conditions a continuation of my employment at the Academy is at all possible, or desirable." Planck probably intervened to ensure that Einstein was saved for the academy at least for the summer semester. Einstein on his own initiative proposed to the ministry a reduction by half of his annual salary—a gesture which, despite his prolonged and well-paid visits abroad over the past few years, he had not previously made. When it was reported that he would move to the United States altogether, he corrected the reports: "I will not leave Germany. My permanent place of residence will continue to be Berlin."

The California Institute of Technology, on the other hand, was immediately informed of Einstein's association with Flexner's new institute. In the circumstances, Einstein expected that Caltech would now do without his agreed visit to Pasadena during the coming winter. Millikan was disappointed, believing that he had a right to Einstein's presence exclusively at Caltech, even though he still had not offered Einstein a long-term contract. However, he did not wish to do without the famous man and therefore confirmed his invitation for the winter. Millikan was hoping that Einstein

3. Abraham Flexner had money to set up an institute for advanced study and asked Einstein to be a member when it opened. 4. Paul von Hindenburg was president of the Weimar Republic.

might, in the future, divide his visits to America between Pasadena and Princeton. Einstein left this open as a vague possibility, but Flexner condescendingly rejected it.

CONSERVATIVE AMERICANS SUSPICIOUS OF EINSTEIN'S POLITICS

Much as Einstein was in demand, both Millikan and Flexner were continually worried about his political activity, which they not only personally disapproved of but had to defend, halfheartedly, to their wealthy patrons. Since Einstein's triumphal arrival in America in December 1930, irritation had been growing in the conservative camp about this strange professor, who did not confine himself to reporting amazing things about the universe but was raising his voice in pacifist and socialist speeches on very terrestrial—and, worse, domestic American—issues.

When Flexner proudly announced that he was about to inaugurate his Institute for Advanced Study with Einstein as its most prominent member, some conservative groups believed that this questionable foreigner represented a danger to the United States. The board of a "National Patriotic Council" felt it necessary to issue a warning against this "German bolshevist" with his dubious theories and scandalous opinions; and its female branch, the American Women's League, addressed a formal petition to the visa section of the State Department. These patriotic women condemned Einstein's pacifist activities on sixteen pages, complaining—and here they were factually correct—that he supported communist associations such as the International Workers' Help, which was an organ of the Comintern. This, along with some rank nonsense about how relativity theory would undermine the church, the state, and science, culminated in a demand that Einstein should be prohibited from entering the United States of America.

The State Department sent the pamphlet of the patriotic women to the United States consulate in Berlin, where Einstein had in the past always received his visa without any problems, but where he was now to be questioned on the complaints. "Wouldn't it be funny if they didn't let me in?" Einstein scoffed to the Berlin reporter of *The New York Times.* "The whole world would be laughing at America." And to make sure there would be something to laugh about, he improvised a sarcastic comment for the press:

Never before have I been spurned so vigorously by the fair sex, or if this did ever happen, then not by so many at a time. But aren't they right, those vigilant women citizens? Why should one admit a person who devours hard-boiled capitalists with the same appetite and pleasure as the Minotaur monster in Crete devoured toothsome Greek virgins, and who moreover is mean enough to reject any kind of war, except the inevitable war with one's own wife? Listen therefore to your clever patriotic little women and remember that the Capitol of mighty Rome was once saved by the chatter of its loyal geese.

EINSTEIN SUBDUES HIS POLITICS

The American consul, however, did not find the conflict at all amusing and summoned Einstein for a talk on December 5. When he had cautiously worked his way around to the question whether Einstein was a communist or an anarchist, Einstein—according to reports in the press—lost his patience and, in the form of an ultimatum, demanded a visa, which was promptly provided the following day. According to recently released American government papers, however, Einstein did something different. He signed the declaration demanded of him, confirming that he was not a member of any radical organization. Thus there was no further obstacle to his departure for California.

Nothing about Einstein's preparations for the journey had suggested a final farewell, and he had told the academy and his friends that he would be back in Berlin in April. But he was haunted by dark premonitions. "Take a very good look at it," he said calmly to his wife as they locked up their villa in Caputh for the winter. "You will never see it again."

On December 10, Einstein and his wife boarded a ship in Antwerp, which would again take them directly to California through the Panama Canal. To Millikan's relief, nothing spectacular accompanied their arrival in the port of Los Angeles. Einstein had evidently resolved to restrain his political impulses, possibly out of consideration for his hosts, but possibly also because his experience at the consulate in Berlin was giving him pause. After Einstein's first, exceedingly reserved, meeting with journalists, Millikan was very pleased with his guest's remarks, which "supplied no additional ammunition for those who are spreading grotesque and silly stories about his links with groups aiming to subvert American institutions and ideals." Besides, the president of Caltech was anxious to shield his guest from the public—and perhaps to his own surprise, he succeeded in doing so.

Through an ironical turn of fate, Millikan had this time acquired Einstein's fee of $7,000 from the Oberlaender Trust in Philadelphia, a foundation of a family of German extraction, and in return had agreed that Einstein would make a speech that would be "helpful to American-German relations," to be broadcast by the National Broadcasting Corporation on January 23.

That evening Millikan gave a formal dinner at the Athenaeum; afterward, the guests moved in procession to the Pasadena Civic Auditorium, where Einstein was to speak at a symposium on "America and the World." In the pleasant style of an after-dinner talk, Einstein poked gentle fun at social taboos, beginning with dress, and criticized the use of negative labels such as "communist" in America, "Jew" among the right wing in Germany, and "bourgeois" in the Soviet Union. Millikan was satisfied with those irrelevant remarks, but not so *The New York Times*, which observed that Einstein's speech "had not thrown any new light on a dark situation."

Meanwhile, in Berlin, Adolf Hitler was getting ready to take over the government, and a week later he was appointed Reich chancellor. Einstein's premonitions had not deceived him. He was not to see his house in the country ever again, or Berlin, or Germany.

Einstein at Princeton

Peter A. Bucky

Peter A. Bucky presents snapshots of Einstein's life
in Princeton, New Jersey, where Einstein spent his
last twenty years. At the time Princeton was a conservative, gracious college town, and Einstein's
home was a simple colonial on Mercer Street. Bucky
offers glimpses of Einstein's negotiation for salary,
his job assignment at the Institute for Advanced
Study, and his daily routine. Peter A. Bucky, a family
friend of the Einsteins for two decades, often drove
the Einstein family by car to vacation places. During
those long drives Bucky held extended conversations
with Einstein, which he afterward recorded in notes.

Resettling from the Old World to the New has usually been a
shocking experience for most cultivated Europeans. The
brash, robust, noisy, energetic panorama that prevailed always presented a clash with the more proper, staid, tradition-
alist, and slow-moving Continental style. Everything must appear totally alien to such a sensibility. This was as true in the
pre-World War II days as it still is [in the 1990s]. . . .

Princeton—of all New Jersey towns, this is the one that
would appeal most to those who appreciate a European
aura. From its serene business streets (all two of them) to
the regal English-style architecture of the university's older
campus buildings to the hilly roads winding through en-
claves of privilege, to the cultural amenities and French
restaurants so alien to most other New Jersey suburban
communities, Princeton carries a European flavor found in
few other American cities, as if Oxford [University, England]
had been lifted and transported whole across the ocean. . . .

EINSTEIN NEGOTIATES A SALARY IN A NEW COUNTRY

What was it like for Albert Einstein, putting down roots in a
strange land at the age of fifty-four? First of all, it wasn't a

poor life—though no thanks to Einstein's business acumen. Einstein had been offered a position at the Institute for Advanced Studies [at Princeton] by Dr. Abraham Flexner, the director, who gave Einstein virtually a blank check to write his own salary. Einstein carefully figured out how much money he would require to live in his new country. Translating his knowledge of German currency into American dollars, Einstein computed that he would require $3,000 a year, and it was this figure that he suggested to Dr. Flexner.

Fortunately for Einstein, the Institute did not accept his suggestion. Einstein, perplexed by their refusal, and assuming that he had asked for too much, quickly asked Dr. Flexner, "Could I live on less?" Flexner, astutely sizing up the situation, suggested that the matter be arranged with Mrs. Einstein, who was more adept at business affairs. At the time, Einstein's adviser and accountant, Samuel D. Leidesdorf, spent at least an hour explaining to Einstein the difference in buying power and the greater expenses of living in the United States compared with Germany. But Einstein, despite the fact that he nodded and agreed, was not entirely convinced.

Finally, the Institute offered $17,000, or almost six times his original request. Einstein couldn't understand how he could possibly spend such an amount of money during a year's time. After many more discussions, the Institute finally agreed to set his salary at about $16,000—a handsome sum a half-century ago, when the average per capita income in the area was about $1,500. . . .

EINSTEIN'S NEW JOB AND HOME

Einstein's obligations to the Institute were really only to himself. He was committed to be there only between October and April, and he wasn't required to teach. His main function was to research and develop his theories and ideas. Actually, the one drawback to this arrangement was that Einstein missed the collision of young intellects in the classroom environment. His work at the Institute, which has no students, threatened to isolate him from the younger college set. For this reason, he established a standing rule that allowed students from Princeton University to come to him at any time with their problems.

This underscored one of Einstein's most amazing qualities, that is, the ability to concentrate at a moment's notice on the most abstract of thoughts, to be interrupted in his work, and then to continue with his own problem without losing one strand of his thoughts.

Einstein did not attain true permanency in his new land for the first two years of his residency. He was first given quarters on the Princeton campus until he and his wife were moved to a rented house at 2 Library Place, a few hundred yards from the campus. From there, Einstein easily walked to the headquarters of the Institute, on Alexander Street, which juts out from Nassau Street, the main Princeton roadway. Finally, in August of 1935, the Einsteins bought the house at 112 Mercer Street, a simple, clapboard white colonial house on a pleasant street with quiet country-like surroundings, where Einstein was to live out the last twenty years of his life.

Anyone driving along Mercer Street today would find it difficult to imagine that here lived one of the greatest scientists of the twentieth century. The house at 112 Mercer, where Einstein's stepdaughter Margot continued to live until her own death in 1986, is modest, and old-fashioned, in keeping with Einstein's disdain for luxury. But it is easy to see that this unprepossessing house gave Einstein what he so craved—a privacy that enabled him to carry on with his work.

Einstein was determined that his house should not be preserved as a museum after his death. Indeed, it hasn't been and, in fact, Helen Dukas also continued to live there until her own death in 1982, and very little has changed to this day.

So what was it really like to be there in those exciting days when Einstein filled the house with his ideas, his mirth, and his music? . . .

DAILY LIFE IN PRINCETON

One can well imagine the serenity that this simple home and garden provided for Einstein. Indeed, most of his days were spent here on Mercer Street. Since Einstein's duties at the Institute did not involve teaching, his schedule was his own to make. Usually, he would work at the Institute's headquarters only in the morning. Then, around noontime, he and his associates would walk back together to Mercer Street in a neighborhood where most of his colleagues also lived. Dr. Alan Schenstone, chairman of the Princeton Physics Department, lived directly opposite Einstein on Mercer.

Schenstone once described a typical noon-time scene on
the street, with Einstein and several colleagues walking up
Mercer, engaged in intense conversation. In front of Einstein's house they continued to talk, hands and arms in motion. Suddenly, the discussion ended, the group broke up to
go their separate ways and Einstein, still deep in a trance of
concentration, forgetting his surroundings, turned around
and began to walk back to the Institute until Miss Dukas, observing from a window, ran out and dragged the professor
back to his house for lunch.

Lunch for Einstein in Princeton, as in Germany, was his

EINSTEIN'S IMPRESSIONS OF AMERICA

In his book The Private Albert Einstein, *Peter A. Bucky
records a conversation regarding Einstein's first impressions of America. Einstein, gracious toward his host country,
only reluctantly admits a few things he does not like.*

BUCKY: Professor, you spent more than the first fifty years of
your life living in Europe. To suddenly emigrate to the
United States must have been a traumatic experience. What
were your first impressions?

EINSTEIN: Actually, I always felt very happy living in America,
because I think that it is a wonderful country to live in. I have
always considered myself fortunate to be here and also to have
been given the privilege of becoming an American citizen.

 Probably my greatest impression when I first arrived was
one of gratification to see that so much money was made
available for scientific research here. To me this demonstrated that the United States was not just content to develop
the country as a whole but had an honest and true desire to
explore the natural sciences. In fact, the longer I live here
the more I truly believe that this is one of the greatest assets
that we possess—the will to learn and to understand the
natural wonders of this world.

BUCKY: You say: "One of the greatest assets." What do you
count as some of the other assets of America—the country
or its people?

EINSTEIN: Oh, of course, there are many others. As individuals, for example, everyone feels assured of his worth as
an individual, no matter what level of wealth or poverty.
Nobody in America bows down to another person or class.
Certainly, there are great discrepancies of wealth, as in
other countries, and this wealth means superior power

main meal of the day, at which he usually enjoyed Italian food, a holdover from boyhood days when he lived in Milan with his parents. Spaghetti or macaroni often sufficed to satisfy him.

After lunch, Einstein would go to his study either to take a nap or to resume work. In the evening, he would take a light supper, consisting of sandwiches with no warm foods. Then, he would either entertain guests for conversation or music or return to his study, sometimes not to emerge until far into the night.

Einstein, of course, was famous in his community, although

to those who possess it.

But somehow, in America, this isn't allowed to undermine the healthy self-confidence and natural respect for the dignity of each individual. And yet, this strong individualistic current is well-balanced by the need for community. In fact, it is my impression that in the United States, "we" is much more stressed than "I," which is exactly the opposite than in Europe. This is a basic American strength, I think. Generally speaking, Americans are kinder to each other than the average European and there is more unity in their philosophies.

BUCKY: Surely, though, you must have some criticisms to make of America and Americans?

EINSTEIN: Well, of course, I see things that I do not care for, but everything cannot be perfect. I actually find it difficult to criticize anything in America publicly because I am, after all, a guest of this country and for this reason would not like to have my criticisms misunderstood. But yes, naturally, there are imperfections that I see. For example, I think the United States is considerably more materialistic than European countries.

This materialism fosters a certain mentality that I have carefully avoided. There is, for instance, a certain amount of superficiality that is predominant in the United States. This external quest for material comfort and economic security contributes to this superficiality of thought and feelings. It takes a strong will for a foreigner to avoid being sucked into this maelstrom. Another weakness of this country is the tendency to try to legislate moral principles. For example, I think that Prohibition was definitely a bad thing for this country.

Peter A. Bucky, in collaboration with Allen G. Weakland. *The Private Albert Einstein.*

there was not the constant frenzy of celebrity that we have come to expect now. And this was how Einstein liked it. He loved the quiet town and went to it because he felt that he could live and, most important, do his work there free from the rush of the big city It suited him fine that he could walk to and from the Institute without attracting crowds of curiosity-seekers and autograph-hunters.

In the early days, it is true, he encountered a certain coldness. Princeton, an Ivy League school, was an enclave of WASP-dom [white Anglo-Saxon Protestant] and Einstein was a Jew—and an eccentric Jew, at that, with his long hair and his lack of concern about matters of dress. But time convinced Princetonians that Einstein only enhanced their community.

So, the man who for many years had floated between Italy, Germany, and Switzerland, settled finally in this tiny, eastern corner of the United States, for the first time putting down true roots. There he worked and played and observed his new homeland, trying to make sense of a society that had attracted so many millions of Europeans like himself for so many years. His observations were always frank, but one could always be sure that they stemmed from his eternal quest for truth and logic.

Einstein and the Atomic Bomb

Hilaire Cuny

Hilaire Cuny defends Einstein against the charge
that he was responsible for the atomic bomb. Cuny
identifies the scientists who developed the theory
that nuclear energy could be released by using en-
riched uranium. Since projects to develop a nuclear
reaction were going forward in Nazi Germany, scientists thought America should also be working on
the project and chose Einstein to recommend nuclear research to President Franklin D. Roosevelt. After the bomb was developed, Einstein signed a letter
warning Roosevelt not to drop it on cities in Japan,
but Roosevelt died without seeing the letter and the
new President, Harry Truman, ignored the esteemed
physicist's warning. Hilaire Cuny, a biographer, is
the author of *Ivan Pavlov: The Man and His Theories*
and *Louis Pasteur: The Man and His Theories*.

No pacifist ever expended more in the cause of peace than
Albert Einstein, and yet it was undoubtedly he who in 1939,
before the United States had entered the war—although
everyone knew that this was a matter of time—suggested to
Roosevelt that the odious nuclear bomb could be made.
Without him, let us face it, the crime would still have been
committed. Moreover, anyone who had "an uneasy conscience" knows that he has no right to accuse Einstein. Only
someone who has never made a mistake has this right, and
we know that such a being does not exist anywhere in the
world and that he never will exist.

Einstein was never the father of the release of nuclear energy, as has so often been maintained. As early as 1906, after
the discovery of natural radioactivity by [nuclear physicist
Antoine Henri] Becquerel and the subsequent experiments

Excerpted from *Albert Einstein: The Man and His Theories*, by Hilaire Cuny (New York:
Paul S. Ericksson, trans. Mervyn Savill, 1965). Copyright © 1962 by Pierre Seghers,
publisher of the series *Savants du Monde Entier*, Paris. Translation © Souvenir Press.
Reprinted with permission of the publishers.

carried out by Pierre and Marie Curie, he showed that matter is no more than concentrated energy, and that in theory this energy can be released.

A whole galaxy of scientists worked on the fulfillment of this astonishing prophecy: [Ernest] Rutherford, Niels Bohr, Frédéric and Irène Joliot-Curie, Otto Hahn, [Fritz] Strassmann, Lise Meitner, and Enrico Fermi, to quote only a few of the illustrious names which spring to mind.

EINSTEIN'S WORRY ABOUT THE HITLERITES

This does not mean to say that Einstein did not "press the button" to release the bomb. He did not deny this himself, but it was the sorrow of his old age that he had done it[1]. But there was the great fear—not for himself, but for the future of the human race—of Nazi domination. The Hitlerites would not have hesitated for a moment to make the bomb and to use it to the maximum had they possessed the material means of bringing about the essential chain reaction. [German physicist Werner] Heisenberg had received precise orders on this subject. It is true that Heisenberg—no more than Frédéric Joliot-Curie in Paris—did not dispose of enough fissile [possible to split] material to obtain reactions on the industrial plane, prior to the realization of a plutonium bomb. Above all he "retarded" the plan as much as he could because he was far from appreciating Hitlerian methods. He could, however, have been replaced by one of the 200 specialists working under his direction, who were not necessarily anti-Nazi, that is to say as opposed to Heisenberg, and who would have continued their research to the maximum. It would also have been possible for Germany to perfect a "revolutionary" method of isotopic separation of the eminently fissile U-235 [Uranium 235, an isotope of uranium], eliminating the intermediary stage of construction of a plutonium reactor. In short Einstein feared that the Nazis would perfect a nuclear bomb before the Allies; this would naturally have completely changed the outcome of the war—in other words, have given them the victory with all the consequences it implied for the freedom of the world. Moreover, it was legitimate to suppose that the Americans would use the monstrous weapon

1. "Had I known that the Nazis would not succeed in making the bomb before the Allies," he repeated several times, "I should have abstained from any participation."

in a less barbarous way than the Germans. It was in this context that he wrote to Roosevelt, at the express wish of other physicists, his colleagues.

THE FUNDAMENTALS FOR MAKING A NUCLEAR BOMB

It was primarily a question of drawing the President's attention to the terrifying reality—the possibility of transforming matter into energy by a process of fission[2] of an atom nucleus of an explosive nature. Joliot-Curie, [Hans] von Halban, and [Lew] Kowarski in Paris had established this possibility in theory. The plans were in the hands of the Americans, showing how this could be realized. Fermi had just perfected a satisfactory principle of chain reaction[3] to produce plutonium from uranium metal. It was now only a question of finding the uranium. . . .

This demanded enormous investment beyond the scope of any industrial concern. Moreover, the "business" was too specialized to interest any particular financial group, however adventurous.

A chain reaction in a bomb (explosive fission) can only be realized with what is called "eminently fissile matter," such as the isotope 235 of uranium or plutonium.

At the time no one was very sure of the quantity of the material necessary to make a bomb, since the figures ranged between 10 and 100 kilos. In any case, no one possessed more than a few grams of Uranium 235 and practically no plutonium.

The isotope 235 of uranium pre-exists only in the proportion of 7 per 1,000 in a volume of uranium metal (the major part being U-238). The separation has to be effected by chemical (gaseous diffusion) or physical (electromagnetic selection) methods. Plutonium does not exist in the natural state and appears only as the result of transmutations that take place in the fission of nuclear reactors.

But in common with many other elements, uranium metal is not found in a pure state. It therefore has to be extracted from ores such as pitchblende [a variety of the mineral uraninite]. In very rich lodes it is found only in the proportion of 1 to 100 and in poor ores, which are still worth

2. a nuclear reaction in which an atomic nucleus splits into fragments, usually two fragments of comparable mass, with the evolution of from 100 million to several hundred million electron volts of energy. 3. a multistage nuclear reaction, especially a self-sustaining series of fissions in which the release of neutrons from the splitting of one atom leads to the splitting of others.

exploiting, in the proportion of 1 to 1,000.

Before the war no factory was equipped to produce an acceptable output. Uranium was only considered a worthless byproduct of the extraction of radium, which also originated from the same pitchblende.

THE MANHATTAN PROJECT

On account of his fame, Einstein was chosen by his colleagues to encourage Roosevelt to persuade Congress to vote the enormous funds needed for what was known in code as the "Manhattan Project." At the outset these monetary allowances were small, but eventually no expense was spared, and not only was the extraction of pitchblende organized on a vast scale, notably in the Belgian Congo and later in Canada; not only were industrial stations built for the refinement of uranium metal, but, purely and simply extrapolating laboratory methods to speed up the project, there were built—(a) a factory for separating the isotope of Uranium 235 by the use of huge electromagnets (the electromagnetic process) and (b) a factory for the isotopic separation of this same uranium by gaseous diffusion.

But the most gigantic effort (due to Fermi and [Leo] Szilard) was the building of the Hanford reactors on the model of the

---

EINSTEIN WARNS PRESIDENT ROOSEVELT

In his essay, "Einstein the Pacifist Warrior," Joseph Rotblat includes a copy of Einstein's 1939 letter to President Roosevelt, explaining research on the bomb and recommending that the American Administration become involved.

Some recent work by E. Fermi and L. Szilard, which has been communicated to me in manuscript, leads me to expect that the element uranium may be turned into a new and important source of energy in the immediate future. Certain aspects of the situation seem to call for watchfulness and, if necessary, quick action on the part of the Administration. I believe, therefore, that it is my duty to bring to your attention the following facts and recommendations.

In the course of the last four months it has been made probable—through the work of Joliot in France as well as Fermi and Szilard in America—that it may become possible to set up nuclear chain reactions in a large mass of uranium, by which vast amounts of power and large quantities of new radium-like

first Chicago "pile" and designed for the elaboration of plutonium. For the cooling system of these reactors America even
went so far as to change the course of the Columbia River. . . .

A controversy now started as to whether Einstein simply
signed the letter to Roosevelt or composed it himself. The
question is no longer of importance, but it is almost certain
that he merely appended his signature to a letter composed
by Szilard. The tragedy was that no one listened either to
Einstein, Szilard, or the vast majority of scientists who supported them, when after the Nazi capitulation they entreated
that the bomb should not be used against the innocent inhabitants of Hiroshima and Nagasaki. The war had been
won in any case and as has been clearly established today
the monstrous hecatomb [a large-scale sacrifice or slaugh-
ter] was not inevitable. *Einstein signed the second warning
letter to Roosevelt,* accompanied by a very detailed memo-
randum from Szilard informing him of the monstrous consequences of a nuclear explosion but, according to [journal-
ist] Robert Jungk, "the two letters were still pending on the
President's desk when he died suddenly on April 12, 1945."

Truman and his advisers ignored the warnings and pleas
of the scientists and gave the military *carte blanche* [unre-
stricted power to act]. . . .

---

elements would be generated. Now it appears almost certain
that this could be achieved in the immediate future.

This new phenomenon would also lead to the construction
of bombs, and it is conceivable—though much less certain—
that extremely powerful bombs of a new type may thus be
constructed. A single bomb of this type, carried by boat or ex-
ploded in a port, might very well destroy the whole port together with some of the surrounding territory. However, such
bombs might very well prove to be too heavy for transporta-
tion by air. . . .

In view of this situation you may think it desirable to have
some permanent contact maintained between the Administration and the group of physicists working on chain reactions in
America. One possible way of achieving this might be for you
to entrust with this task a person who has your confidence
and who could perhaps serve in an unofficial capacity.

Joseph Rotblat, "Einstein the Pacifist Warrior." In *Einstein: The First Hundred
Years.* Ed. by Maurice Goldsmith, Alan Mackay, and James Woudhuysen. New
York: Pergamon, 1980.

Before setting ourselves up as implacable judges we should have to search our own consciences. We should have to forget our cowardly relief at the cessation of the carnage. We should remember that we cried victory at the period without bothering about the price that this victory had cost the others. . . . We should also have to explain why we did not have the courage to make a gesture, however small, in recent times and within the framework of our own country, to reprove and try to repress certain other massacres and certain other barbarities which, although they were not "nuclear," were no less infamous.

CHAPTER 5

ASSESSING EINSTEIN'S CONTRIBUTIONS

ALBERT EINSTEIN

The Person of the Century

Walter Isaacson

Walter Isaacson gives several reasons for identifying
Einstein as the most important person of the twentieth century. He maintains that Einstein's insights
and theories changed science forever. Moreover, Einstein did important work for charity, contributed to
causes of peace and freedom, and influenced morality, art, and politics. In spite of all of his contributions, Isaacson declares, Einstein also best exempli-
fies the qualities of humility and dignity. Walter
Isaacson, a journalist, was a reporter for the Sunday
Times of London and senior editor for *Time* magazine. He is the author of *Pro and Con, The Wise Men:
Six Friends and the World They Made,* and *Kissinger:
A Biography.*

In a century that will be remembered foremost for its science
and technology—in particular for our ability to understand
and then harness the forces of the atom and the universe—
one person stands out as both the greatest mind and paramount icon of our age: the kindly, absentminded professor
whose wild halo of hair, piercing eyes, engaging humanity
and extraordinary brilliance made his face a symbol and his
name a synonym for genius: Albert Einstein.

Slow in learning to talk as a child, expelled by one headmaster and proclaimed by another unlikely to amount to anything, Einstein has become the patron saint of distracted
schoolkids. But even at age five, he later recalled, he was puz-
zling over a toy compass and the mysteries of nature's forces.

EINSTEIN'S MAJOR DISCOVERIES

During his spare time as a young technical officer in a Swiss
patent office in 1905, he produced three papers that changed
science forever. The first, for which he was later to win the

Nobel Prize, described how light could behave not only like a wave but also like a stream of particles, called quanta or photons. This wave-particle duality became the foundation of what is known as quantum physics. It also provided theoretical underpinnings for such 20th century advances as television, lasers and semiconductors.

The second paper confirmed the existence of molecules and atoms by statistically showing how their random collisions explained the jerky motion of tiny particles in water. Important as both these were, it was his third paper that truly upended the universe.

It was based, like much of Einstein's work, on a thought experiment: if you could travel at the speed of light, what would a light wave look like? If you were in a train that neared the speed of light, would you perceive time and space differently?

Einstein's conclusions became known as the special theory of relativity. No matter how fast one is moving toward or away from a source of light, the speed of that light beam will appear the same, a constant 186,000 miles per second. But space and time will appear relative. As a train accelerates to near the speed of light, time on the train will slow down from the perspective of a stationary observer, and the train will get shorter and heavier. O.K., it's not obvious, but that's why we're no Einstein and he was.

Einstein went on to show that energy and matter were merely different faces of the same thing, their relationship described by the most famous equation in all of physics: energy equals mass multiplied by the speed of light squared, $E=mc^2$. Although not exactly a recipe for an atomic bomb, it explained why one was possible. He also helped resolve smaller mysteries, such as why the sky is blue (it has to do with how the molecules of air diffuse sunlight).

His crowning glory, perhaps the most beautiful theory in all of science, was the general theory of relativity, published in 1916. Like the special theory, it was based on a thought experiment: imagine being in an enclosed lab accelerating through space. The effects you'd feel would be no different from the experience of gravity. Gravity, he figured, is a warping of space-time. Just as Einstein's earlier work paved the way to harnessing the smallest subatomic forces, the general theory opened up an understanding of the largest of all things, from the formative Big Bang of the universe to its mysterious black holes.

EINSTEIN BECOMES A CELEBRITY

It took three years for astronomers to test this theory by measuring how the sun shifted light coming from a star. The results were announced at a meeting of the Royal Society in London presided over by J.J. Thomson, who in 1897 had discovered the electron. After glancing up at the society's grand portrait of Sir Isaac Newton, Thomson told the assemblage, "Our conceptions of the fabric of the universe must be fundamentally altered." The headline in the next day's *Times* of London read: "Revolution in Science . . . Newtonian Ideas Overthrown." The New York *Times*, back when it knew how to write great headlines, was even more effusive two days later: "Lights All Askew in the Heavens/ Men of Science More or Less Agog Over Results of Eclipse Observations/ Einstein's Theory Triumphs."

Einstein, hitherto little known, became a global celebrity and was able to sell pictures of himself to journalists and send the money to a charity for war orphans. More than a hundred books were written about relativity within a year.

EINSTEIN AND QUANTUM

Einstein also continued his contributions to quantum physics by raising questions that are still playing a pivotal role in the modern development of the theory. Shortly after devising general relativity, he showed that photons have momentum, and he came up with a quantum theory of radiation explaining that all subatomic particles, including electrons, exhibit characteristics of both wave and particle.

This opened the way, alas, to the quantum theories of Werner Heisenberg and others who showed how the wave-particle duality implies a randomness or uncertainty in nature and that particles are affected simply by observing them. This made Einstein uncomfortable. As he famously and frequently insisted, "God does not play dice." (Retorted his friendly rival Niels Bohr: "Einstein, stop telling God what to do.") He spent his later years in a failed quest for a unified theory that would explain what appeared to be random or uncertain.

Does Einstein's discomfort with quantum theory make him less a candidate for Person of the Century? Not by much. His own work contributed greatly to quantum theory and to the semiconductor revolution it spawned. And his belief in the existence of a unified field theory could well be proved right in the new century.

EINSTEIN'S INFLUENCE EXPANDS

More important, he serves as a symbol of all the scientists—such as [Werner] Heisenberg, [Niels] Bohr, Richard Feynman and Stephen Hawking, even the ones he disagreed with—who built upon his work to decipher and harness the forces of the cosmos. As [physicist] James Gleick wrote earlier this year in the TIME 100 series, "The scientific touchstones of our age—the Bomb, space travel, electronics—all bear his fingerprints." Or, to quote a TIME cover story from 1946 (produced by [journalist] Whittaker Chambers): "Among 20th-Century men, he blends to an extraordinary degree those highly distilled powers of intellect, intuition and imagination which are rarely combined in one mind, but which, when they do occur together, men call genius. It was all but inevitable that this genius should appear in the field of science, for 20th-Century civilization is first & foremost technological."

Einstein's theory of relativity not only upended physics, it also jangled the underpinnings of society. For nearly three centuries, the clockwork universe of Galileo and Newton—which was based on absolute laws and certainties—formed the psychological foundation for the Enlightenment, with its belief in causes and effects, order, rationalism, even duty.

Now came a view of the universe in which space and time were all relative. Indirectly, relativity paved the way for a new relativism in morality, arts and politics. There was less faith in absolutes, not only of time and space but also of truth and morality. "It formed a knife," historian Paul Johnson says of relativity theory, "to help cut society adrift from its traditional moorings." Just as Darwinism became, a century ago, not just a biological theory but also a social theology, so too did relativity shape the social theology of the 20th century.

The effect on arts can be seen by looking at 1922, the year that Einstein won the Nobel Prize, [novelist] James Joyce published *Ulysses* and [poet] T.S. Eliot published *The Waste Land*. There was a famous party in May for the debut of the ballet *Renard*, composed by [Igor] Stravinsky and staged by [Sergey] Diaghilev. They were both there, along with [Pablo] Picasso (who had designed the sets), [Marcel] Proust (who had been proclaimed Einstein's literary interpreter) and Joyce. The art of each, in its own way, reflected the breakdown of mechanical order and of the sense that space and time were absolutes.

In early 1933, as [Adolf] Hitler was taking power, Einstein immigrated to the U.S., settling in Princeton as the world's first scientific supercelebrity. That year he helped found a group to resettle refugees, the International Rescue Committee. Thus he became a symbol of another of the great themes of the century: how history was shaped by tides of immigrants, so many of them destined for greatness, who fled oppressive regimes for the freedom of democratic climes.

As a humanist and internationalist, Einstein had spent most of his life espousing a gentle pacifism, and he became one of [Indian pacifist Mahatma] Gandhi's foremost admirers. But in 1939 he signed one of the century's most important letters, one that symbolizes the relationship between science and politics. "It may become possible to set up nuclear chain reactions," he wrote President [Franklin] Roosevelt. "This new phenomenon would also lead to the construction of bombs." When Roosevelt read the letter, he crisply ordered, "This requires action."

EINSTEIN BEST EXEMPLIFIES HUMILITY

Roosevelt, Gandhi, Einstein. Three inspiring characters, each representing a different force of history in the past century. They were about as different as any three men are likely to be. Yet each in his own way, both intentionally and not, taught us the century's most important lesson: the value of being both humble and humane.

Roosevelt, scarcely an exemplar of humility, nonetheless saved the possibility of governmental humility from the forces of utopian and dystopian arrogance. Totalitarian systems—whether fascist or communist—believe that those in charge know what's best for everyone else. But leaders who nurture democracy and freedom—who allow folks to make their own choices rather than dictating them from on high—are being laudably humble, an attitude that the 20th century clearly rewarded and one that is necessary for creating humane societies.

Gandhi, unlike Roosevelt, was the earthly embodiment of humility, so much so that at times it threatened to become a conceit. He taught us that we should value the civil liberties and individual rights of other human beings, and he lived for (and was killed for) preaching tolerance and pluralism.

By exhibiting these virtues, which the century has amply taught us are essential to civilization, we express the humility and humanity that come from respecting people who are different from us.

Einstein taught the greatest humility of all: that we are but a speck in an unfathomably large universe. The more we gain insight into its mysterious forces, cosmic and atomic, the more reason we have to be humble. And the more we harness the huge power of these forces, the more such humility becomes an imperative. "A spirit is manifest in the laws of the universe," he once wrote, "in the face of which we, with our modest powers, must feel humble."

Einstein often invoked God, although his was a rather depersonalized deity. He believed, he said, in a "God who reveals himself in the harmony of all that exists." His faith in this divine harmony was what caused him to reject the view that the universe is subject to randomness and uncertainty. "The Lord God is subtle, but malicious he is not." Searching for God's design, he said, was "the source of all true art and science." Although this quest may be a cause for humility, it is also what gives meaning and dignity to our lives.

As the century's greatest thinker, as an immigrant who fled from oppression to freedom, as a political idealist, he best embodies what historians will regard as significant about the 20th century. And as a philosopher with faith both in science and in the beauty of God's handiwork, he personifies the legacy that has been bequeathed to the next century.

In a hundred years, as we turn to another new century— nay, ten times a hundred years, when we turn to another new millennium—the name that will prove most enduring from our own amazing era will be that of Albert Einstein: genius, political refugee, humanitarian, locksmith of the mysteries of the atom and the universe.

The Greatness of Einstein

Cornelius Lanczos

Cornelius Lanczos argues that Einstein is great because he possessed the insight and imagination to penetrate the core workings of the universe and because his theories changed the view of the universe forever. Lanczos shows how Einstein departed from hundreds of years of traditional physics by beginning with speculation about basic problems rather than with experimentation. Einstein united the concepts of time, space, and matter in relativity, and for the last thirty years of his life, he tried to find a complete unified field theory. Cornelius Lanczos taught mathematics at the School of Theoretical Physics in Dublin, Ireland, and at Purdue University in Indiana. He is the author of *Linear Differential Operators*.

Somebody mentions the name Einstein and immediately our reaction is: "This is it. He is the man to whom we should turn."

But why? Why Einstein and not somebody else? Since the end of the last century a whole galaxy of great geniuses have appeared in physics: Here are Marie and Pierre Curie, the discoverers of radium. Here is Max Planck, the discoverer of a new radiation law which initiated an era of physics and became the basis of quantum theory. Here is Ernest Rutherford, who with his ingenious experiments demonstrated the commutability of chemical elements and at the same time paved the way toward a better understanding of the structure of the atom. Here is Niels Bohr, who created the theoretical edifice by which Rutherford's experiments became explainable. Here is Louis de Broglie, the discoverer of the strange "matter waves" which accompany the world of elementary particles. And finally here are the three great founders of the modern theory of matter, called "wave me-

Excerpted from *Albert Einstein and the Cosmic World Order*, by Cornelius Lanczos. Copyright © 1965 by John Wiley & Sons, Inc. This material is used by permission of John Wiley & Sons, Inc.

chanics," or "quantum mechanics": [Werner] Heisenberg, [Erwin] Schroedinger, and [Paul] Dirac.

Why then should we single out Einstein as *the* great physicist of our age?

PROFESSIONALS AND LAYMEN RECOGNIZE EINSTEIN'S GREATNESS

Yet if we should have asked any one of these great physicists which man made the most fundamental contribution to the physics of the twentieth century, they would have answered without hesitation: Albert Einstein. The overwhelming importance of Einstein's physical discoveries and his unique place in the history of science is universally recognized and can hardly be contested. Nobody intends to diminish the merits of other great men of science, but there was something in Einstein's mental make-up which distinguished him as a personality without peers. He wrote his name in the annals of science with indelible ink which will not fade as long as men live on earth. There is a finality about his discoveries which cannot be shaken. Theories come, theories go. Einstein did more than formulate theories. He listened with supreme devotion to the silent voices of the universe and wrote down their message with unfailing certainty.

What was so astonishing in his manner of thinking was that he could discover the underlying principle of a physical situation, undeceived by the details, and penetrate straight down to the very core of the problem. Thus he was never deceived by appearances and his findings had to be acknowledged as irrefutable.

What can the educated layman grasp of the phenomenon Einstein? Is it possible that such a deep thinker can be understood only by his technically trained colleagues while the great bulk of humanity is left out in the cold? Is it true that the technical difficulties of the subject are so overwhelming that his findings cannot be put in a language understandable to the large group of people who have a good general education, although they have not been specifically trained in the exact sciences?

It is improbable that the findings of such a deep thinker could not be translated into a universally comprehensible language without losing too much of their substance. This is corroborated by the further circumstance that Einstein was never too much attracted to his technically trained colleagues, who spoke outwardly the same language but had a widely different approach to the deeper exploration of the mysteries of the universe. He considered himself more a philosopher than a professional physicist; he was more at home with visionary people—artists, writers, poets, actors— than with many of his professional associates. They followed the well-trodden path, laid out by the well-established rules of the game. Einstein never played the game according to the traditional rules. To him the universe was important and not the game we play with the universe. This distinction separated him from most of his contemporaries, to whom science is an occupation and not a religion of highest devotion and abandonment.

If we mention the name Einstein anywhere in the world, the response is unmitigated reverence and admiration. "Yes, Einstein, of course, the great physicist and mathematician." But then we ask the question: What do you know of him? What made this Einstein a world figure of such incomparable dimensions that he was held in mystical awe by millions of people as the revered voice of the universe? The answer is usually: "That I cannot tell you. You know, I was never too good in mathematics and to study Einstein you require so much higher mathematics that I am, of course, lost if it comes to really understanding what he has accomplished. I only know that he discovered something very important and that the name of this discovery is relativity."

This answer certainly seems reasonable enough, yet there is a flaw in it. Of course it is impossible to describe in a few sentences what such a great genius accomplished in a long life of ceaseless and devoted meditation. But by spending several hours in serious effort, it is by no means impossible to gain a fairly adequate concept of his achievements. There is so much in the line of general ideas in his investigations which can be stated without any (or with a minimum of) mathematical symbols that one can go a long way in pointing out the specific nature of his reasoning, without being hampered by the technicalities of the mathematical language. . . .

THE BREADTH AND DEPTH OF EINSTEIN'S MIND

Einstein was not merely the creator of the theory of relativity. He discovered a host of other basic results in theoretical physics and it has been pointed out more than once that if somebody asked: "Who is the greatest modern physicist after Einstein?" the answer would be: Einstein again. And why? Because, although the theory of relativity in itself would have established his fame forever, had somebody else discovered relativity, his other discoveries would still make him the second greatest physicist of his time.

Nevertheless, it is not an accident that in the popular mind his fame rests on the theory of relativity. His other discoveries could have been made by others. Moreover, they are discoveries which may be modified as science progresses. The theory of relativity, however, was an astonishing discovery which opened an entirely new door in our understanding of the physical universe and it is a door which will never be shut again. Our concepts of space and time have been radically changed by Einstein's first formulation of the principle of relativity, now called "special relativity." This happened when Einstein was only twenty-six years of age. But our most fundamental physical concepts, involving space, time, *and matter*, have been even more radically altered by Einstein's second formulation of the principle of relativity, called "general relativity," which came to its fruition ten years later, during the years 1915-16. Now not only space and time, but *space, time* and *matter* were amalgamated into one fundamental and inseparable unity. His discovery of this unity had a tremendous impact on Einstein's scientific philosophy. From now on he lost interest in the bewildering variety of physical phenomena and focused on one theme only: to find the unifying law which is the basis of all physical events. In the eyes of his colleagues he changed from a "physicist" to a "metaphysicist," a man out for the ultimates—and why should a scientist care for the ultimates?

To Einstein himself it made little difference by what label he was called. For him the watertight compartments in which we customarily classify our intellectual endeavors did not exist. As a true disciple of [German astronomer Johannes] Kepler, he too listened to the secret music of the celestial spheres. Is that mathematics, or physics, or alchemy, or astronomy, or philosophy—what does it matter? To his colleagues the difference was that, whereas before he tackled—and how successfully!—all kinds of physical phenomena, now he shut himself up in the half-shadow of his study-room and lost touch with the contemporary problems of science. . . .

[Einstein's 1905] papers were written in a peculiar style,

very characteristic of Einstein's manner of thinking. They did not contain a great deal of mathematical formalism. There was a great deal of text and little in the line of formal manipulations. In the end the startling conclusion was there, obtained apparently with the greatest of ease, and by a reasoning which could not be refuted. Outside sources were hardly ever quoted; it looked as if the author had arrived at his results practically unaided, as if he had conjured up the whole procedure out of thin air, by a wave of his magic wand. This made Einstein suspicious in the eyes of his colleagues. A man who writes so clearly and with so few technicalities cannot be taken too seriously. Something must be wrong with him. It is not proper that he should deduce important results so elegantly, apparently without laborious efforts, and without consulting the opinions of others. And thus it happened that the majority of physicists ignored his work, while a few first-class minds, particularly [Max] Planck, [H.] Rubens, [Walther] Nernst, and [Max] von Laue, accepted this amazing fledgeling as a full-grown member of their august community, in spite of the fact that he was much younger.

It is thus understandable that as early as 1909 Einstein received a call to a professorship at the University of Zürich. At that time he was employed as a minor consultant at the Swiss Patent Office in Berne. When he announced his resignation because he was going to Zürich as a professor of the university, his boss got red in the face and blurted out: "Now, Mr. Einstein, don't make any silly jokes. Nobody would believe such an absurdity." Yet the absurdity was true, as were so many of the apparent "absurdities" which were encountered in Einstein's theories, and Einstein's fame spread more and more. In 1914 he was called to Berlin as director of the Physics Section of the world-famous Kaiser-Wilhelm-Institut, the highest honor that Germany could bestow on him. In the meantime he pursued his studies concerning the nature of radiation. These profound researches contributed fundamentally toward the development of quantum theory and the deeper understanding of the structure of the atom. Between the years 1905 and 1925 he was the undisputed leader of a whole generation of theoretical physicists. Nobody could compete with him in the depth of comprehension and the uncanny simplicity with which he could derive fundamental results from a few basic experimental results.

In the meantime he was in the grip of a mighty idea which germinated slowly. Almost from the beginning he realized that his space-time theory of 1905 could not be considered as the final solution but only as a first step to something much more comprehensive. After ten years of incessant ponderings which led him to many false leads and cul-de-sacs, he arrived at his "general theory of relativity," which was hailed as his masterpiece and which Einstein himself considered as his most fundamental discovery. This theory showed that our customary ideas concerning geometry do not correspond to the geometry actually realized in the physical universe. The geometry which we have learned in school for thousands of years—it is called "Euclidean geometry," because it was the Greek geometer Euclid who put this geometry in a remarkably exact, scientific system—is in fact *not* the geometry of nature. It is true that Einstein's paper of 1905 had already demonstrated that our traditional ideas about space and time fall down if motions of high velocities are involved. . . .

RELATIVITY REPLACES NEWTONIAN PHYSICS

The new discovery of 1915 modified this picture very decisively by showing that the geometry of Euclid, even if extended from three to four dimensions, does not do full justice to the physical world because it pictures it geometrically in the form of a completely *flat* country. In actual fact we should imagine the universe as a *hilly* country with mountains and valleys, instead of as a monotonous plane which extends from infinity to infinity, free of any imperfections. Let us imagine bumps on this plane, like mole-hills which cover a field infested by rodents. What are these mole-hills? They appear to us as *matter*. Whenever we perceive matter at some place in the universe, we actually perceive a mole-hill on a generally flat field. These mole-hills were left out in Euclid's geometry but in fact they are the most important agents of the universe, since anything that happens in the universe is somehow related to the action of matter.

This theory was of tremendous abstraction and tremendous boldness. Never has the human mind perceived such astonishing constructions. We knew, of course, that geometry is important. We all learn geometry in school, even if later we forget almost everything of this truly fascinating subject. And why do we learn geometry? Because it is recognized that the laws of space are important, because, after all, it is this space in which physical action takes place. But notice the extraordinary change which came to our geometrical thinking through the meditations of a single man: Albert Einstein. In Newton's physics we had an empty space like a huge empty box, into which matter is put from the outside. In addition, we had time in which physical action takes place. We thus had three basic entities which were apparently completely independent of each other: space, time, and matter. But Minkowski's interpretation of Einstein's theory of special relativity showed that space and time are not independent of each other but form one inseparable unit, the world of space-time. This four-dimensional space-time world now took over the role of Newton's empty receptacle into which matter was put from the outside.

Then came Einstein's great discovery of 1915 which carried the synthesis to the ultimate. Matter is not put from the outside into an empty box but forms an integral part of geometry. Matter belongs to geometry. What we observe as matter is in fact a hill in a generally flat country. We can measure such a hill by its curvature. Curvature is a strictly geometrical quantity which apparently has nothing to do with physics. For example, we can measure the curvature of our globe by determining the radius of the earth, which is about 4000 miles. Now, if we put a certain amount of matter, such as a lump of steel, on a balance and found that it weighs, let us say, a pound, we would certainly not think that this pound has anything to do with a length. But Einstein's theory has shown that this pound can be converted into length because we can figure out the exact amount by which the generally flat Euclidean world has been indented by the presence of that pound of steel.

But then if time is nothing but length, and mass is nothing but length, what else do we have in physics? Space, time, matter—these are the three basic entities of the physical universe. Time has been absorbed by space as an added dimension. Matter has been absorbed by space as a curvature property of space. What is left? Is it possible that space is everything? Is it possible that if only we understood the proper geometry of space, we would understand *all* physics, since the whole physical universe is nothing but the manifestation of a certain kind of geometry?

This was an intoxicating thought which caught Einstein

and never let him go again. Up to the discovery of general relativity he was a sober physicist like anybody else. . . .

EINSTEIN DEFIES THE USUAL PROCEDURE

The amazing thing about Einstein's discovery was that he did not follow the usual sequence. His theory was not motivated by some new gravitational experiments. He started on essentially *speculative* grounds, although on the firm basis of some well-known experimental facts whose correctness could not be doubted. He felt that these facts expressed more than some accidental relations, that in fact they were the emanation of some basic *principles* realized in the physical world. From here, by higher and higher abstractions and by making use of the most advanced tools of mathematics, he came to the formulation of certain equations, the celebrated "Einstein gravitational equations.". . .

To stare in empty air and pull out results from nothing as a result of speculations, as the old Greek philosophers were wont to do, was disdained since the time of Galileo as a nonsensical proccdure. One had to experiment first and see what happened. Then one tried to codify these experiments by a mathematical equation. This had been the well-established rule for hundreds of years. And now Einstein dared to challenge this procedure by reverting to the dreams of the ancients who tried to *understand* nature on the basis of logical deductions rather than *describe* it on the basis of carefully conducted experiments. The magical thing about Einstein was, however, that he succeeded where the ancients failed. He had the mighty tools of mathematics at his disposal, developed in a slow evolution of more than two thousand years since the time of Plato and Aristotle. . . .

EINSTEIN CONTINUES TO SEARCH

But Einstein was not a man who could rest on his laurels. He was too much wedded to the universe to care too much for human recognition. The psychological impact of the success of his theory was quite profound on Einstein himself, because it had shown him that inspired mathematical speculation can soar into heights that mere experimentation could never achieve. The idea that we may not merely *describe* the physical universe but *understand* its inner workings had an intoxicating effect on his thinking. If it was possible to achieve such a speculative victory in the field of gravitation, why should we stop here? . . .

During the last thirty years of his life he became more and more a recluse who lost touch with the contemporary development of physics. His eyes were glued on the universe and the possibility of penetrating to the ultimate core where all secrets would be resolved and understood as the emanation of a single world law. In his great paper of 1916 he showed how the replacement of Euclidean geometry by the more advanced geometry developed by the great German mathematician [Bernard] Riemann—and thus called Riemannian geometry—was able to explain all the gravitational phenomena. But electricity did not seem to find its natural place in this geometry and thus he attempted to give it up in favor of a still more comprehensive form of geometry. Again and again he jubilantly felt that he had found the final answer, but again and again he admitted his defeat, returning to his starting point. In the last ten years of his life he settled for a certain "unified field theory" which he considered the final answer and the true fulfillment of all his hopes. Yet we have good reasons to doubt that he truly achieved his goal.

Nor is this point of any importance in the evaluation of Einstein as a man and a scientist. He has given us a new picture of the universe and he has demonstrated the power of inspired abstract thinking. Never before had any human being attained such marvelous insights into the inner heart of the physical universe. Never before would it have been possible even to hope that some day our minds may clearly recognize the master plan according to which the universe is constructed. What he accomplished in a single lifetime is stupendous and a sufficient basis for research for hundreds of years to come. In an era of unprecedented aggressiveness and destruction he held up a mirror to the human mind which demonstrated its greatness and its boundless possibilities if turned toward inspired constructive reasoning. He thus occupies a place in the history of civilization which is unique and may never be duplicated.

The Stature of Einstein

By Leopold Infeld

Writing five years before Einstein's death, Leopold Infeld portrays the importance of Einstein as a human being—a genius, aloof and detached, funny and kind. Infeld writes from personal experience: Einstein befriended him when he was a lonely Polish student in Berlin and later collaborated with Infeld at the Institute for Advanced Study in Princeton. Leopold Infeld taught physics at the University of Lvov in Poland before he emigrated to America. He is the author of *Quest: The Evolution of a Scientist* and with Einstein coauthor of *The Evolution of Physics*.

How important is Einstein's life story for the understanding of Einstein? Books have been written about genius. Endless discussions have been held to decide in what degree a genius is formed by heredity or environment. Although I do not know the literature on this subject, I am inclined to think that the problem is to a great degree meaningless. Even if it were possible to distinguish between heredity and environment I do not see how any rules could be applied to a genius. It seems to me equally silly to try to give a definition of a genius. Genius is a very rare phenomenon. It is characterized just by the fact that it escapes classification. There isn't any other common denominator of genius. This, as I see it, is its only characteristic feature. To be more specific: I worked for a few years with Einstein and during this time I had the unforgettable experience of observing and admiring him. I believe I know and understand him as well as anyone does. For another four years, through the pages of history, I studied and tried to understand the working of another genius, Evariste Galois.[1] Whatever definition of a genius one might give, there seems little doubt that both Galois and Einstein

---

1. French mathematician who made valuable contributions to number theory algebra before being killed in a duel at the age of twenty-one.

would be regarded by every scientist as geniuses. Yet they seem as different from each other as two men can be. In the tragic life of Galois we see the strong ties by which he was bound to the society in which he lived. He was caught, as in a deadly spider net from which there was no escape. He suffered from the impact of the external world, from its injustice; his heart bled and his life burned out quickly. How different from him is Einstein! His heart never bleeds and he moves through life with mild enjoyment and emotional indifference. For Einstein, life is an interesting spectacle that he views with only slight interest, never torn by the tragic emotions of love or hatred. He is an objective spectator of human folly, and feelings do not impair his judgments. His interest is intellectual and when he takes sides (and he does take them!) he can be trusted more than anyone else because in his decision the "I" is not involved. The great intensity of Einstein's thought is directed outside toward the world of phenomena. No one expressed more clearly this aloofness toward the world of human affairs than Einstein himself in *The World As I See It*:

> My passionate interest in social justice and social responsibility has always stood in curious contrast to a marked lack of desire for direct association with men and women. I am a horse for single harness, not cut out for tandem or team work. I have never belonged wholeheartedly to country or state, to my circle of friends, or even to my own family. These ties have always been accompanied by a vague aloofness, and the wish to withdraw into myself increases with the years.

> Such isolation is sometimes bitter, but I do not regret being cut off from the understanding and sympathy of other men. I lose something by it, to be sure, but I am compensated for it in being rendered independent of the customs, opinions, and prejudices of others, and am not tempted to rest my peace of mind upon such shifting foundations.

EINSTEIN IS INTROSPECTIVE

Therefore, the external scenery of Einstein's life is of little importance.

He must have been shy and withdrawn as a child. The capability to wonder must have appeared early. In Einstein's memory, the greatest impression left from his childhood is the observation of a magnetic needle. It is this fact that he so often recalls when he speaks of his early years. He was not exceptionally brilliant as a student, neither at high school nor at the university. If I did not know this from Einstein I could easily have deduced it for myself. The most characteristic feature of his work is originality and obstinacy, the capability of travelling a lonely path for years and years, not the capability of learning, but of thinking and understanding. Schools and universities all over the world reward men who can easily tread a well-beaten path. The one who knows has an advantage over the one who wonders.

As a child and as a youth he wished to be left alone. The ideal life was, for him, that of least interference from the outside world. He was comparatively happy in Switzerland because there men are left to themselves and privacy is respected. The results of the thoughts he started when he was sixteen were published in 1905.[2] This is the year in which his four celebrated papers appeared. His fame among physicists began some four years later. Einstein told me, "Before I was thirty, I never met a real physicist." In Einstein's case it was luck that he did not. There was no one to discourage him, though I doubt whether anyone would have been successful, anyway.

The rest is the story of increasing success and rising fame. To give a few dates: he graduated from the Zürich Polytechnical School in Switzerland in 1901[3], then he worked in the Swiss Patent Office. Four years after special relativity theory was formulated he became an associate professor at the University of Zürich; then, in quick succession, a full professor in Prague and again a professor in Zürich. In 1913 he became a member of the Prussian Academy of Science and moved to Berlin. There he remained for the next seventeen years. Since 1933 he has lived in Princeton, New Jersey. He was married twice, once divorced and once widowed.

Of course, the rising fame was annoying to Einstein. It took much of his time; but it was not too important because nothing was ever important to him besides the understanding of the phenomena of nature.

CONSERVATIVES ATTACK EINSTEIN'S THEORY

In 1921, when I went to study in Berlin, I saw with amazement the disgraceful spectacle which attended Einstein's fame. It was still twelve years before Hitler. I saw conservative

---

2. He wondered what a light beam would look like if he could travel along side at the same speed; the idea developed into the 1905 paper on the theory of special relativity.
3. Most sources identify 1900 as the year he graduated.

daily papers with editorials attacking Einstein's theory: "If he believes in his theory, let him answer our arguments. We shall be fair and we shall print his reply." I saw placards announcing lectures against Einstein's theory in one of Berlin's greatest concert halls. I was curious enough to buy a ticket and witness the performance. It was a double feature with two professors scheduled to speak. A man with a small beard and a monotonous voice read a manuscript to an overflowing audience, telling them how silly was special relativity theory with its paradox of the twins, that it was the greatest hoax in the history of science, that the attention paid to this subject was foreign to the truly German spirit. At that time, it still was not the right thing to attack Einstein openly as being Jewish, yet this was done not once, but hundreds of times in a more veiled form. On the surface there was the Weimar Republic in Germany, but beneath this thin wretched surface one could detect the seeds of coming turmoil.[4]

I remember, too, that during the interval between two consecutive lectures, everyone was looking at the box in which Einstein sat. I don't know why he came, but he seemed to have a wonderful time greeting people and smiling broadly with a loud giggle and stealing the show just by his presence.

An amazing spectacle developed. All over the world popular lectures on relativity theory were delivered. There was even money in it. An American magazine—I don't remember the name—announced a prize of a few thousand dollars for an article on relativity theory that would explain it in three thousand words. For students in a country with inflation, such a great sum was almost beyond the imagination. I helped my friend with his entry and in my wretched room we put the finishing touches on an essay. As we counted the words, we dreamed about the rain of gold that relativity theory and the U.S.A. would bestow upon us. No, we did not win.

DEBATES AND LECTURES ON RELATIVITY DRAW LARGE CROWDS

When later I went back to Poland, to my surprise I found the same atmosphere. The fame of relativity theory crossed all national frontiers. It was as vastly and passionately debated then as Communism is today. My professor in mathematics,

4. The Weimar Republic was liberal, but the Nazis and radical conservatives were rising under Hitler's leadership.

Zaremba—and a very distinguished mathematician he was— gave a graduate lecture and many popular lectures against relativity theory. He argued that relativity theory is inconsistent with the definition of a rigid body. A rigid body is a body that does not contract. How, therefore, can a rigid stick contract when in motion? Of course, it was a trivial argument although my professor put it in heavy and learned language. The simple point, that the same bodies that we regard as rigid behave differently according to classical physics and special relativity theory, was not understood by the old professor nor would I have dared explain it to him. He was attacked in a very brutal way by another professor, also a distinguished mathematician and astronomer (his name was Banachiewicz), who called Zaremba blind and his arguments foolish. What happened in Cracow, my small university town, is interesting only because similar things happened all over the world. Popular lectures about relativity theory drew great crowds and bewildered audiences listened to the arguments pro and con. Even Einstein was persuaded to give public lectures on relativity theory. He was not a very good popularizer of his own doctrine, yet the public was charmed to see Einstein and to listen to his fine voice. During one of his lectures he played with a stick that lay on the table. One lady asked another, "Why doesn't he leave the stick alone?" But she soon saw the point. When Einstein showed by gestures how a stick moves and contracts, the relieved lady whispered to her neighbor, "I did not know that this is the contracting stick."

I, myself, was ready and willing to take part in these discussions and suffered when I was not asked to do so. A year later, in 1922, I was a high school teacher in a small Polish town. The excitement of relativity theory reached even there and I had the rare distinction of being the only man in this town who knew anything about relativity theory. I gave a series of four lectures and many had to be sent away because the room could not accommodate the crowd. Afterward one of my friends wisecracked, "I would much prefer to listen to Einstein lecturing about Infeld."

INTEREST IN EINSTEIN AND RELATIVITY CONTINUE IN THE 1930S AND BEYOND

Slowly the arguments against relativity theory subsided. Nowadays no physicist doubts that the axioms of special and general relativity theory are superior to those of Newton's classical physics. He may doubt whether the revolution is radical enough, but no one in his proper senses believes that a retreat into the position of classical physics is possible. Even later, when Hitler came to power, papers on relativity theory were still printed in Germany. This was considered all right as long as the name of the creator of relativity theory was omitted.

Even if one understands why Einstein's fame started suddenly one does not understand so easily why it still prevails. There are different reasons. I believe one is that some of the Herren Professoren fought him just a little too bitterly for their own good. The other reason is that Einstein is colorful. You sense it when you glance at any of his pictures. If Einstein were to enter your room at a party and be introduced to you as Mr. Eisenstein of whom you knew nothing, you would still be fascinated by the brilliance of his eyes, by his shyness and gentleness, by his delightful sense of humor, by the fact that he can twist platitudes into wisdom, and that whatever he might say would be the product of his own mind uninfluenced by the shrieks of the outside world. You feel that before you is a man who thinks for himself. He has influenced millions, but in a deeper sense he can be influenced by no one.

EINSTEIN'S INVOLVEMENT IN POLITICS SPANS FOUR DECADES

During the First World War and later, one saw Einstein entering the arena of politics, or rather being pushed into it. He takes sides. He has contempt for violence, for bullying, for aggression, for injustice. "Contempt" is, I believe, the right word. It would be wrong to use the word "hatred," instead. He is always kind and because of the strong impact of the external world he learns to go through the motions of being interested and of concealing his inner detachment. His appearance helps. His striking face of a great artist or prophet, his eyes that seem to radiate, may deceive you if you talk to Einstein. Their radiation is directed far into the world and the laws that govern it and not toward your personal problems. Yet he will gladly, with a witty remark and loud laugh, sign a letter of recommendation as long as he has not a definite proof that you are a crook or incompetent. He believes what you tell him because he is kind, because he wishes to be kind and because it is much simpler to believe than to disbelieve.

You may think that one can convince Einstein of anything, but he will become stubborn and unbending if he finds out that you are a Fascist. He will become suspicious if you come with a project that seems to benefit him and not you.

In 1914, he refused to sign the Manifesto of the German scientists. After the First World War he was the first German scientist to be invited to France.

His most important participation in the affairs of our world came in 1939. The story of how physicists tried unsuccessfully to interest the Army and Navy in the Atomic Project is told in the Smyth report with subtle understatements and omissions. It was the famous letter of Einstein to Roosevelt that broke the rigidity of the military mind. Einstein, who has contempt for violence and for wars, is regarded as the father of the Atomic Bomb. This is so because the modern history of the development of atomic energy starts with Einstein's equivalence relation between mass and energy. This is also so because the history of the Atomic Bomb starts with Einstein's letter.

In these dark times when the air is filled with empty platitudes, silly arguments, tales of little men, it is refreshing to listen to the clear voice that speaks for reason. It is the aloof conscience of the world that tells us (*Only Then Shall We Find Courage*):

> Science has brought forth this danger, but the real problem is in the minds and hearts of men. We will not change the hearts of other men by mechanisms, but by changing *our* hearts and speaking bravely.
>
> We must be generous in giving to the world the knowledge we have of the forces of nature, after establishing safeguards against abuse.
>
> We must be not merely willing but actively eager to submit ourselves to binding authority necessary for world security.
>
> We must realize we cannot simultaneously plan for war and peace.
>
> When we are clear in heart and mind—only then shall we find courage to surmount the fear which haunts the world.

EINSTEIN'S APPEAL TO THE IMAGINATION

In seeking to understand Einstein's appeal to the imagination of so many of his fellow men, a strange comparison comes to my mind. In a village in India there is a wise old saint. He sits under a tree and never speaks. The people look at his eyes directed toward heaven. They do not know the thoughts of this old man because he is always silent. But they form their own image of the saint, a picture that comforts them. They sense deep wisdom and kindness in his eyes. They bring food to the tree where the man sits, happy that by this small sacrifice they form a communion with the lofty thoughts of their saint.

In our civilization we do not have primitive villagers and silent, contemplating saints. Yet we see in our newspapers a picture of a man who does not go to the barber, who does not wear a tie or socks, whose eyes seem to be directed away from the little things of our world. He does not toil for personal comfort. He cares little for all the things that mean so much in our lives. If he speaks in defense of a cause he does not do it for his personal glory. It is comforting for us to know that such a man still exists, a man whose thoughts are directed toward the stars. We give him admiration because in admiring him we prove to ourselves that we, too, yearn for the distant stars.

Einstein has become a symbol for many, a monument people have built, a symbol that they need for their own comfort.

And perhaps, in the last analysis, these people are right. Perhaps the real greatness of Einstein lies in the simple fact that, though in his life he has gazed at the stars, yet he also tried to look at his fellow men with kindness and compassion.

Reflections on the Legendary Einstein

Abraham Pais

Abraham Pais reflects on the legendary view of Einstein as held by the physicists at the Institute for Advanced Study at Princeton, New Jersey. Based on conversations during his regular walks with Einstein, Pais emphasizes Einstein's preoccupation with quantum mechanics and unified field theory, topics that made Einstein a legend among his colleagues. Pais also reveals the subtle awe in which even the most renowned physicists held Einstein. Abraham Pais taught physics at Rockefeller University and the Institute for Advanced Study. He is the author of *Inward Bound*, a history of twentieth-century physics.

It must have been around 1950. I was accompanying Einstein on a walk from The Institute for Advanced Study to his home, when he suddenly stopped, turned to me, and asked me if I really believed that the moon exists only if I look at it. The nature of our conversation was not particularly metaphysical. Rather, we were discussing the quantum theory,[1] in particular what is doable and knowable in the sense of physical observation. The twentieth century physicist does not, of course, claim to have the definitive answer to this question. He does know, however, that the answer given by his nineteenth century ancestors will no longer do. They were almost exactly right, to be sure, as far as conditions of everyday life are concerned, but their answer cannot be extrapolated to things moving nearly as fast as light, or to things that are as small as atoms, or—in some respects—to things that are as heavy as stars. We now know better than

1. The theory that light is emitted in discrete units; the particles may behave like waves and the waves like particles. The position and velocity of a particle can never be predicted, except statistically. Einstein never accepted this theory as final.

Reprinted from *Subtle Is the Lord: The Science and Life of Albert Einstein* by Abraham Pais (1982) by permission of Oxford University Press. Copyright © Oxford University Press 1982.

before that what man can do under the best of circumstances depends on a careful specification of what those circumstances are. That, in very broad terms, is the lesson of
the theory of relativity, which Einstein created, and of quantum mechanics, which he eventually accepted as (in his
words) the most successful theory of our period but which,
he believed, was none the less only provisional in character.

We walked on and continued talking about the moon and
the meaning of the expression *to exist* as it refers to inani-
mate objects. When we reached 112 Mercer Street, I wished
him a pleasant lunch, then returned to the Institute. As had
been the case on many earlier occasions, I had enjoyed the
walk and felt better because of the discussion even though it
had ended inconclusively. I was used to that by then, and as
I walked back I wondered once again about the question,
Why does this man, who contributed so incomparably much
to the creation of modern physics, remain so attached to the
nineteenth century view of causality?

To make that question more precise, it is necessary to understand Einstein's credo in regard not just to quantum
physics but to all of physics. That much I believe I know, and
will endeavor to explain in what follows. However, in order
to answer the question, one needs to know not only his beliefs but also how they came to be adopted. My conversations
with Einstein taught me little about that. The issue was not
purposely shunned; it simply was never raised. Only many
years after Einstein's death did I see the beginnings of an answer when I realized that, nearly a decade before the discovery of modern quantum mechanics, he had been the first
to understand that the nineteenth century ideal of causality
was about to become a grave issue in quantum physics.
However, while I know more now about the evolution of his
thinking than I did when I walked with him, I would not go
so far as to say that I now understand why he chose to believe what he did believe. When Einstein was fifty years old,
he wrote in the introduction to the biography by his son-in-
law Rudolph Kayser, 'What has perhaps been overlooked is
the irrational, the inconsistent, the droll, even the insane,
which nature, inexhaustibly operative, implants in an individual, seemingly for her own amusement. But these things
are singled out only in the crucible of one's own mind.' Perhaps this statement is too optimistic about the reach of self-
knowledge. Certainly it is a warning, and a fair one, to any

biographer not to overdo answering every question he may legitimately raise.

MEETING NIELS BOHR AND EINSTEIN

I should briefly explain how it happened that I went on that walk with Einstein and why we came to talk about the moon. I was born in 1918 in Amsterdam. In 1941 I received my PhD with Léon Rosenfeld in Utrecht. Some time thereafter I went into hiding in Amsterdam. Eventually I was caught and sent to the Gestapo prison there. Those who were not executed were released shortly before VE Day. Immediately after the war I applied for a postdoctoral fellowship at the Niels Bohr Institute in Copenhagen and at The Institute for Advanced Study in Princeton where I hoped to work with [physicist Wolfgang] Pauli. I was accepted at both places and first went to Copenhagen for one year. Soon thereafter, I worked with Bohr for a period of several months. The following lines from my account of that experience are relevant to the present subject: 'I must admit that in the early stages of the collaboration I did not follow Bohr's line of thinking a good deal of the time and was in fact often quite bewildered. I failed to see the relevance of such remarks as that [physicist Erwin] Schroedinger was completely shocked in 1927 when he was told of the probability interpretation of quantum mechanics or a reference to some objection by Einstein in 1928, which apparently had no bearing whatever on the subject at hand. But it did not take very long before the fog started to lift. I began to grasp not only the thread of Bohr's arguments but also their purpose. just as in many sports a player goes through warming-up exercises before entering the arena, so Bohr would relive the struggles which it took before the content of quantum mechanics was understood and accepted. I can say that in Bohr's mind this struggle started all over every single day. This, I am convinced, was Bohr's inexhaustible source of identity. Einstein appeared forever as his leading spiritual partner—even after the latter's death he would argue with him as if Einstein were still alive'.

In September 1946 I went to Princeton. The first thing I learned was that, in the meantime, Pauli had gone to Zürich. Bohr also came to Princeton that same month. Both of us attended the Princeton Bicentennial Meetings. I missed my first opportunity to catch a glimpse of Einstein as he walked next to President Truman in the academic parade. However, shortly thereafter, Bohr introduced me to Einstein, who greeted a rather awed young man in a very friendly way. The conversation on that occasion soon turned to the quantum theory. I listened as the two of them argued. I recall no details but remember distinctly my first impressions: they liked and respected each other. With a fair amount of passion, they were talking past each other. And, as had been the case with my first discussions with Bohr, I did not understand what Einstein was talking about.

WALKS AND CONVERSATION

Not long thereafter, I encountered Einstein in front of the Institute and told him that I had not followed his argument with Bohr and asked if I could come to his office some time for further enlightenment. He invited me to walk home with him. So began a series of discussions that continued until shortly before his death. I would visit with him in his office or accompany him (often together with [physicist] Kurt Gödel) on his lunchtime walk home. Less often I would visit him there. In all, I saw him about once every few weeks. We always spoke in German, the language best suited to grasp both the nuances of what he had in mind and the flavor of his personality. Only once did he visit my apartment. The occasion was a meeting of the Institute faculty for the purpose of drafting a statement of our position in the 1954 Oppenheimer affair.

Einstein's company was comfortable and comforting to those who knew him. Of course, he well knew that he was a legendary figure in the eyes of the world. He accepted this as a fact of life. There was nothing in his personality to promote his mythical stature; nor did he relish it. Privately he would express annoyance if he felt that his position was being misused. I recall the case of Professor X, who had been quoted by the newspapers as having found solutions to Einstein's generalized equations of gravitation. Einstein said to me, 'Der Mann ist ein Narr,' the man is a fool, and added that, in his opinion, X could calculate but could not think. X had visited Einstein to discuss this work, and Einstein, always courteous, had said to him that his, X's, results would be important if true. Einstein was chagrined to have been quoted in the papers without this last provision. He said that he would keep silent on the matter but would not receive X again. According to Einstein, the whole thing started because X, in his enthusiasm, had repeated Einstein's opinion to some colleagues who saw the value of it as publicity for their university.

PHYSICISTS TREAT EINSTEIN AS A LEGEND

To those physicists who could follow his scientific thought and who knew him personally, the legendary aspect was never in the foreground—yet it was never wholly absent. I remember an occasion in 1947 when I was giving a talk at the Institute about the newly discovered π and μ mesons. Einstein walked in just after I had begun. I remember being speechless for the brief moment necessary to overcome a sense of the unreal. I recall a similar moment during a symposium held in Princeton on March 19, 1949, on the occasion of Einstein's seventieth birthday. Most of us were in our seats when Einstein entered the hall. Again there was this brief hush before we stood to greet him.

Nor do I believe that such reactions were typical only of those who were much younger than he. There were a few occasions when Pauli and I were both with him. Pauli, not known for an excess of awe, was just slightly different in Einstein's company. One could perceive his sense of reverence. Bohr, too, was affected in a similar way, differences in scientific outlook notwithstanding.

PHYSICS TOPICS, MAINLY QUANTUM MECHANICS

Whenever I met Einstein, our conversations might range far and wide but invariably the discussion would turn to physics. Such discussions would touch only occasionally on matters of past history. We talked mainly about the present and the future. When relativity was the issue, he would often talk of his efforts to unify gravitation and electromagnetism and of his hopes for the next steps. His faith rarely wavered in the path he had chosen. Only once did he express a reservation to me when he said, in essence, 'I am not sure that differential geometry is the framework for further progress, but, if it is, then I believe I am on the right track.' (This remark must have been made some time during his last few years.)

The main topic of discussion, however, was quantum physics. Einstein never ceased to ponder the meaning of the quantum theory. Time and time again, the argument would turn to quantum mechanics and its interpretation. He was explicit in his opinion that the most commonly held views on this subject could not be the last word, but he also had more subtle ways of expressing his dissent. For example, he would never refer to a wave function as *die Wellenfunktion* but would always use mathematical terminology: *die Psi-funktion*. I was never able to arouse much interest in him about the new particles which appeared on the scene in the late 1940s and especially in the early 1950s. It was apparent that he felt that the time was not ripe to worry about such things and that these particles would eventually appear as solutions to the equations of a unified theory. In some sense, he may well prove to be right.

The most interesting thing I learned from these conversations was how Einstein thought and, to some extent, who he was. Since I never became his co-worker, the discussions were not confined to any particular problem. Yet we talked physics, often touching on topics of a technical nature. We did not talk much about statistical physics, an area to which he had contributed so much but which no longer was the center of his interests. If the special and the general theory of relativity came up only occasionally, that was because at that time the main issues appeared to have been settled. Recall that the renewed surge of interest in general relativity began just after his death. However, I do remember him talking about [physicist Hendrik] Lorentz, the one father figure in his life; once we also talked about [physicist Henri] Poincaré. If we argued so often about the quantum theory, that was more his choice than mine. It had not taken long before I grasped the essence of the Einstein-Bohr dialogue: complementarity versus objective reality. It became clear to me from listening to them both that the advent of quantum mechanics in 1925 represented a far greater break with the past than had been the case with the coming of special relativity in 1905 or of general relativity in 1915. That had not been obvious to me earlier, as I belong to the generation which was exposed to 'ready-made' quantum mechanics. I came to understand how wrong I was in accepting a rather widespread belief that Einstein simply did not care anymore about the quantum theory. On the contrary, he wanted nothing more than to find a unified field theory which not only would join together gravitational and electromagnetic forces but also would provide the basis for a new interpretation of quantum phenomena. About relativity he spoke with detachment, about the quantum theory with passion. The quantum was his demon. I learned only much later that Einstein had once said to his friend [physicist] Otto Stern, 'I have thought a hundred times as much about the quantum problems as I have about general relativity theory'. From my own experiences I can only add that this statement does not surprise me.

EINSTEIN REVEALED IN HIS CONVERSATION AND HIS PAPERS

We talked of things other than physics: politics, the bomb, the Jewish destiny, and also of less weighty matters. One day I told Einstein a Jewish joke. Since he relished that, I began to save good ones I heard for a next occasion. As I told these stories, his face would change. Suddenly he would look much younger, almost like a naughty schoolboy. When the punch line came, he would let go with contented laughter, a memory I particularly cherish.

An unconcern with the past is a privilege of youth. In all the years I knew Einstein, I never read any of his papers, on the simple grounds that I already knew what to a physicist was memorable in them and did not need to know what had been superseded. Now it is obvious to me that I might have been able to ask him some very interesting questions had I been less blessed with ignorance. I might then have learned some interesting facts, but at a price. My discussions with Einstein never were historical interviews. They concerned live physics. I am glad it never was otherwise.

I did read Einstein's papers as the years went by, and my interest in him as an historical figure grew. Thus it came about that I learned to follow his science and his life from the end to the beginnings. I gradually became aware of the most difficult task in studying past science: to forget temporarily what came afterward.

DISCUSSION QUESTIONS

1. How would you characterize Einstein's experiences at the Luitpold Gymnasium? Identify attitudes and feelings that Einstein developed there and explain what effect they had on his life as a whole. Was Einstein better off or worse off for having attended this school?

2. According to what Einstein remembers of his childhood, was he thinking like an ordinary boy or did he show unusual insight at an early age? In light of your own experience, what elements in Einstein's experience and thought seemed ordinary or extraordinary?

3. Was Marcel Grossmann justified in letting Einstein study his notes? What might have been the short-term and the long-term ramifications had he chosen not to let Einstein study his notes?

CHAPTER TWO

1. Heinz R. Pagels quotes Einstein as saying, "Space is what we measure with a measuring rod and time is what we measure with clocks." How does this statement form the basis for special relativity?

2. What is curved space? Why did Einstein need a new geometry to complete his theory of general relativity?

3. Einstein rejected quantum mechanics and spent thirty years searching unsuccessfully for a unified field theory. What fundamental belief motivated him to take these two actions? Do you think he made the right or wrong decisions? Why or why not?

CHAPTER THREE

1. What words describe the tone of Anton Reiser's essay on Einstein's fame? Select words, phrases, and anecdotes that support your opinion. What fact might have biased Reiser's attitude toward Einstein?

2. What personal and public conditions led Einstein to sup-

port political causes but refrain from joining organizations? Was Einstein justified in spending time on nonscientific issues, or should he have narrowed his focus to science only?

3. According to Gerald Holton, in what sense was Einstein's theory of relativity misinterpreted as "relative" in the popular imagination? What elements in the social, intellectual, and artistic community changed because of this misinterpretation?

CHAPTER FOUR

1. What accounts for the outpouring of attention given to Einstein on his 1931–1932 visit to America: that the media had made him a hero? that Americans are attracted to new and bizarre ideas? that Americans genuinely respected Einstein's relativity theories? or another reason?

2. Why were Princeton and the Institute for Advanced Study good fits for Einstein given his personality, scientific interests, and political beliefs? What might have happened had he chosen to remain in Germany?

3. Did Einstein do the right or wrong thing by recommending to President Franklin D. Roosevelt that the U.S. government begin research on the development of an atomic bomb? What might have resulted had the government chosen not to go ahead with this research? How might the dropping of atomic bombs on Japan have been averted?

CHAPTER FIVE

1. Walter Isaacson and Cornelius Lanczos both praise Einstein for his achievements. Compare and contrast the arguments the two writers make in drawing their conclusions.

2. Leopold Infeld says that Einstein and the theories of relativity were "vastly and passionately debated." According to Infeld, what arguments did Einstein's opponents use to undermine him and his theories? What reasons does he give for Einstein's popularity and fame that arose suddenly and then continued?

3. Evaluate the use of Einstein's image as a symbol. Does this use have serious effects, or does it amount to nothing more than harmless fun? Cite examples to support your opinion.

GENERAL QUESTIONS

1. What do you think are the most important reasons for identifying Einstein as a person "who made history"?

2. Why was Einstein so popular during his lifetime and after his death? Was it his personality or his achievements?

APPENDIX OF DOCUMENTS

EINSTEIN'S ETHICAL AND INTELLECTUAL IDEAS

DOCUMENT 1: EINSTEIN AND THE MEDIA

At the height of Einstein's fame, reporters sought Einstein wherever he went and asked his opinions on all manner of topics beyond science. In a short piece written in 1934, Einstein expresses, in his characteristic good humor, the dilemma reporters cause him.

To be called to account publicly for everything one has said, even in jest, in an excess of high spirits or in momentary anger, may possibly be awkward, yet up to a point it is reasonable and natural. But to be called to account publicly for what others have said in one's name, when one cannot defend oneself, is indeed a sad predicament. "But to whom does such a thing happen?" you will ask. Well, everyone who is of sufficient interest to the public to be pursued by interviewers. You smile incredulously, but I have had plenty of direct experience and will tell you about it.

Imagine the following situation. One morning a reporter comes to you and asks you in a friendly way to tell him something about your friend N. At first you no doubt feel something approaching indignation at such a proposal. But you soon discover that there is no escape. If you refuse to say anything, the man writes: "I asked one of N's supposedly best friends about him. But he prudently avoided my questions. This in itself enables the reader to draw the inevitable conclusions." There is, therefore, no escape, and you give the following information: "Mr. N is a cheerful, straightforward man, much liked by all his friends. He can find a bright side to any situation. His enterprise and industry know no bounds; his job takes up his entire energies. He is devoted to his family and lays everything he possesses at his wife's feet. . . ."

Now for the reporter's version: "Mr. N takes nothing very seriously and has a gift for making himself liked, particularly as he carefully cultivates a hearty and ingratiating manner. He is so completely a slave to his job that he has no time for the considerations of any non-personal subject or for any extracurricular mental activity. He spoils his wife unbelievably and is utterly under her thumb. . . ."

186

A real reporter would make it much more spicy, but I expect this will be enough for you and your friend N. He reads the above, and some more like it, in the paper next morning, and his rage against you knows no bounds, however cheerful and benevolent his natural disposition may be. The injury done to him gives you untold pain, especially as you are really fond of him.

What's your next step, my friend? If you know, tell me quickly so that I may adopt your method with all speed.

Ideas and Opinions by Albert Einstein. Based on *Mein Weltbild,* edited by Carl Seelig. New translations and revisions by Sonja Bargmann. New York: Wings, 1954.

DOCUMENT 2: THE MEANING OF FREEDOM

Einstein valued freedom. In an essay published in Freedom, Its Meaning, *he identifies three elements he feels are necessary for a satisfactory existence: the freedom to express intellectual ideas and opinions, the freedom to have enough leisure for personal activities, and the inner spiritual freedom to think.*

I know that it is a hopeless undertaking to debate about fundamental value judgments. For instance, if someone approves, as a goal, the extirpation of the human race from the earth, one cannot refute such a viewpoint on rational grounds. But if there is agreement on certain goals and values, one can argue rationally about the means by which these objectives may be attained. Let us, then, indicate two goals which may well be agreed upon by nearly all who read these lines.

1. Those instrumental goods which should serve to maintain the life and health of all human beings should be produced by the least possible labor of all.

2. The satisfaction of physical needs is indeed the indispensable precondition of a satisfactory existence, but in itself it is not enough. In order to be content, men must also have the possibility of developing their intellectual and artistic powers to whatever extent accords with their personal characteristics and abilities.

The first of these two goals requires the promotion of all knowledge relating to the laws of nature and the laws of social processes, that is, the promotion of all scientific endeavor. For scientific endeavor is a natural whole, the parts of which mutually support one another in a way which, to be sure, no one can anticipate. However, the progress of science presupposes the possibility of unrestricted communication of all results and judgments—freedom of expression and instruction in all realms of intellectual endeavor. By freedom I understand social conditions of such a kind that the expression of opinions and assertions about general and particular matters of knowledge will not involve dangers or serious disadvantages for him who expresses them. This freedom of communication is indispensable for the development and extension of scientific knowledge, a consideration of much practical import. In the first instance it must be guaranteed by law. But laws alone cannot secure freedom of expression; in order that every man may present his views without penalty, there must be a spirit of tolerance in the entire population. Such an ideal of external liberty can never be fully attained but must be sought unremittingly if scientific thought, and philosophical and creative thinking in general, are to be advanced as far as possible.

If the second goal, that is, the possibility of the spiritual development of all individuals, is to be secured, a second kind of outward freedom is necessary. Man should not have to work for the achievement of the necessities of life to such an extent that he has neither time nor strength for personal activities. Without this second kind of outward liberty, freedom of expression is useless for him. Advances in technology would provide the possibility of this kind of freedom if the problem of a reasonable division of labor were solved.

The development of science and of the creative activities of the spirit in general requires still another kind of freedom, which may be characterized as inward freedom. It is this freedom of the spirit which consists in the independence of thought from the restrictions of authoritarian and social prejudices as well as from unphilosophical routinizing and habit in general. This inward freedom is an infrequent gift of nature and a worthy objective for the individual. Yet the community can do much to further this achievement, too, at least by not interfering with its development. Thus schools may interfere with the development of inward freedom through authoritarian influences and through imposing on young people excessive spiritual burdens; on the other hand, schools may favor such freedom by encouraging independent thought. Only if outward and inner freedom are constantly and consciously pursued is there a possibility of spiritual development and perfection and thus of improving man's outward and inner life.

From *Freedom, Its Meaning*, edited by Ruth Nanda Anshen. New York: Harcourt, Brace, 1940. Translated by James Guthmann. Reprinted in *Ideas and Opinions by Albert Einstein*. Based on *Mein Weltbild*, edited by Carl Seelig. New translations and revisions by Sonja Bargmann. New York: Wings, 1954.

DOCUMENT 3: HUMAN RIGHTS

In a speech to the Chicago Decalogue Society on February 20, 1954, Einstein said that the struggle for the ideals of human rights must go on constantly. He identified human rights as personal safety, the right to work with adequate earnings, freedom of expression, the right to participate in government, and the right to abstain from activities that go against one's conscience.

In a long life I have devoted all my faculties to reach a somewhat deeper insight into the structure of physical reality. Never have I made any systematic effort to ameliorate the lot of men, to fight injustice and suppression, and to improve the traditional forms of human relations. The only thing I did was this: in long intervals I have expressed an opinion on public issues whenever they appeared to me so bad and unfortunate that silence would have made me feel guilty of complicity.

The existence and validity of human rights are not written in the stars. The ideals concerning the conduct of men toward each other and the desirable structure of the community have been conceived and taught by enlightened individuals in the course of history. Those ideals and convictions which resulted from historical experience, from the craving for beauty and harmony, have been readily accepted in theory by man—and at all times, have been trampled upon by the same people under the pressure of their animal instincts. A large part of history is therefore replete with the struggle for those human rights, an eternal struggle in which a final victory can never be won. But to tire in that struggle would mean the ruin of society.

In talking about human rights today, we are referring primarily to the following demands: protection of the individual against arbitrary infringement by other individuals or by the government; the right to work and to adequate earnings from work; freedom of discussion and teaching; adequate participation of the individual in the formation of his government. *These* human rights are nowadays recognized theoretically, although, by abundant use of formalistic, legal maneuvers, they are being violated to a much greater extent than even a generation ago. There is, however, one other human right which is infrequently mentioned but which seems to be destined to become very important: this is the right, or the duty, of the individual to abstain from cooperating in activities which he considers wrong or pernicious. The first place in this respect must be given to the refusal of military service. I have known instances where individuals of unusual moral strength and integrity have, for that reason, come into conflict with the organs of the state.

Ideas and Opinions by Albert Einstein. Based on *Mein Weltbild,* edited by Carl Seelig. New translations and revisions by Sonja Bargmann. New York: Wings, 1954.

DOCUMENT 4: A SCIENTIST'S RELIGION

In a statement published in 1934, Einstein says that for a scientist the future and the past are equally determined because of nature's laws. A scientist's religious feelings stem from his amazement at the superior order of natural law, and those feelings guide his life and work.

The scientist is possessed by the sense of universal causation. The future, to him, is every whit as necessary and determined as the past. There is nothing divine about morality; it is a purely human affair. His religious feeling takes the form of a rapturous amazement at the harmony of natural law, which reveals an intelligence of such superiority that, compared with it, all the systematic thinking and acting of human beings is an utterly insignificant reflection. This feeling is the guiding principle of his life and work, in so far as he succeeds in keeping himself from the shackles of selfish desire. It is beyond question closely akin to that which has possessed the religious geniuses of all ages.

Ideas and Opinions by Albert Einstein. Based on *Mein Weltbild*, edited by Carl Seelig. New translations and revisions by Sonja Bargmann. New York: Wings, 1954.

DOCUMENT 5: THE RELATIONSHIP BETWEEN SCIENCE AND RELIGION

In a 1941 symposium on science, philosophy, and religion, Einstein argues that science and religion can enhance each other. Central to his argument, however, is the elimination of the concept of a personal God that interferes in nature because such a concept is incompatible with today's knowledge. Better, he says, is the concept of a God as a force for "cultivating the Good, the True, and the Beautiful" in human beings because this concept is compatible with the goals of science.

The main source of the present-day conflicts between the spheres of religion and of science lies in this concept of a personal God. It is the aim of science to establish general rules which determine the reciprocal connection of objects and events in time and space. For these rules, or laws of nature, absolutely general validity is required—not proven. It is mainly a program, and faith in the possibility of its accomplishment in principle is only founded on partial successes. But hardly anyone could be found who would deny these partial successes and ascribe them to human self-deception. The fact that on the basis of such laws we are able to predict the temporal behavior of phenomena in certain domains with great precision and certainty is deeply embedded in the consciousness of the modern man, even though he may have grasped very little of the contents of those laws. He need only consider that planetary courses within the solar system may be calculated in advance with great exactitude on the basis of a limited number of simple laws. In a similar way, though not with the same precision, it is possible to calculate in advance the mode of operation of an electric motor, a transmission system, or of a wireless apparatus, even when dealing with a novel development.

To be sure, when the number of factors coming into play in a phenomenological complex is too large, scientific method in most cases fails us. One need only think of the weather, in which case prediction even for a few days ahead is impossible. Nevertheless no one doubts that we are confronted with a causal connection whose causal components are in the main known to us. Occurrences in this domain are beyond the reach of exact prediction because of the variety of factors in operation, not because of any lack of order in nature.

We have penetrated far less deeply into the regularities obtain-

ing within the realm of living things, but deeply enough nevertheless to sense at least the rule of fixed necessity. One need only think
of the systematic order in heredity, and in the effect of poisons, as
for instance alcohol, on the behavior of organic beings. What is still
lacking here is a grasp of connections of profound generality, but
not a knowledge of order in itself.

The more a man is imbued with the ordered regularity of all
events the firmer becomes his conviction that there is no room left
by the side of this ordered regularity for causes of a different nature. For him neither the rule of human nor the rule of divine will
exists as an independent cause of natural events. To be sure, the
doctrine of a personal God interfering with natural events could
never be *refuted*, in the real sense, by science, for this doctrine can
always take refuge in those domains in which scientific knowledge
has not yet been able to set foot.

But I am persuaded that such behavior on the part of the repre-
sentatives of religion would not only be unworthy but also fatal. For
a doctrine which is able to maintain itself not in clear light but only
in the dark, will of necessity lose its effect on mankind, with incalculable harm to human progress. In their struggle for the ethical
good, teachers of religion must have the stature to give up the doctrine of a personal God, that is, give up that source of fear and hope
which in the past placed such vast power in the hands of priests. In
their labors they will have to avail themselves of those forces which
are capable of cultivating the Good, the True, and the Beautiful in
humanity itself. This is, to be sure, a more difficult but an incomparably more worthy task. After religious teachers accomplish the
refining process indicated they will surely recognize with joy that
true religion has been ennobled and made more profound by scientific knowledge.

If it is one of the goals of religion to liberate mankind as far as
possible from the bondage of egocentric cravings, desires, and
fears, scientific reasoning can aid religion in yet another sense. Although it is true that it is the goal of science to discover rules which
permit the association and foretelling of facts, this is not its only
aim. It also seeks to reduce the connections discovered to the
smallest possible number of mutually independent conceptual elements. It is in this striving after the rational unification of the manifold that it encounters its greatest successes, even though it is precisely this attempt which causes it to run the greatest risk of falling
a prey to illusions. But whoever has undergone the intense experience of successful advances made in this domain is moved by profound reverence for the rationality made manifest in existence. By
way of the understanding he achieves a far-reaching emancipation
from the shackles of personal hopes and desires, and thereby at-
tains that humble attitude of mind toward the grandeur of reason
incarnate in existence, and which, in its profoundest depths, is in-
accessible to man. This attitude, however, appears to me to be reli-

gious, in the highest sense of the word. And so it seems to me that science not only purifies the religious impulse of the dross of its anthropomorphism but also contributes to a religious spiritualization of our understanding of life.

The further the spiritual evolution of mankind advances, the more certain it seems to me that the path to genuine religiosity does not lie through the fear of life, and the fear of death, and blind faith, but through striving after rational knowledge. In this sense I believe that the priest must become a teacher if he wishes to do justice to his lofty educational mission.

From *Science, Philosophy and Religion,* A Symposium, published by the Conference on Science, Philosophy and Religion in their Relation to the Democratic Way of Life, Inc., New York, 1941. In *Ideas and Opinions by Albert Einstein.* Based on *Mein Weltbild,* edited by Carl Seelig. New translations and revisions by Sonja Bargmann. New York: Wings, 1954.

DOCUMENT 6: CREATING AN ETHICAL CULTURE

In a letter read to the New York Ethical Culture Society in January 1951 on the society's seventy-fifth anniversary, Einstein says that overemphasis on science and intellectual thought impairs ethical values. Art and religion (as long as it is without superstition) are better able to instill sympathy for other human beings, a quality necessary for an ethical society. Educational institutions need to put greater emphasis on this kind of training.

I believe, indeed, that overemphasis on the purely intellectual attitude, often directed solely to the practical and factual, in our education, has led directly to the impairment of ethical values. I am not thinking so much of the dangers with which technical progress has directly confronted mankind, as of the stifling of mutual human considerations by a "matter-of-fact" habit of thought which has come to lie like a killing frost upon human relations.

Fulfillment on the moral and esthetic side is a goal which lies closer to the preoccupations of art than it does to those of science. Of course, *understanding* of our fellow-beings is important. But this understanding becomes fruitful only when it is sustained by sympathetic feeling in joy and in sorrow. The cultivation of this most important spring of moral action is that which is left of religion when it has been purified of the elements of superstition. In this sense, religion forms an important part of education, where it receives far too little consideration, and that little not sufficiently systematic.

The frightful dilemma of the political world situation has much to do with this sin of omission on the part of our civilization. Without "ethical culture" there is no salvation for humanity.

Ideas and Opinions by Albert Einstein. Based on *Mein Weltbild,* edited by Carl Seelig. New translations and revisions by Sonja Bargmann. New York: Wings, 1954.

DOCUMENT 7: EDUCATION FOR A HEALTHY SOCIETY

Speaking in Albany, New York, in 1936, three hundred years after the founding of higher education in America, Einstein told his audience that a school should not be a place simply to transfer knowledge to the next generation nor a place achieving its discipline by fear or force. Because a healthy society is dependent on the school system, a school should instill love of work and the satisfaction it provides and train minds for independent thinking and judgment.

The school has always been the most important means of transferring the wealth of tradition from one generation to the next. This applies today in an even higher degree than in former times, for through modern development of the economic life, the family as bearer of tradition and education has been weakened. The continuance and health of human society is therefore in a still higher degree dependent on the school than formerly.

Sometimes one sees in the school simply the instrument for transferring a certain maximum quantity of knowledge to the growing generation. But that is not right. Knowledge is dead; the school, however, serves the living. It should develop in the young individuals those qualities and capabilities which are of value for the welfare of the commonwealth. But that does not mean that individuality should be destroyed and the individual become a mere tool of the community, like a bee or an ant. For a community of standardized individuals without personal originality and personal aims would be a poor community without possibilities for development. On the contrary, the aim must be the training of independently acting and thinking individuals, who, however, see in the service of the community their highest life problem. So far as I can judge, the English school system comes nearest to the realization of this ideal.

But how shall one try to attain this ideal? Should one perhaps try to realize this aim by moralizing? Not at all. Words are and remain an empty sound, and the road to perdition has ever been accompanied by lip service to an ideal. But personalities are not formed by what is heard and said, but by labor and activity.

The most important method of education accordingly always has consisted of that in which the pupil was urged to actual performance. This applies as well to the first attempts at writing of the primary boy as to the doctor's thesis on graduation from the university, or as to the mere memorizing of a poem, the writing of a composition, the interpretation and translation of a text, the solving of a mathematical problem or the practice of physical sport.

But behind every achievement exists the motivation which is at the foundation of it and which in turn is strengthened and nourished by the accomplishment of the undertaking. Here there are the greatest differences and they are of greatest importance to the educational value of the school. The same work may owe its origin to fear and compulsion, ambitious desire for authority and distinction, or loving interest in the object and a desire for truth and understanding, and thus to that divine curiosity which every healthy child possesses, but which so often is weakened early. The educational influence which is exercised upon the pupil by the accomplishment of one and the same work may be widely different, depending upon whether fear of hurt, egoistic passion, or desire for pleasure and satisfaction is at the bottom of this work. And nobody will maintain that the administration of the school and the attitude of the teachers do not have an influence upon the molding of the psychological foundation for pupils.

To me the worst thing seems to be for a school principally to work with methods of fear, force, and artificial authority. Such treatment destroys the sound sentiments, the sincerity, and the self-confidence of the pupil. It produces the submissive subject. It is no wonder that such schools are the rule in Germany and Russia. I know that the schools in this country are free from this worst evil; this also is so in Switzerland and probably in all democratically governed countries. It is comparatively simple to keep the school free from this worst of all evils. Give into the power of the teacher the fewest possible coercive measures, so that the only source of the pupil's respect for the teacher is the human and intellectual qualities of the latter.

The second-named motive, ambition or, in milder terms, the aiming at recognition and consideration, lies firmly fixed in human nature. With absence of mental stimulus of this kind, human cooperation would be entirely impossible; the desire for the approval of one's fellow-man certainly is one of the most important binding powers of society. In this complex of feelings, constructive and destructive forces lie closely together. Desire for approval and recognition is a healthy motive; but the desire to be acknowledged as better, stronger, or more intelligent than a fellow being or fellow scholar easily leads to an excessively egoistic psychological adjustment, which may become injurious for the individual and for the community. Therefore the school and the teacher must guard against employing the easy method of creating individual ambition, in order to induce the pupils to diligent work. . . .

Therefore one should guard against preaching to the young man success in the customary sense as the aim of life. For a successful man is he who receives a great deal from his fellowmen, usually incomparably more than corresponds to his service to them. The value of a man, however, should be seen in what he gives and not in what he is able to receive.

The most important motive for work in the school and in life is the pleasure in work, pleasure in its result, and the knowledge of the value of the result to the community. In the awakening and strengthening of these psychological forces in the young man, I see the most important task given by the school. Such a psychological foundation alone leads to a joyous desire for the highest possessions of men, knowledge and artistlike workmanship.

The awakening of these productive psychological powers is certainly less easy than the practice of force or the awakening of individual ambition but is the more valuable for it. The point is to develop the childlike inclination for play and the childlike desire for recognition and to guide the child over to important fields for society; it is that education which in the main is founded upon the desire for successful activity and acknowledgment. If the school succeeds in working successfully from such points of view, it will be highly honored by the rising generation and the tasks given by the school will be submitted to as a sort of gift. I have known children who preferred schooltime to vacation.

Such a school demands from the teacher that he be a kind of artist in his province. What can be done that this spirit be gained in the school? For this there is just as little a universal remedy as there is for an individual to remain well. But there are certain necessary conditions which can be met. First, teachers should grow up in such schools. Second, the teacher should be given extensive liberty in the selection of the material to be taught and the methods of teaching employed by him. For it is true also of him that pleasure in the shaping of his work is killed by force and exterior pressure.

If you have followed attentively my meditations up to this point, you will probably wonder about one thing. I have spoken fully about in what spirit, according to my opinion, youth should be instructed. But I have said nothing yet about the choice of subjects for instruction, nor about the method of teaching. Should language predominate or technical education in science?

To this I answer: in my opinion all this is of secondary importance. If a young man has trained his muscles and physical endurance by gymnastics and walking, he will later be fitted for every physical work. This is also analogous to the training of the mind and the exercising of the mental and manual skill. Thus the wit was not wrong who defined education in this way: "Education is that which remains, if one has forgotten everything he learned in school." For this reason I am not at all anxious to take sides in the struggle between the followers of the classical philologic-historical education and the education more devoted to natural science.

On the other hand, I want to oppose the idea that the school has to teach directly that special knowledge and those accomplishments which one has to use later directly in life. The demands of life are much too manifold to let such a specialized training in school appear possible. Apart from that, it seems to me, moreover, objectionable to treat the individual like a dead tool. The school should always have as its aim that the young man leave it as a harmonious personality, not as a specialist. This in my opinion is true in a certain sense even for technical schools, whose students will devote themselves to a quite definite profession. The development of general ability for independent thinking and judgment should always be placed foremost, not the acquisition of special knowledge. If a person masters the fundamentals of his subject and has learned to think and work independently, he will surely find his way and besides will better be able to adapt himself to progress and changes than the person whose training principally consists in the acquiring of detailed knowledge.

Finally, I wish to emphasize once more that what has been said here in a somewhat categorical form does not claim to mean more than the personal opinion of a man, which is founded upon *nothing but* his own personal experience, which he has gathered as a student and as a teacher.

Ideas and Opinions by Albert Einstein. Based on *Mein Weltbild,* edited by Carl Seelig. New translations and revisions by Sonja Bargmann. New York: Wings, 1954.

DOCUMENT 8: EDUCATING THE YOUNG TO UPHOLD THE CULTURE

In an article printed in the October 5, 1952, New York Times, Einstein emphasizes the importance of educating the young to appreciate what is beautiful and good and to develop independent critical thinking. This task is not accomplished in a competitive and specialized system.

It is not enough to teach man a specialty. Through it he may become a kind of useful machine but not a harmoniously developed personality. It is essential that the student acquire an understanding of and a lively feeling for values. He must acquire a vivid sense of the beautiful and of the morally good. Otherwise he—with his specialized knowledge—more closely resembles a well-trained dog than a harmoniously developed person. He must learn to understand the motives of human beings, their illusions, and their sufferings in order to acquire a proper relationship to individual fellow-men and to the community.

These precious things are conveyed to the younger generation through personal contact with those who teach, not—or at least not in the main—through textbooks. It is this that primarily constitutes and preserves culture. This is what I have in mind when I recommend the "humanities" as important, not just dry specialized knowledge in the fields of history and philosophy.

Overemphasis on the competitive system and premature specialization on the ground of immediate usefulness kill the spirit on which all cultural life depends, specialized knowledge included.

It is also vital to a valuable education that independent critical thinking be developed in the young human being, a development that is greatly jeopardized by overburdening him with too much and with too varied subjects (point system). Overburdening necessarily leads to superficiality. Teaching should be such that what is offered is perceived as a valuable gift and not as a hard duty.

Ideas and Opinions by Albert Einstein. Based on *Mein Weltbild,* edited by Carl Seelig. New translations and revisions by Sonja Bargmann. New York: Wings, 1954.

EINSTEIN'S IDEAS ON PEACE AND WAR

DOCUMENT 9: SUPPORT FOR CONSCIENTIOUS OBJECTORS

As an internationalist and a pacifist, Einstein hated nationalism and compulsory military training: He thought that they interacted and promoted moral decay. In an article for the Nation *in 1931, published prior to the Disarmament Conference of 1932, he advocates safety and support for conscientious objectors.*

The greatest obstacle to international order is that monstrously exaggerated spirit of nationalism which also goes by the fair-sounding but misused name of patriotism. During the last century and a half this idol has acquired an uncanny and exceedingly pernicious power everywhere.

To estimate this objection at its proper worth, one must realize that a reciprocal relation exists between external machinery and internal states of mind. Not only does the machinery depend on traditional modes of feeling and owe its origin and its survival to them, but the existing machinery in its turn exercises a powerful influence on national modes of feeling.

The present deplorably high development of nationalism everywhere is, in my opinion, intimately connected with the institution of compulsory military service or, to call it by its sweeter name, national armies. A state which demands military service of its inhabitants is compelled to cultivate in them a nationalistic spirit, thereby laying the psychological foundation for their military usefulness. In its schools it must idolize, alongside with religion, its instrument of brutal force in the eyes of the youth.

The introduction of compulsory military service is therefore, to my mind, the prime cause of the moral decay of the white race, which seriously threatens not merely the survival of our civilization but our very existence. This curse, along with great social blessings, started with the French Revolution, and before long dragged all the other nations in its train.

Therefore, those who desire to cultivate an international spirit and to combat chauvinism must take their stand against compulsory military service. Is the severe persecution to which conscientious objectors to military service are subjected today a whit less disgraceful to the community than those to which the martyrs of religion were exposed in former centuries? Can you, as the Kellogg Pact does, condemn war and at the same time leave the individual to the tender mercies of the war machine in each country?

If, in view of the Disarmament Conference, we are not merely to restrict ourselves to the technical problems of organization, but also to tackle the psychological question more directly from the standpoint of educational motives, we must try along international lines to create legal means by which the individual can refuse to serve in the army. Such a regulation would undoubtedly produce a great moral effect.

Let me summarize my views: Mere agreements to limit arma-
ments furnish no sort of security. Compulsory arbitration must be
supported by an executive force, guaranteed by all the participating
countries, which is ready to proceed against the disturber of the
peace with economic and military sanctions. Compulsory military
service, as the hotbed of unhealthy nationalism, must be combated;
most important of all, conscientious objectors must be protected on
an international basis.

Ideas and Opinions by Albert Einstein. Based on *Mein Weltbild,* edited by Carl Seelig.
New translations and revisions by Sonja Bargmann. New York: Wings, 1954.

DOCUMENT 10: AN URGENT PLEA FOR INTERNATIONALISM

Between World War I and World War II, Einstein spoke passionately
for disarmament and the cause of peace. He worked actively for the
League of Nations and in a 1934 essay urges America to reject isola-
tionism and work hard to help Europe to restore peace and order.

Few of us still cling to the notion that acts of violence in the shape
of wars are either advantageous or worthy of humanity as a
method of solving international problems. But we are not consistent enough to make vigorous efforts on behalf of the measures
which might prevent war, that savage and unworthy relic of the age
of barbarism. It requires some power of reflection to see the issue
clearly and a certain courage to serve this great cause resolutely
and effectively.

Anybody who really wants to abolish war must resolutely declare
himself in favor of his own country's resigning a portion of its sover-
eignty in favor of international institutions: he must be ready to
make his own country amenable, in case of a dispute, to the award
of an international court. He must, in the most uncompromising
fashion, support disarmament all round, as is actually envisaged in
the unfortunate Treaty of Versailles; unless military and aggressively
patriotic education is abolished, we can hope for no progress.

No event of the last few years reflects such disgrace on the leading civilized countries of the world as the failure of all disarmament conferences so far; for this failure is due not only to the intrigues of ambitious and unscrupulous politicians but also to the
indifference and slackness of the public in all countries. Unless this
is changed we shall destroy all the really valuable achievements of
our predecessors.

I believe that the American people are only imperfectly aware of
the responsibility which rests with them in this matter.

They no doubt think "Let Europe go to the dogs, if she is destroyed by the quarrelsomeness and wickedness of her inhabitants.
The good seed of our Wilson[1] has produced a mighty poor crop in

1. At the 1919 Paris Peace Conference following World War I President Woodrow Wilson included the establishment of the League of Nations, but the U.S. Senate refused
to ratify the treaty. The league's purpose was to prevent war, oversee peace treaties,
and improve social and economic conditions.

the stony group of Europe. We are strong and safe and in no hurry to mix ourselves up in other people's affairs."

Such an attitude is neither noble nor far-sighted. America is partly to blame for the difficulties of Europe. By ruthlessly pressing her claims she is hastening the economic and therewith the moral decline of Europe; she has helped to Balkanize Europe and therefore shares the responsibility for the breakdown of political morality and the growth of that spirit of revenge which feeds on despair. This spirit will not stop short of the gates of America—I had almost said, has not stopped short. Look around, and beware!

The truth can be briefly stated:—The Disarmament Conference comes as a final chance, to you no less than to us, of preserving the best that civilized humanity has produced. And it is on you, as the strongest and comparatively soundest among us, that the eyes and hopes of all are focused.

Ideas and Opinions by Albert Einstein. Based on *Mein Weltbild,* edited by Carl Seelig. New translations and revisions by Sonja Bargmann. New York: Wings, 1954.

DOCUMENT 11: THE MILITARY MENTALITY

Writing in The American Scholar *in 1947, Einstein describes the danger of the military mentality, the mind-set that elevates all matters connected with military power to the place of highest importance. When such an attitude prevails, Einstein believes, human factors are diminished and individuals degraded.*

It is characteristic of the military mentality that non-human factors (atom bombs, strategic bases, weapons of all sorts, the possession of raw materials, etc.) are held essential, while the human being, his desires and thoughts—in short, the psychological factors—are considered as unimportant and secondary. Herein lies a certain resemblance to Marxism, at least in so far as its theoretical side alone is kept in view. The individual is degraded to a mere instrument; he becomes "human matériel." The normal ends of human aspiration vanish with such a viewpoint. Instead, the military mentality raises "naked power" as a goal in itself—one of the strangest illusions to which men can succumb.

In our time the military mentality is still more dangerous than formerly because the offensive weapons have become much more powerful than the defensive ones. Therefore it leads, by necessity, to preventive war. The general insecurity that goes hand in hand with this results in the sacrifice of the citizen's civil rights to the supposed welfare of the state. Political witch-hunting, controls of all sorts (e.g., control of teaching and research, of the press, and so forth) appear inevitable, and for this reason do not encounter that popular resistance, which, were it not for the military mentality, would provide a protection. A reappraisal of all values gradually takes place in so far as everything that does not clearly serve the utopian ends is regarded and treated as inferior.

I see no other way out of prevailing conditions than a farseeing, honest, and courageous policy with the aim of establishing security on supranational foundations.

From *The American Scholar,* New York, Summer 1947. In *Ideas and Opinions by Albert Einstein.* Based on *Mein Weltbild,* edited by Carl Seelig. New translations and revisions by Sonja Bargmann. New York: Wings, 1954.

DOCUMENT 12: AN OPEN LETTER TO THE JAPANESE PEOPLE

Those who hated Einstein blamed him for the atomic bomb and criticized him openly. Personally he opposed its use against Japanese civilians and had sent a letter to the American president urging him not to drop the bombs, but the advice was not heeded. In 1952 he wrote a letter to the Japanese people which was published in Kaizo, *a Japanese magazine. In it he explains his part in producing the bomb and urges the abolition of all war as a means of curbing an arms race.*

My part in producing the atomic bomb consisted in a single act: I signed a letter to President Roosevelt, pressing the need for experiments on a large scale in order to explore the possibilities for the production of an atomic bomb.

I was fully aware of the terrible danger to mankind in case this attempt succeeded. But the likelihood that the Germans were working on the same problem with a chance of succeeding forced me to this step. I could do nothing else although I have always been a convinced pacifist. To my mind, to kill in war is not a whit better than to commit ordinary murder.

As long, however, as the nations are not resolved to abolish war through common actions and to solve their conflicts and protect their interests by peaceful decisions on a legal basis, they feel compelled to prepare for war. They feel obliged to prepare all possible means, even the most detestable ones, so as not to be left behind in the general armament race. This road necessarily leads to war, a war which under the present conditions means universal destruction.

Under these circumstances the fight against *means* has no chance of success. Only the radical abolition of wars and of the threat of war can help. This is what one has to work for. One has to be resolved not to let himself be forced to actions that run counter to this goal. This is a severe demand on an individual who is conscious of his dependence on society. But it is not an impossible demand.

Gandhi, the greatest political genius of our time, has pointed the way. He has shown of what sacrifices people are capable once they have found the right way. His work for the liberation of India is a living testimony to the fact that a will governed by firm conviction is stronger than a seemingly invincible material power.

Ideas and Opinions by Albert Einstein. Based on *Mein Weltbild,* edited by Carl Seelig. New translations and revisions by Sonja Bargmann. New York: Wings, 1954.

EINSTEIN'S IDEAS ON JEWISHNESS AND ZIONISM

DOCUMENT 13: WHAT IT MEANS TO BE A JEW

In an article published in Collier's Magazine *in 1938, Einstein says that a Jew who abandons his faith is still a Jew because he has Jewish qualities deeply instilled. Jews have long been united around a tradition of social justice, of helping others and tolerating others' differences, and they have a long tradition of respect for intellectual aspirations and endeavors.*

The bond that has united the Jews for thousands of years and that unites them today is, above all, the democratic ideal of social justice, coupled with the ideal of mutual aid and tolerance among all men. Even the most ancient religious scriptures of the Jews are steeped in these social ideals, which have powerfully affected Christianity and Mohammedanism and have had a benign influence upon the social structure of a great part of mankind. The introduction of a weekly day of rest should be remembered here—a profound blessing to all mankind. Personalities such as Moses, Spinoza, and Karl Marx, dissimilar as they may be, all lived and sacrificed themselves for the ideal of social justice; and it was the tradition of their forefathers that led them on this thorny path. The unique accomplishments of the Jews in the field of philanthropy spring from the same source.

The second characteristic trait of Jewish tradition is the high regard in which it holds every form of intellectual aspiration and spiritual effort. I am convinced that this great respect for intellectual striving is solely responsible for the contributions that the Jews have made toward the progress of knowledge, in the broadest sense of the term. In view of their relatively small number and the considerable external obstacles constantly placed in their way on all sides, the extent of those contributions deserves the admiration of all sincere men. I am convinced that this is not due to any special wealth of endowment, but to the fact that the esteem in which intellectual accomplishment is held among the Jews creates an atmosphere particularly favorable to the development of any talents that may exist. At the same time a strong critical spirit prevents blind obeisance to any mortal authority.

I have confined myself here to these two traditional traits, which seem to me the most basic. These standards and ideals find expression in small things as in large. They are transmitted from parents to children; they color conversation and judgment among friends; they fill the religious scriptures; and they give to the community life of the group its characteristic stamp. It is in these distinctive ideals that I see the essence of Jewish nature. That these ideals are but imperfectly realized in the group—in its actual everyday life—is only natural. However, if one seeks to give brief expression to the essential character of a group, the approach must always be by the way of the ideal.

202   *Albert Einstein*

Ideas and Opinions by Albert Einstein. Based on *Mein Weltbild,* edited by Carl Seelig.
New translations and revisions by Sonja Bargmann. New York: Wings, 1954.

DOCUMENT 14: EINSTEIN SUPPORTS ZIONISM

*Writing in response to a 1929 article by Professor Hellpach, Einstein
proclaims his support for Zionism, the establishment of a Jewish center in Palestine. Because Jews had no place, no community to unite
them, they lacked the support they needed when they were humili-
ated by the majority community. Thus, Einstein believed, establishing a home or center in Palestine was a worthy cause.*

Dear Mr. Hellpach:

I have read your article on Zionism and the Zurich Congress
and feel, as a strong devotee of the Zionist idea, that I must answer
you, even if only shortly.

The Jews are a community bound together by ties of blood and
tradition, and not of religion only: the attitude of the rest of the
world toward them is sufficient proof of this. When I came to Germany fifteen years ago I discovered for the first time that I was a
Jew, and I owe this discovery more to Gentiles than Jews.

The tragedy of the Jews is that they are people of a definite historical type, who lack the support of a community to keep them together. The result is a want of solid foundations in the individual
which amounts in its extremer forms to moral instability. I realized
that salvation was only possible for the race if every Jew in the
world should become attached to a living society to which he as an
individual might rejoice to belong and which might enable him to
bear the hatred and the humiliations that he has to put up with
from the rest of the world.

I saw worthy Jews basely caricatured, and the sight made my
heart bleed. I saw how schools, comic papers, and innumerable
other forces of the Gentile majority undermined the confidence
even of the best of my fellow-Jews, and felt that this could not be allowed to continue.

Then I realized that only a common enterprise dear to the heart
of Jews all over the world could restore this people to health. It was
a great achievement of [Theodor] Herzl's to have realized and proclaimed at the top of his voice that, the traditional attitude of the
Jews being what it was, the establishment of a national home or,
more accurately, a center in Palestine, was a suitable object on
which to concentrate our efforts.

All this you call nationalism, and there is something in the accu-
sation. But a communal purpose without which we can neither live
nor die in this hostile world can always be called by that ugly name.
In any case it is a nationalism whose aim is not power but dignity
and health. If we did not have to live among intolerant, narrow-
minded, and violent people, I should be the first to throw over all
nationalism in favor of universal humanity.

The objection that we Jews cannot be proper citizens of the German state, for example, if we want to be a "nation," is based on a misunderstanding of the nature of the state which springs from the intolerance of national majorities. Against that intolerance we shall never be safe, whether we call ourselves a people (or nation) or not.

I have put all this with brutal frankness for the sake of brevity, but I know from your writings that you are a man who stands to the sense, not the form.

Ideas and Opinions by Albert Einstein. Based on *Mein Weltbild*, edited by Carl Seelig. New translations and revisions by Sonja Bargmann. New York: Wings, 1954.

DOCUMENT 15: RELATIONS WITH ARABS IN PALESTINE

From 1920 on Einstein strongly supported the Zionist movement because he saw a growing anti-Semitism in Germany after World War I. On his American visit in 1931–32, he spoke to young people about Zionism and the importance of building good relations with the Arabs as preparation for the establishment of a Jewish community in Palestine.

I am delighted to have the opportunity of addressing a few words to the youth of this country which is faithful to the common aims of Jewry. Do not be discouraged by the difficulties which confront us in Palestine. Such things serve to test the will to live of our community.

Certain proceedings and pronouncements of the English administration have been justly criticized. We must not, however, let the matter rest at that, but draw what lesson we can from the experience.

We need to pay great attention to our relations with the Arabs. By cultivating these carefully we shall be able in future to prevent things from becoming so dangerously strained that people can take advantage of them to provoke acts of hostility. This goal is perfectly within our reach, because our work of construction has been, and must continue to be, carried out in such a manner as to serve the real interests of the Arab population also.

In this way we shall be able to avoid getting ourselves quite so often into the position, disagreeable for Jews and Arabs alike, of having to call in the mandatory power as arbitrator. We shall thereby be following not merely the dictates of Providence but also our traditions, which alone give the Jewish community meaning and stability. For our community is not, and must never become, a political one; this is the only permanent source whence it can draw new strength and the only ground on which its existence can be justified.

Ideas and Opinions by Albert Einstein. Based on *Mein Weltbild*, edited by Carl Seelig. New Translations and revisions by Sonja Bargmann. New York: Wings, 1954.

DOCUMENT 16: IN HONOR OF THE HEBREW UNIVERSITY

In 1949 Einstein spoke in honor of the Hebrew University of Jerusalem, which had opened in the early 1920s. He expressed his pride in the accomplishments of the Jewish people in their establishment of a state and a university. He also expressed his disappointment that use of arms had been necessary against the Arab people and his hope that a trusting relation would grow between Jews and Arabs.

The little that I could do, in a long life favored by external circumstances to deepen our physical knowledge, has brought me so much praise that for a long time I have felt rather more embarrassed than elated. But from you there comes a token of esteem that fills me with pure joy—joy about the great deeds that our Jewish people have accomplished within a few generations, under exceptionally difficult conditions, by itself alone, through boundless courage and immeasurable sacrifices. The University which twenty-seven years ago was nothing but a dream and a faint hope, this University is today a living thing, a home of free learning and teaching and happy brotherly work. There it is, on the soil that our people have liberated under great hardships; there it is, a spiritual center of a flourishing and buoyant community whose accomplishments have finally met with the universal recognition they deserved.

In this last period of the fulfilment of our dreams there was but one thing that weighed heavily upon me: the fact that we were compelled by the adversities of our situation to assert our rights through force of arms; it was the only way to avert complete annihilation. The wisdom and moderation the leaders of the new state have shown gives me confidence, however, that gradually relations will be established with the Arab people which are based on fruitful cooperation and mutual respect and trust. For this is the only means through which both peoples can attain true independence from the outside world.

Albert Einstein, *Out of My Later Years.* Secaucus, NJ: Citadel, 1956.

EINSTEIN IN SONG AND VERSE

DOCUMENT 17: A HYMN TO EINSTEIN

Following Einstein's overnight fame when his general theory was validated in 1919, physicist A.A. Robb wrote a "hymn" spoofing the praise Einstein was receiving. The verses are meant to be sung to the tune of "Deutschland Uber Alles."

Scientists so unbelieving
   Have completely changed their ways;
Now they humbly sing to Einstein
   Everlasting hymns of praise.
Journalists in search of copy
   First request an interview;
Then they boost him, boost him, boost him;
   Boost him until all is blue.

He the universe created;
  Spoke the word and it was there.
Now he reigns in radiant glory
  On his professorial chair.
Editions of daily papers,
  Yellow red and every hue
Boost him, boost him, boost him, boost him;
  Boost him until all is blue.

Philosophic speculators
  Stand in awe around his throne.
University professors
  Blow upon his loud trombone.
Praise him on the Riemann symbols
  On Christoffel symbols too
They boost him, boost him, boost him;
  Boost him until all is blue.

Other scientists neglected
  May be feeling somewhat sick;
And imagine that the butter
  Is laid on a trifle thick.
Heed not such considerations
  Be they false, or be they true;
Boost him, boost him, boost him, boost him;
  Boost him until all is blue.

Ronald W. Clark, *Einstein: The Life and Times.* New York: Avon, 1971.

Document 18: "St. Francis Einstein of the Daffodils"

William Carlos Williams's poem, "St. Francis Einstein of the Daffodils," was first published shortly after Einstein's first visit to America in April 1921. Williams identifies Einstein with spring and a new season of knowledge. The poem contains elements of relativity: observation from different referent points and relative time—"at last, in the end of time (old, absolute time),/ Einstein has come by force of/ complicated mathematics."

In March's black boat
Einstein and April
have come at the time in fashion
up out of the sea
through the rippling daffodils
in the foreyard of
the dead Statue of Liberty
whose stonearms
are powerless against them
the Venusremembering wavelets
breaking into laughter—

Sweet Land of Liberty,
at last, in the end of time,
Einstein has come by force of
complicated mathematics
among the tormented fruit trees
to buy freedom
for the daffodils
till the unchained orchards
shake their tufted flowers—
Yiddishe springtime!

At the time in fashion
Einstein has come
bringing April in his head
up from the sea
in Thomas March Jefferson's
black boat bringing
freedom under the dead
Statue of Liberty
to free the daffodils in
the water which sing:
Einstein has remembered us
Savior of the daffodils!

A twig for all the dead!
shout the dark maples
in the tearing wind, shaking
pom-poms of green flowers—
April Einstein has come
to liberate us
here among
the Venusremembering daffodils
Yiddishe springtime of the mind
and a great pool of rainwater
under
the blossomy peachtrees.

April Einstein
through the blossomy waters
rebellious, laughing
under liberty's dead arm
has come among the daffodils
shouting
that flowers and men
were created
relatively equal.
Oldfashioned knowledge is
dead under the blossoming peachtrees.

Einstein, tall as a violet
in the latticearbor corner
is tall as a blossomy
peartree! The shell
of the world is split
and from under the sea
Einstein has emerged
triumphant, St. Francis
of the daffodils!

O Samos, Samos
dead and buried. Lesbia is
a black cat in the freshturned
garden. All dead.
All flesh that they have sung
is long since rotten.
Sing of it no longer.

Sing of Einstein's
Yiddishe peachtrees, sing of
sleep among the cherryblossoms.
Sing of wise newspapers
that quote the great mathematician:
A little touch of
Einstein in the night—

Side by side the young and old
trees take the sun together,
the maples, green and red
according to their kind,
yellowbells and the
vermillion quinceflower together—
The tall peartree with
foetid blossoms
sways its high topbranches
with contrary motions and green
has come out of the wood
upon them also—

The mathematics grow complex:
there are both pinkflowered
and coralflowered peachtrees
in the bare chickenyard
of the old negro
with white hair who hides
poisoned fish-heads
here and there
where stray cats find them—

find them—find them.

O spring days, swift
and mutable, wind blowing
four ways, hot and cold.
Now the northeast wind,
moving in fogs, leaves the grass
cold and dripping. The night
is dark but in the night
the southeast wind approaches.
It is April and Einstein!
The owner of the orchard
lies in his bed
with the windows wide
and throws off his covers
one by one.

It is Einstein
out of complicated mathematics
among the daffodils—
spring winds blowing
four ways, hot and cold,
shaking the flowers!

Alan J. Friedman and Carol C. Donley, *Einstein: As Myth and Muse.* New York: Cambridge University Press, 1985.

CHRONOLOGY

1879

Albert Einstein is born in Ulm, Germany, on March 14.

1880

The Einsteins move to Munich, Germany.

1881

Einstein's sister, Maja, is born.

1884

Einstein is fascinated with a pocket compass, his first "wonder."

1885

Begins violin lessons and continues until age thirteen.

1886

Attends the neighborhood Catholic school.

1888

Enters Luitpold Gymnasium.

1889

Meets Max Talmey, who brings him science and philosophy books.

1891

Studies Euclid's geometry.

1894

The Einsteins move to Milan, Italy; Einstein stays in Munich to finish school.

1895

Drops out of school to join family in Milan; fails entrance exams for Zurich Polytechnic school; finishes high school in Aarau, Switzerland.

1896

Receives document certifying that he is no longer a German citizen.

1900

Receives diploma from Zurich Polytechnic; sends first paper to the *Annalen der Physik.*

1901

After five years without citizenship, Einstein becomes a Swiss citizen; assumes temporary teaching position in Winterthur, Switzerland.

1902

Begins work on a trial basis at patent office in Bern, Switzerland; father dies in Milan.

1903

Marries Mileva Maric.

1904

Einstein's son Hans Albert is born; Einstein's job at the patent office is made permanent.

1905

Completes paper on the light-quantum hypothesis; completes Ph.D. thesis, which is accepted; sends paper on Brownian motion to *Annalen der Physik;* sends first paper on special relativity to *Annalen;* sends second paper on special relativity to *Annalen* (contains $E=MC^2$); sends second paper on Brownian motion to *Annalen.*

1906

Is promoted to technical expert at the patent office; completes paper on specific heats of solids.

1908

Is admitted as a privatdocent at the University of Bern.

1909

Resigns from the patent office; begins job as associate professor at the University of Zurich.

1910

Einstein's sister, Maja, marries Paul Winterler; Einstein's son Eduard is born.

1911

Is appointed full professor at the University of Prague; gives address at Solvay conference.

1912

Is appointed professor at Zurich Polytechnic.

1912–1913

Collaborates with Marcel Grossmann on mathematics for the general theory of relativity.

1914

Moves to Berlin to begin tri-part job at Prussian Academy of Sciences, the University of Berlin, and the Kaiser Wilhelm Institute for Physics; Mileva and boys return to Zurich; outbreak of World War I in August.

1915

Completes general theory of relativity.

1916

General theory of relativity is published in *Annalen der Physik;* writes *Relativity: The Special and the General Theory.*

1917

Suffers from stomach problems and exhaustion; is cared for by his cousin Elsa.

1919

Divorces Mileva; general relativity theory is verified during solar eclipse; marries Elsa Einstein Lowenthal, who has two daughters, Ilse and Margot; verification of general theory is announced at the meeting of the Royal Society and the Royal Astronomical Society in London; London *Times* announces "Revolution in Science, New Theory of the Universe, Newtonian Ideas Overthrown."

1920

Mother dies; mass meetings against the general relativity theory are held in Berlin.

1921

Visits the United States to raise funds for the proposed Hebrew University in Jerusalem; is received at the White House by President Warren Harding; lectures in Princeton, Chicago, and Boston.

1922

Completes first paper on unified field theory; accepts invitation to membership of the League of Nations Committee on Intellectual Cooperation; visits Japan, with stops at Colombo, Singapore, Hong Kong, and Shanghai on the way; is awarded the Nobel Prize for discovery of the law of the photoelectric effect.

1923

On return from Japan, stops in Palestine and Spain; lectures on relativity in Goteborg in acknowledgment of the Nobel Prize.

1924

Opening of the Einstein Institute, housed in the Einstein Tower in Potsdam; Einstein's stepdaughter Ilse marries Rudolf Kayser.

1925

Einstein travels to South America; signs manifesto against obligatory military service.

1927

Son Hans Albert marries Frida Knecht; Einstein begins dialogue with Niels Bohr on quantum mechanics.

1928

Suffers temporary physical collapse from overexertion and heart problems, requiring four months of bed rest; hires Helen Dukas as his secretary.

1930

Visits the United States and Cuba.

1931

Spends winter term at the California Technological Institute (Cal Tech) in Pasadena, California.

1932

Spends winter term at Cal Tech in Pasadena, California.

1933

Nazis under Adolf Hitler come to power in Germany; Nazis raid Einstein's apartment and summer home; he resigns from the Prussian Academy and the Bavarian Academy of Sciences; gives up German citizenship and German passport; hides in Belgium and England; Ilse, Margot, Helen Dukas, and his assistant, Walther Mayer, escape from Germany; accepts position at the Institute for Advanced Study and moves to Princeton, New Jersey.

1934

Einstein's stepdaughter Ilse dies in Paris; Margot and her husband join family in Princeton.

1935

Moves to 112 Mercer Street in Princeton.

1936

Elsa dies; Hans Albert receives his Ph.D. from Zurich Polytechnic.

1939

Einstein's sister, Maja, moves to Mercer Street; Einstein sends letter to President Franklin Roosevelt drawing attention to military implications of atomic energy.

1940

Along with Margot and Helen Dukas, Einstein receives American citizenship; retains Swiss citizenship.

1941

America enters World War II.

1943

Becomes consultant for Research and Development Division of the U.S. Navy Bureau of Ordnance.

1945

American military drops atomic bombs on Hiroshima and Nagasaki; World War II ends; Einstein gives address in New York, "The War Is Won but Peace Is Not."

1946

Is appointed chairman of the Emergency Committee for Atomic Scientists; sends letter to United Nations urging world government.

1947

Hans Albert is appointed professor of engineering at the University of California, Berkeley.

1948

Einstein's former wife, Mileva, dies in Zurich.

1950

The Hebrew University is named as official repository of Einstein's letters and manuscripts.

1951

Maja dies in Princeton.

1952

Einstein is offered the presidency of Israel.

1955

Dies on April 18; his body is cremated, and his ashes are scattered at an undisclosed place.

FOR FURTHER RESEARCH

ABOUT ALBERT EINSTEIN

Pamela Zanin Bradbury, *Albert Einstein.* New York: Julian Messner, 1988.

Denis Brian, *Einstein: A Life.* New York: John Wiley and Sons, 1996.

William Cahn, *Einstein: A Pictorial Biography.* New York: Citadel, 1955.

Ronald W. Clark, *Einstein: The Life and Times.* New York: World, 1971.

Milton Dank, *Albert Einstein.* New York: Franklin Watts, 1983.

Aylesa Forsee, *Albert Einstein: Theoretical Physicist.* New York: Macmillan, 1963.

Phillip Frank, *Einstein: His Life and Times.* Trans. George Rosen. Ed. and rev. Shuichi Kusaka. New York: Alfred A. Knopf, 1953.

Maurice Goldsmith, Alan Mackay, and James Woudhuysen, eds., *Einstein: The First Hundred Years.* New York: Pergamon, 1980.

Roger Highfield and Paul Carter, *The Private Lives of Albert Einstein.* New York: St. Martin's, 1993.

Banesh Hoffmann and Helen Dukas, *Albert Einstein: Creator and Rebel.* New York: Penguin, 1972.

Abraham Pais, *"Subtle Is the Lord . . ." The Science and Life of Albert Einstein.* Oxford: Clarendon, 1982.

Anton Reiser, *Albert Einstein: A Biographical Portrait.* New York: Albert and Charles Boni, 1930.

James Sayen, *Einstein in America: The Scientist's Conscience in the Age of Hitler and Hiroshima.* New York: Crown, 1985.

Michael White and John Gribbin, *Einstein: A Life in Science.* New York: Dutton, 1993.

ABOUT EINSTEIN'S PHYSICS

Necia H. Apfel, *It's All Relative: Einstein's Theory of Relativity.* New York: Lothrop, Lee & Shepard, 1981.

J. Bronowski and Milicent E. Selsam, *Biography of an Atom.* New York: Harper and Row, 1963.

Nigel Calder, *Einstein's Universe.* New York: Greenwich House, 1979.

Eric Chaisson, *Relatively Speaking: Relativity, Black Holes, and the Fate of the Universe.* New York: W.W. Norton, 1988.

Timothy Ferris, *Coming of Age in the Milky Way.* New York: William Morrow, 1988.

George Gamow, *Thirty Years That Shook Physics: The Story of Quantum Theory.* New York: Doubleday, 1966.

Martin Gardner, *Relativity Simply Explained.* Mineola, NY: Dover, 1997.

Donald Goldsmith, *Einstein's Greatest Blunder? The Cosmological Constant and Other Fudge Factors in Physics.* Cambridge, MA: Harvard University Press, 1995.

John Gribbin, *Q Is for Quantum: An Encyclopedia of Particle Physics.* New York: Free, 1998.

Gerald Holton, *The Advancement of Science, and Its Burdens.* New York: Cambridge University Press, 1986.

Leopold Infeld, *Albert Einstein: His Work and Its Influence on Our World.* Rev. ed. New York: Charles Scribner's Sons, 1950.

Herbert Kondo, *Adventures in Space and Time: The Story of Relativity.* New York: Holiday House, 1966.

Heinz R. Pagels, *The Cosmic Code: Quantum Physics as the Language of Nature.* New York: Simon and Schuster, 1982.

Barry Parker, *Einstein's Dream: The Search for a Unified Theory of the Universe.* New York: Plenum, 1987.

Rudy Rucker, *The Fourth Dimension.* Boston: Houghton Mifflin, 1980.

Edwin E. Slosson, *Easy Lessons in Einstein: A Discussion of the More Intelligible Features of the Theory of Relativity.* New York: Harcourt Brace, 1920.

James S. Trefil, *Physics as a Liberal Art.* New York: Pergamon, 1978.

Spencer R. Weart and Melba Phillips, eds., *History of Physics.* New York: American Institute of Physics, 1985.

Steven Weinberg, *Dreams of a Final Theory.* New York: Pantheon, 1992.

ABOUT EINSTEIN'S TIMES

Lucy S. Dawidowicz, *The War Against the Jews: 1933–1945.* New York: Holt, Rinehart, and Winston, 1975.

Anne Frank, *Diary of a Young Girl.* Trans. B.M. Mooyaart. New York: Pocket Books, 1967.

Mary Fulbrook, *The Divided Nation: A History of Germany: 1918–1990.* New York: Oxford University Press, 1992.

Martin Gilbert, *Holocaust Journey: Travelling in Search of the Past.* New York: Columbia University Press, 1997.

John Hersey, *Hiroshima.* New York: Alfred A. Knopf, 1985.

Edward Jablonski, *A Pictorial History of World War I Years.* Garden City, NY: Doubleday, 1979.

Don Nardo, ed., *The Rise of Nazi Germany.* San Diego: Greenhaven, 1999.

Benjamin Netanyahu, *A Place Among the Nations: Israel and the World.* New York: Bantam, 1993.

Detlev J.K. Peukert, *Inside Nazi Germany: Conformity, Opposition, and Racism in Everyday Life.* Trans. Richard Deveson. New Haven, CT: Yale University Press, 1982.

A.J.P. Taylor, *Illustrated History of the First World War.* New York: G.P. Putnam's Sons, 1964.

Ben Wicks, *Dawn of a Promised Land.* New York: Hyperion, 1997.

BY EINSTEIN

Albert Einstein, *Autobiographical Notes.* Trans. and ed. Paul Schilpp. 1949. Reprint. La Salle, IL: Open Court, 1979.

———, *Ideas and Opinions*. Ed. Carl Seelig. Trans. and rev. Sonja Bargmann. New York: Wings, 1954.

———, *The Meaning of Relativity*. 1922. Reprint. Princeton, NJ: Princeton University Press, 1955.

———, *Out of My Later Years*. 1950. Reprint. Westport, CT: Greenwood, 1970.

———, *Relativity: The Special and the General Theory*. Trans. Robert W. Lawson. New York: Crown, 1961.

INDEX

About the Editor

After many years of teaching British literature to high school students, Clarice Swisher now devotes her time to research and writing. She is the author of *The Age of Monarchs, Pablo Picasso, Genetic Engineering, Victorian England, The Glorious Revolution,* and editor of *Spread of Islam* and *Galileo.* She is currently working on a new series, *Understanding Great Literature.* She lives in St. Paul, Minnesota.